RECIPES FOR
SURFACES

RECIPES FOR
SURFACES

•

DECORATIVE PAINT
FINISHES MADE SIMPLE

•

TEXT BY MINDY DRUCKER
AND
PIERRE FINKELSTEIN

PHOTOGRAPHS BY
TONY CENICOLA

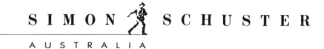

SIMON **SCHUSTER**

AUSTRALIA

RECIPES FOR SURFACES

First published in Australasia in 1990 by Simon & Schuster Australia
7 Grosvenor Place, Brookvale NSW 2100

A division of Paramount Communications Inc.

RECIPES FOR SURFACES
was produced and conceived by
Running Heads Incorporated
55 West 21st Street
New York, New York 10010
U.S.A.

Senior Editor: Sarah Kirshner
Designer: Liz Trovato
Production Manager: Linda Winters
Managing Editor: Lindsey Crittenden

All paint finishes designed and executed by Pierre Finkelstein.
Drawings by Clarisse Thomas.

10   9   8   7   6   5   4   3   2

National Library of Australia
Cataloguing in Publication data

Drucker, Mindy.
    Recipes for surfaces : decorative paint finishes made
    simple.

    Bibliography.
    Includes index.
    ISBN 0 7318 0156 3.

    1. House painting — Amateurs' manuals.   2. Interior
    decoration — Amateurs' manuals.   3. Decoration and
    ornament — Amateurs' manuals.   I. Finkelstein, Pierre.
    II. Cenicola, Tony.   III. Title.
698.14

Typeset by Trufont Typographers
Color separations by Hong Kong Scanner Craft Co., Ltd.
Printed and bound in Hong Kong by C&C Offset Printing Co., Ltd.

To the memory of my grandparents—Max, Anne, Gertrude, and Monroe

—M.D.

To Clarisse, for her support, patience, and encouragement

—P.F.

CONTENTS

• KEY TO SYMBOLS •

= easy

= intermediate

= difficult

= advanced

· FOREWORD ·

HOW TO USE THIS BOOK

Sponging, marbling, stencilling, ragging, graining—you've probably admired decorative painting effects such as these in a magazine or in someone's home. Creating these effects may have seemed beyond your ability—but it's not! With practice and *Recipes for Surfaces* as your guide, you can easily master many of today's most popular finishes.

A true how-to book, this volume offers a wealth of information on everything you'll need to produce decorative finishes— from where to find inspiration to developing colour schemes to the materials you'll require to directions for readying a room for painting. But the main purpose of *Recipes for Surfaces* is to supply clear, concise step-by-step instructions for mixing paints and executing more than forty decorative painting techniques.

The format of the book suits its goal. Instead of concentrating on elaborate interiors, it focuses on the finishes themselves, including close-ups of crucial stages and of the completed effects. This helps eliminate distractions and aids you in studying the techniques. It also encourages you to adapt the techniques to your space instead of trying to reproduce them exactly as they appear on the page in a room setting (a frustrating experience because the architecture, lighting, and furnishings—all of which contribute to its look—will undoubtedly differ from your own).

Once you learn a technique presented in the book, you will be able to vary the colour and pattern so as to devise many other looks in addition to those pictured. The chapters on colour and mixing paint will aid you in developing hues to complement your interiors. In the introductions to the techniques, you'll often find suggestions for varying an effect by using another tool, type of paint, or colour scheme as well as ideas on locating patterns or creating your own.

In many ways, decorative painting is close in spirit to cooking: In cooking, you have basic recipes, such as how to make a pie crust or prepare a sauce, as well as general guidelines, like how to plan a menu or store leftovers. The same is true of decorative painting: There are recipes for mixing a base coat and tinting a glaze as well as rules for planning a colour scheme and storing paints. Thus, *Recipes for Surfaces* has much in common with a well-designed cookbook: It features a tempting array of great colour photographs that make you want to try techniques for yourself. And it includes all the basic recipes, general guidelines, and detailed directions you'll need to complete each one.

Also as in a cookbook, each recipe stands on its own. Just review Part I for a grounding in colour, supplies, and preparation. Then turn to Part II, and for each recipe you'll find a materials list—including tools, paints, recommended surfaces, and more—painting tips, instructions, and clear step-by-step photos. You will want to read through the introduction to the chapter your technique is in as well as the introductions to similar techniques within each chapter for an even more thorough understanding of a particular decorative finish.

The chapters are arranged roughly from simple to difficult. If you're browsing through the book and see a technique you like, just locate the paint can symbol 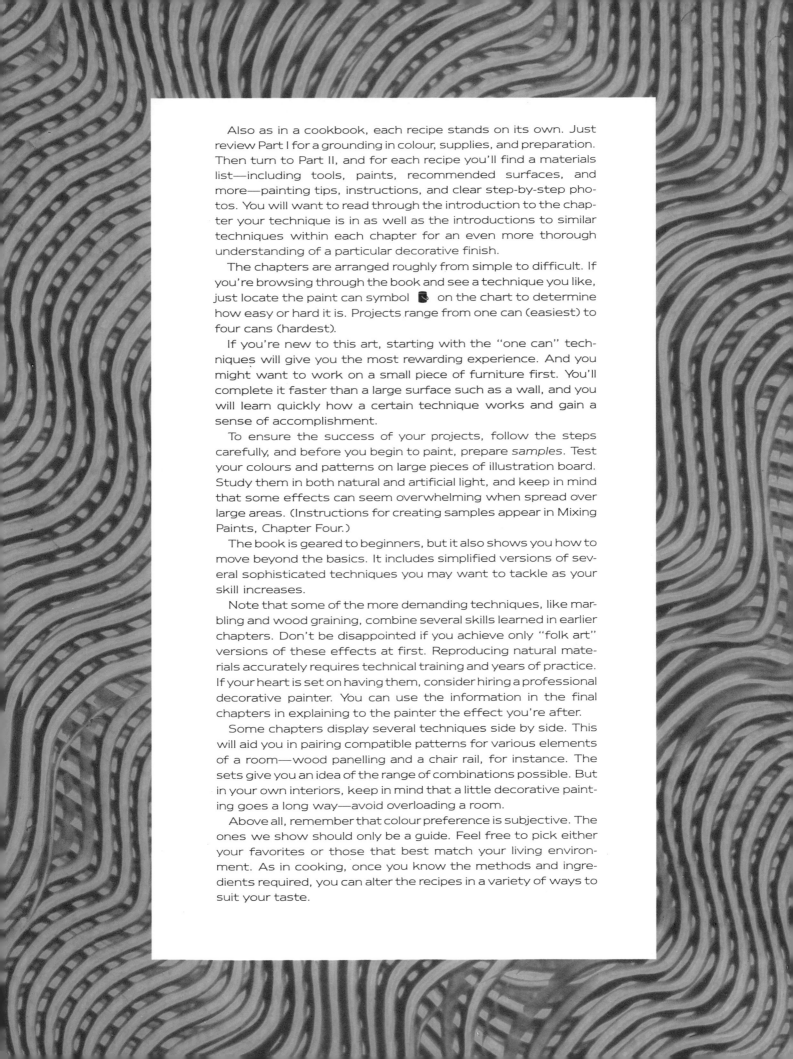 on the chart to determine how easy or hard it is. Projects range from one can (easiest) to four cans (hardest).

If you're new to this art, starting with the "one can" techniques will give you the most rewarding experience. And you might want to work on a small piece of furniture first. You'll complete it faster than a large surface such as a wall, and you will learn quickly how a certain technique works and gain a sense of accomplishment.

To ensure the success of your projects, follow the steps carefully, and before you begin to paint, prepare *samples*. Test your colours and patterns on large pieces of illustration board. Study them in both natural and artificial light, and keep in mind that some effects can seem overwhelming when spread over large areas. (Instructions for creating samples appear in Mixing Paints, Chapter Four.)

The book is geared to beginners, but it also shows you how to move beyond the basics. It includes simplified versions of several sophisticated techniques you may want to tackle as your skill increases.

Note that some of the more demanding techniques, like marbling and wood graining, combine several skills learned in earlier chapters. Don't be disappointed if you achieve only "folk art" versions of these effects at first. Reproducing natural materials accurately requires technical training and years of practice. If your heart is set on having them, consider hiring a professional decorative painter. You can use the information in the final chapters in explaining to the painter the effect you're after.

Some chapters display several techniques side by side. This will aid you in pairing compatible patterns for various elements of a room—wood panelling and a chair rail, for instance. The sets give you an idea of the range of combinations possible. But in your own interiors, keep in mind that a little decorative painting goes a long way—avoid overloading a room.

Above all, remember that colour preference is subjective. The ones we show should only be a guide. Feel free to pick either your favorites or those that best match your living environment. As in cooking, once you know the methods and ingredients required, you can alter the recipes in a variety of ways to suit your taste.

INTRODUCTION

•

WHAT IS DECORATIVE PAINTING?

Familiarity breeds indifference. We have seen too much pure, bright colour at Woolworth's to find it intrinsically transporting.

—*Aldous Huxley*

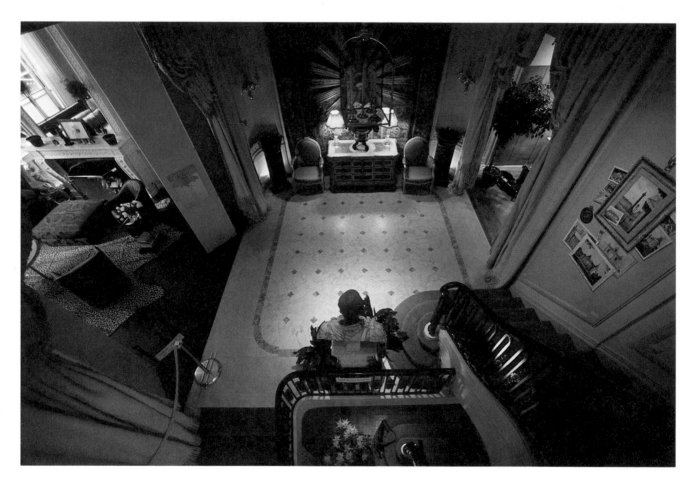

An elegant faux marble floor is a classical focal point for this stairway landing.

TODAY WE ARE MORE TUNED IN TO INTERIOR DESIGN THAN EVER before. We've tired of solid-colour surfaces and are ready for unique and sophisticated ways to embellish our homes. Perhaps you're looking for an alternative to the opaque paint colours on the market. Or maybe you're seeking a more personalized substitute for wallpaper. Or you might want something other than an area rug to dress up your wood floors. The art of decorative painting can meet these desires and more.

Decorative painting differs from standard interior painting in several ways. The first difference is the paints you use. On top of two layers of interior paint, you apply thin coats of transparent paint that you mix yourself and then tint to the hue you desire. This transparent paint is known as glaze. You can buy mixed and coloured glazes in cans, but they are more costly than glazes you mix yourself, and the selection of colours is limited.

This special emphasis on colour is another way decorative painting distinguishes itself. In fact, as the following chapters explain, colour—carefully chosen and properly mixed—is the very heart of decorative painting. The colours that are produced come not only from blending wet paints on an artist's palette, but also from placing translucent layers atop an opaque base. This visual effect yields resonance and depth, almost a glow, as your eye does the mixing.

Pattern, which results from the way you apply the glaze, also contributes to the singularity of decorative painting. With a wide array of tools—sponges, cloth, combs, rollers, and brushes in many shapes and sizes—you manipulate the glaze while it is still wet to form patterns, or different broken-colour effects, like ragging, combing, and colour washing.

The effects range from subtle to bold; so it won't be difficult to find one suited to your taste. Among the softest is stippling (Chapter Seven), which gives a smooth impression at a distance and only reveals its textured look up close. Among the brashest is sponging (Chapter Five), which can enliven the most staid setting.

The condition of your surfaces will also influence your choice of effects. For example, ragrolling (Chapter Six) can hide imperfections in rough old walls, while dragging (Chapter Ten) requires a smooth surface for best results.

In and out of fashion over time, decorative painting was long the province of professionals who kept their "trade secrets"—paint formulas, application techniques, material sources—to themselves. But now, thanks to tried and tested recipes like the ones in this guide, you can avail yourself of these age-old methods for devising unique living environments.

In fact, these recipes are particularly valuable for us today. They turn white-walled modern interiors into warm and personal spaces inspired by the past. They make floors, walls, woodwork, and ceilings focal points in their own right. They transform worn-out furniture into the treasured heirlooms of tomorrow and inexpensive accessories into masterpieces embellished with gilt or precious stones.

These may seem like large claims for decorating techniques. But don't underestimate their power. The "right" surfaces can make a room by underscoring its assets (good proportions, fine detailing) and camouflaging its drawbacks (small size, few windows). Of course, if you're designing from scratch, you can choose the techniques and colours to which you're most drawn. But even if you've already got most of the elements in place, you can find suitable finishes to give your interiors new life. And the challenge of joining old and new can inspire unique solutions.

Another appeal of decorative painting is its ability to make new surfaces appear aged. The creation of a venerable-looking patina takes careful planning: judiciously mixed colour, well-chosen pattern, meticulous execution. Because decorative-painting colours are complex blends instead of "pure" hues, they particularly contribute to the sophisticated "faded-with-age" look. Designers call these colours "dirtied"—and, to them, the expression has only favourable meaning.

You'll also appreciate the individuality that decorative painting bestows on a room. Even though you'll be following recipes, you can put something of yourself into the techniques. For instance, everybody spatters paint a little differently. Your touch might be light or heavy; you might favour a dense or sparse look.

Creating your own finishes is fun, rewarding, and a viable alternative to what would surely be a costly affair if you enlisted a professional decorative painter. In these pages, you'll find many trade secrets to make the process easier. Combine them with patience, practice, and trust in your own talents, and you'll achieve a variety of splendid results.

• COST •

Your budget will depend, of course, on the size of your project. And because many of the tools and materials can be reused, costs for subsequent projects decrease considerably. Here are some guidelines for figuring expenses. But remember that costs may vary greatly across the country; so visit hardware, paint, and art supply shops in your area.

For a large project such as a room, preparation work will be the most expensive part, especially if you hire a professional house painter to do the filling, priming, and base-coating. Call local house painters for estimates, using Preparing to Paint, Chapter Three, to guide you in what to ask them for. They usually charge either by the day or by the square foot.

If you decide to do the preparation yourself, invest in quality tools and materials so that the foundation you create will be worthy of your decorative finish and will help it look great and last. A gallon of primer costs about £20. Preparation materials—dust sheets, sandpaper, filler, masking tape, buckets, containers, rollers—will cost about £25 for a room.

You could put together a good beginner's brush kit consisting of a few base-coat, glazing, round, and fine brushes plus some sponges for about £45; wait to buy more until you need them on future projects. Artist's oils and acrylics range from £1.50 to £3 a tube (38 ml); you need at least a dozen colours for a good decorative-painter's palette.

• POINTERS FROM THE PAST •

In many eras since its humble beginnings, decorative painting has been called upon to work its special charms. A glance at its history can both inspire and instruct us. Not only are the techniques of past artists still valid, but the looks that result from those techniques remain wonderful and affordable ways to beautify our homes.

The earliest "decorative painters" that we know of lived in prehistoric Spain and France. They painted the walls of their caves with figures ranging from simple outlines to depictions suggesting movement and natural color. Their palette was limited. They made paint by grinding plants, clay, and stone into powder and adding water or animal fat. Fine examples of their work survive. Scholars believe the paintings had mystical purposes—to ensure a successful hunt, perhaps, or augment their food supply.

By about 3000 B.C., skilled artisans in India, Egypt, and the Orient began using painted finishes. Then, as now, the finishes were more than decorative: They protected surfaces and, perhaps most important, visually transformed ordinary materials into rich-looking objects. Among the techniques they mastered were marbling, gilding, wood graining, and mural painting. From the ruins of their cities we learn that these artisans embellished not only their temples, palaces, and homes but also furniture, books, and accessories.

The Egyptians particularly enjoyed painted finishes. They augmented their palette by importing plants from India: indigo for blue, madder for red, violet, and brown. Decorative effects even helped them cope with their climate: Inside their homes

of sun-baked brick, they often painted serene outdoor scenes that conveyed a cool feeling, welcome in the Mediterranean heat.

The Greeks and Romans built upon the decorative-painting traditions of the Egyptians, and examples of their work can be seen in the ruins of Pompeii. A signature of their style—trompe l'oeil decorative painting—remains popular today.

In the Middle Ages painting became the province of the monks and served mainly religious purposes. Then, toward the end of this period, came a major breakthrough: Flemish painters invented oil-based paints, prized for their versatility and durability. They also began experimenting with glazes, which they found particularly effective for reproducing subtle shadows and flesh tones.

During the Renaissance, artists throughout Europe began developing new formulas and colors of paint. They guarded their formulas closely—so closely, in fact, that the formulas often died with their creators. Artists trained extensively in gold leafing, stencilling, marbling, wood graining, fresco, and trompe l'oeil offered their services to the wealthy, who commissioned them to embellish everything from pieces of furniture to entire castles. The Palace of Versailles, near Paris, is a classic example.

Unlike European decorative painters, early American artisans usually had little training in fine techniques. Many were itinerants who embellished interiors in exchange for a meal and a bed. Their method of choice was stencilling. The technique, which originated in China and reached great heights in Japan, has a particularly strong legacy in

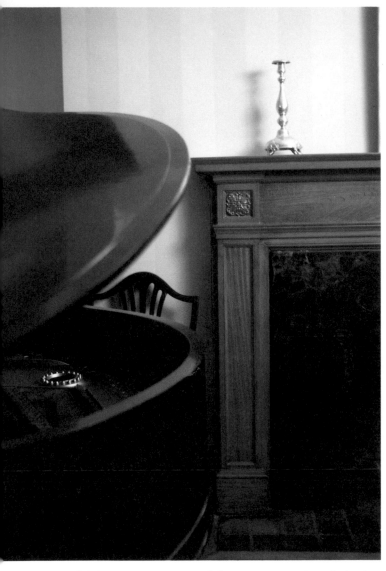

Mahogany wood graining on a wood and plaster fireplace mantel lends warmth to this room.

early nineteenth-century America, where it served as an inexpensive alternative to wallpaper.

In fact, many favourite stencil patterns copied wallpapers of the day. Others adapted classical and natural motifs. Today these patterns make fine complements to traditional country interiors, and we, too, appreciate the ease with which they can be accomplished.

Decorative painting again reached prominence in the Victorian era. Seeking respite from their rapidly changing world, the Victorians embraced the Arts and Crafts movement, which revived respect for handwork such as decorative painting. They turned their homes into shelters elaborately embellished with time-honored techniques. Among their preferences was wood graining, and with it they transformed pine-panelled rooms into sumptuous settings that appeared to feature more costly woods like mahogany and ash.

Inspirations for decorative painting can be found in our own century. Look to the work of English designer John Fowler, who created a wide range of effects using subtly mixed glazes and venerable methods of application. Study interiors from the Art Deco period for examples of elaborate marbling as well as wood graining that simulates exotic varieties like tulipwood and satinwood. (But be prepared to tone down their Hollywood-style opulence to suit today's more relaxed mood.) Examine settings from the 1960s for imaginative effects: a ceiling painted like an azure sky, a trompe l'oeil window that "opens up" a wall.

So keep an eye on history as you plan your decorative effects. At a museum, the faded hues of a medieval tapestry might entrance you. While looking through home-interest books and magazines, a stencilled pattern might catch your eye. Envision how you can bring the enduring spirit of examples like these into your home.

PART I

·

GENERAL INFORMATION

CHAPTER ONE

•

COLOUR:
THE KEY INGREDIENT

REGARDLESS OF WHICH DECORATIVE PAINTING TECHNIQUE YOU

choose, colour will be its most vital component. How the colours you pick look together, suit your space, and harmonize with the existing colours will greatly affect the success of any project. So before you start, take time to learn about colour and its role in interior design.

First, be aware that no two people see colour in the same way—colour is perhaps the most subjective area of design. Choosing colours that you enjoy seeing together is one of the best ways to make your house truly your own. Decorative painting, in particular, lets you fashion a vast array of colours notable for their richness, subtlety, and depth. They can give your rooms an individuality no paint-chart colour can match.

In interior design, the colours you select must always be considered in relation to those around them. The way in which they are distributed throughout a room is called a *colour scheme*.

Deciding which colours to include in your scheme can be fun—it lets you be creative. But like an artist faced

The colours of the cloth-distressed wall and marbleized door trim harmonize with the settee's fabric.

with a blank canvas, you may initially be overwhelmed by the range of options. For help in determining combinations that work well together and bring out the best in your home, you can refer to established principles of interior design as well as guidelines for achieving a pleasing blend of hues.

Many of these rules appear on following pages. In reviewing them, however, bear in mind that, as with any rules, you'll find numerous exceptions. In fact, you could join any two colours in one setting, depending on how much area the hues will cover,

how close together they will be, and whether they will be patterned or solid.

So, since the rules don't cover all contingencies, you must do something you may at first find challenging—*trust your instincts*. How do the colours make *you* feel? Do you like them together? Are they the ones you want to live with? Rest assured that no design professional can answer these questions better than you, and have confidence that if a colour pleases your eye, it has the best chance of looking "right" for your room.

• UNDERSTANDING COLOUR •

Identifying successful colour schemes is not as complicated as you may think. Remember, your instincts are probably right! One way to gain confidence is to review the basics of colour theory.

Our earliest paint-box lessons still apply: Any hue can be made by combining the three primary colours—red, yellow, and blue—plus various amounts of black and white. By mixing pairs of primaries, you form the three secondary colours—red and yellow make orange; yellow and blue make green; blue and red make violet. Then, by blending

the secondaries, you'll get the tertiary colours—olive, for instance, which comes from a mixture of green and violet.

Today, however, thanks to technology, we should probably qualify the basic rule to say that *almost* any colour can be created from the primaries. In reality, the more colours you combine, the less vibrance the resulting hue will have. So manufacturers now produce a wide range of colours whose brilliance would be hard to match by starting with the primaries.

• COLOURS THAT HARMONIZE •

To grasp the relationships among colours, you can use the *colour wheel* pictured below. It has twelve parts, like the face of a clock. You'll find the primary colours at twelve o'clock (yellow), four o'clock (red), and eight o'clock (blue). The secondary colours are at two o'clock (orange), six o'clock (violet), and ten o'clock (green). In the remaining six spaces are the intermediate colours, so called because they lie between the primary and secondary colours.

From the position of colours on the wheel, you can identify harmonious blends. Among recommended combinations are *similar* colours, such as orange and yellow, which appear near each other on the wheel, and *complementaries*, such as red and green, which appear opposite each other. Complementaries serve a special purpose in decorating: They tone each other down to help balance a scheme.

A colour also blends well with the colours flanking its complementary—orange with either blue green or blue violet, for instance. This arrangement is called *split-complementary*. You'll also discover that *triads*—any three colours equidistant on the wheel—harmonize. Exemplifying this are the primary colours.

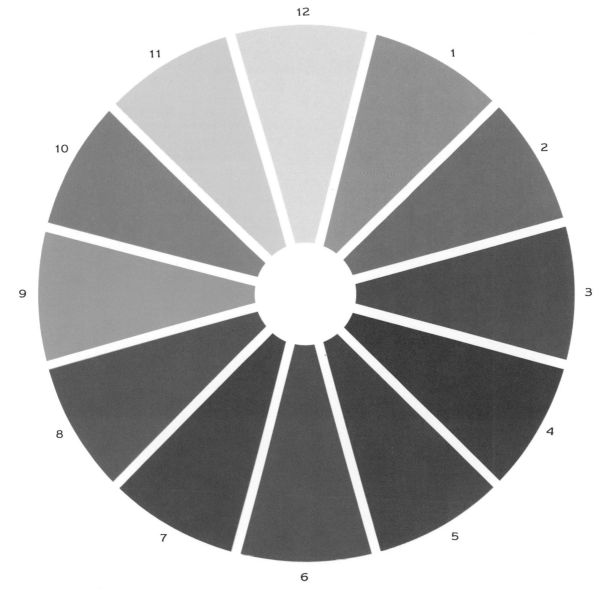

The colour wheel is a helpful tool for understanding how colours relate. Note that although each colour appears on the wheel in its "pure" form, you can apply the same rules to all its values and intensities.

• COLOUR CHARACTERISTICS •

Even though the categories mentioned above might be unfamiliar to you, you'll probably find that many of your favorite colour combinations fit into them naturally. You may not recognize them at first, however, because on the colour wheel they are in their "pure" form, and this is rarely the form in which they are used in decorating.

A colour has three main characteristics: its *hue*, the colour family to which it belongs; its *intensity*, how dull or vivid it is; and its *value*, how dark or light

it is. By varying the intensity and value of the pure colours, we derive a multitude of others. For example, by altering the value of pure red, we can get both rose and pink, which belong to the same colour family and thus share the same position on the colour wheel.

To change the value of a colour, mix black and/or white into it. Mixing a colour with white creates a *tint*; combining it with black produces a *shade*. Blending it with grey, makes a *tone*.

• CLASSIC COLOUR SCHEMES •

Based on these principles, we can devise colour schemes that are pleasing and easily achieved. Using different values of the same colour—mint, medium, and forest green, for instance—will give you a *monochromatic* arrangement. The scheme can be enhanced by decorative painting's two-tone effects. Try, say, walls with a mint base coat and a medium green sponged glaze layer, for example, to add visual interest to a subdued monochromatic setting.

You can also create a harmonious setting with different colours that have the same value: three pastels, for example. The contrast between, say, light peach, pale violet, and soft green enlivens the scene, while their similarity in value ties them together and prevents one colour from dominating and throwing the scheme off balance. Consider soft peach walls trimmed with a stencilled border in pale violet and light green.

You may not be used to thinking of colour in terms of value; so identifying different colours with the same value may take practice. To get a

feel for values, imagine looking at a black-and-white photograph of a room in your house—or better yet, actually take a black-and-white photo of the room and study it. In the photo, all the colours that have the same value will be the same shade of grey. By diminishing the obvious differences in hues, you can more easily spot those of similar value.

Simplicity can be trusted when it comes to colour schemes. Consider employing just a range of neutrals—whites, beiges, greys, browns. You'll be surprised at how many of each there are. A subtle scheme like this makes a fine showcase for intricate painted finishes that might look busy in a brighter setting.

Or you might link your favorite hue with white or a pale neutral. In fact, using your best colour as an accent will produce a scheme that is notable for its versatility. If your taste changes, just switching the accent colour will give your neutral scheme a new look. Employing a light accent with less contrast will imbue your setting with a relaxed air.

• MORE COLOUR-SCHEME OPTIONS •

Interior designers have many methods for developing colour schemes. A simple and effective one is to select the curtains or upholstery fabric first and then create a custom look by painting walls, woodwork, floors, and furnishings in co-ordinating hues.

Picking your fabric before you mix your paints is definitely safer. You can undoubtedly create a hue to match your fabric, but you might not as easily find a fabric to go with a distinctive colour you've specially blended. Professionals usually advise that the background colour of a print fabric and the base coat of your walls be the same. Then you can pull out other hues in the fabric pattern for coordinated accents.

Another method is to select three favorite colours and apply them in varying quantities. Make one colour dominant; include a lot more of it than the others. Use the second colour about half as much, and employ the last as an accent.

A third way is to pick an item for each room that you can't imagine living without and work your scheme around it. You don't have to make its colours the main ones in the room. For example, you might choose neutral shades for walls, floor, and upholstery and use accent colours from a painting.

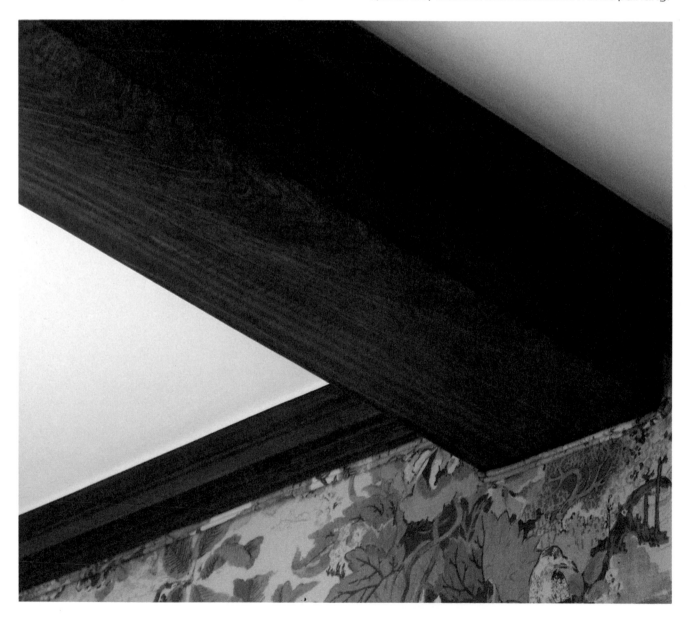

The rich brown tone of the mahogany graining on these beams matches the floral fabric on the walls.

Some of the most satisfying colour combinations occur in nature. Collect items on a walk in the woods and place them beside you as you plan your scheme and mix your colours. Bring the outdoors inside by adopting the brown of a polished stone from a riverbed or the russet of an autumn leaf.

Devise schemes by building on the creativity of others. Do what professional designers do: Travel with a small notebook and jot down elements of interiors—private homes, decorator showhouses, restaurants, public buildings, or historic sites—that please you. Illustrate your notes with quick sketches to help fix an effect in your mind.

And don't be afraid of copying. You'll find that even if you try to reproduce a scheme exactly, your own personality will seep in. And because your space differs from the one that inspired you—whether in the amount of light it receives or the height of its ceiling or what it's used for—you'll naturally adapt the effects for best results.

Assemble a file of photos showing interiors you like from decorating magazines. But also study the advertisements accompanying them. A painted backdrop in a furniture ad might suggest an unusual treatment for your dining room ceiling. Also glance through fashion magazines. Many decorators now look to couture for ideas.

Keep in mind that colour styles change. The Day-Glo colours of the 1960s loom large in memory but find no place in today's decors. Because you'll be putting special effort into your decorative-painting effects, don't let fashion alone dictate your choice. Pick hues that you'll enjoy living with despite the trends next year will surely bring.

Some colours such as pastels and neutrals are perennial decorating favorites because people have long found them comforting to live with. But don't discount your dreams: If magazine clippings of rooms with red walls fill your "wish file," consider using a crimson rich and regal enough to satisfy your personal vision. To this end, decorative painting offers a special bonus: It can have a wonderful softening effect on intense hues.

And what if after you've painted the room it doesn't look quite right? Perhaps the finish is too intense spread over an entire room—even though it looked great on the sample you made. Another real plus of painted finishes is that if you decide the one you've chosen isn't for you, you can paint right over it and start again. Or you might just modify it by, say, adding a neutral border or applying another layer of glaze in a pale colour.

· THE EFFECTS OF COLOUR ·

When planning your scheme, remember that there is more to colour than relationships. Colour is probably the first thing we notice about a room, and subconsciously we feel its influence. Thanks to art, literature, history, nature, and events in our everyday lives, colours—and the different shades and tints of a colour as well—have many associations for us. They can dredge up memories, trigger emotions, and bring strong images to mind. Add your own associations to the following list of conventional symbols linked with colours; they may offer clues to the appeal certain hues hold for you.

Red, the colour of hearts and roses, has deep ties to romance. Yellow, linked to sunshine and the first flowers of spring, is regarded as an uplifting colour. Blue can conjure the sea and sky, the soft pastel blanket of a newborn, or the dignified air of a navy suit. Green, ripe with images of nature, bespeaks tranquility; yet it also symbolizes jealousy. Brown belongs both to rich fertile soil and dying autumn leaves, rustic weathered wood and soft opulent leather. White, the "absence of all colours," expresses not only innocence and purity but also the sterility of hospitals and the cold of winter. Black, the colour of night, death, and evil, also speaks to us of elegance and wealth.

• COLOUR ESTABLISHES MOODS •

Colour can also set the ambience for your interiors. Would you like rooms that convey peacefulness or generate excitement? Do you prefer a casual or elegant air? Classic or country style? Do you dream of a quiet retreat, a striking setting for lively entertaining, or a cool contemporary showplace for a modern art collection? Or would you like to vary the ambience from room to room according to function—a subdued look in the study, a cheery setting for the breakfast nook.

Selecting colours from these categories can help you get the effects you desire:

LIGHT COLOURS.
Whatever hue you choose, light tints of it will give a soft look. This easy-to-live-with quality makes light colours favorites in decorating, especially when livened with accents in a brighter or darker hue.

DARK COLOURS.
Black and other dark hues are less frequent choices for large areas of interiors. Red, purple, green, and blue have regal associations and exude a dignified air. These hues might be at home covering the walls of a formal parlor or dining room, but most often they serve as accents to light colours.

BRIGHT COLOURS.
Even more exuberant than the warm colours, the brights include shades of blue, yellow, black, and white as well as red. They have a contemporary flavour. Except in children's rooms, we rarely see even two of them together. In groups they quickly overwhelm us.

DULL COLOURS.
Shades of grey mellow the dull hues, which can lower stress and evoke a contemplative mood. To keep them from seeming too vague, link them with bright accents.

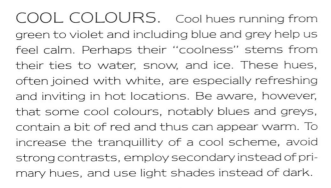

COOL COLOURS.

Cool hues running from green to violet and including blue and grey help us feel calm. Perhaps their "coolness" stems from their ties to water, snow, and ice. These hues, often joined with white, are especially refreshing and inviting in hot locations. Be aware, however, that some cool colours, notably blues and greys, contain a bit of red and thus can appear warm. To increase the tranquillity of a cool scheme, avoid strong contrasts, employ secondary instead of primary hues, and use light shades instead of dark.

WARM COLOURS.

Ranging from red to yellow, these warm, splashy hues demand attention, lend excitement, and help "heat up" even a small, dark, and cold room. Psychologists speculate that they even increase our drive and help us work faster, which might make them a good choice for a kitchen scheme. When combined with cool colours, warm hues always dominate.

NATURAL COLOURS.

Subtle and complex, the natural hues are soothing and, in their simplicity, provide a rich look. As their name suggests, they are the colours found in nature. These natural colours range from pale and clear to dark and muted. They often comprise blends of many hues—a mahogany brown, a driftwood grey, a terra-cotta red. To spice up these colours, complement them with a bright hue also found in nature—the green of a leaf, the blue of the sky. But be careful that the bright hue doesn't overwhelm them.

SURPRISING COLOURS.

Because they are rarely found in nature or teamed in daily life, surprising colours have an attention-getting effect. Among them are hues contrary to their natural brightness—dull orange, for instance. Also in this group are pairs of colours with minimal contrast, such as magenta and purple. Note, however, that the colours in this category change: Many that were once startling have become conventional with frequent use. These colours would be at home in large contemporary living or family rooms.

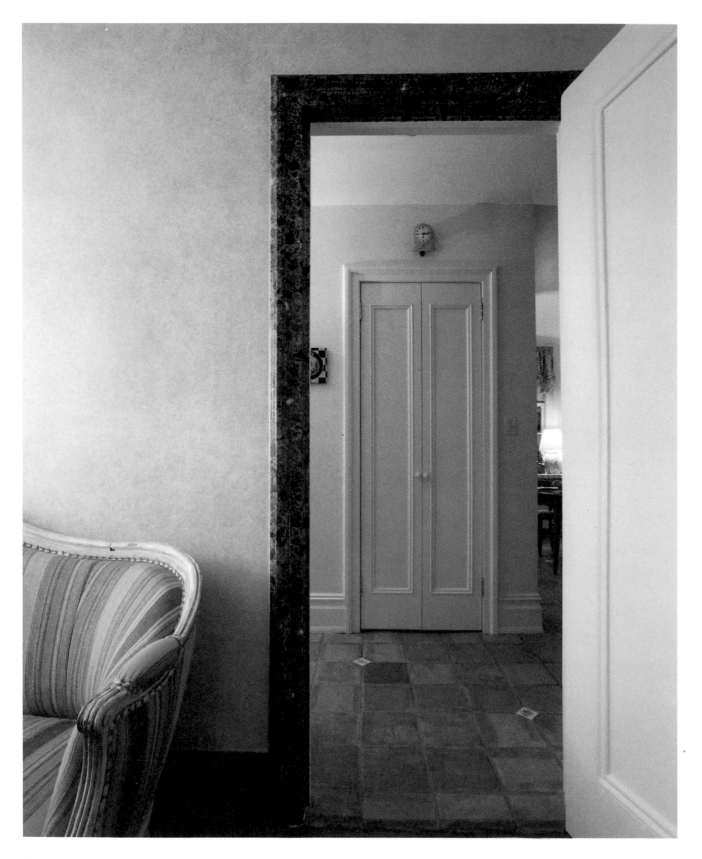

The texture and warm hue of the cloth-distressed walls in this room glow in contrast to the dark green marbleized door trim, giving the room a unique appearance.

• COLOUR TRANSFORMS SPACES •

Colour can work wonders for your interiors in countless ways. Besides imparting your personal stamp and establishing a mood, it can visually alter a room. Answer these questions for each room you plan to paint to determine the kind of "colour therapy" from which it might benefit.

- What size is the room? Remember that painting a room a light colour will make it seem a bit larger; applying a dark hue will give it a cosy feel. A light colour will make a ceiling appear higher; a dark colour will make it seem lower.

- What will the room's focus be—walls, woodwork, furnishings? Varying the value and intensity of colours—that is, combining light or vivid hues with dark or dull ones—lets you place the emphasis where you want it. To make your dark wood furniture stand out, paint other surfaces in pale hues. To stress the architectural quality of a space, use contrasting colours on walls and mouldings.

- Are there elements you want to camouflage? Using the same hue throughout a space will make any awkward angles less evident. Painting a radiator and wall the same shade will help the radiator melt into the background.

- What is the room used for and how often is it used? How much furniture does it contain? A hallway, for example, could take a stimulating colour scheme, since you just pass through it.

But a family room, which is occupied extensively, handles numerous activities at once, and features an array of accoutrements, might demand a neutral scheme.

- What are the colour preferences of those who use the room most? For happiest results, take time to review your choices with those who share the room, and make use of their suggestions.

- Which direction does the room face? Keep in mind that a room receiving colder north or east light might be best served by bright colours.

- How much natural and artificial light does the room get? Prepare paint samples of your colours, and see how they look in the lighting conditions most common to the room. Examine how they look at different times of day. Consider such elements as whether the curtains are usually open or closed and what the view outside the window is like. Sliding glass doors framing a verdant landscape might make your green scheme pale in comparison.

- Will spaces adjacent to the room also display painted finishes? If you can see one room from the other, you might link their colour schemes by employing a common hue—the main colour in one room could be an accent in the next. Also be sure that the textures of the finishes don't clash—an exuberant sponging meeting a brash combing could be unnerving.

CHAPTER TWO

•

PAINTS AND TOOLS

PAINTS
•
•

For centuries, paint making was the province of the artist. Because of the difficulty and expense involved in producing large quantities of paint, decorative effects were long limited to homes of the rich. Only they could afford to employ skilled craftsmen, who prepared paint for each commission in their workshops. Often, these craftsmen had numerous apprentices who spent their days grinding and mixing materials into paint.

Today, thanks to the highly technical paint-manufacturing industry, a vast array of products for diverse jobs is available to all. For decorative painting, you can use either water- or oil-based paints. Both these paints, as well as most others, include:

- pigment: powder ground from natural or synthetic material that gives paint its colour

- binder: vehicle that carries and fixes the pigment and dries to a protective film (linseed oil for oil paint, acrylic resin for emulsion paint)

- diluent: solvents or thinners that dilute paint to workable consistency (white spirit for oil, water for emulsion and acrylics)

For a strong, durable finish, don't mix the two paint types in one project. If, for example, you choose oil-based paints, you should follow an "oil system" for your whole project—primer, base coat, glaze, and solvent for thinning paints and cleaning up. Water-based glaze doesn't "take" well over an oil base—it tends to bead.

An exception to these systems is that you can often top water-based paints with oil because the water-based paints dry quickly and fully, creating a surface that won't repel oil. If your walls already have a good nonporous emulsion base in an appropriate colour (paint must be silk finish to be nonporous), you don't have to re-cover them with an oil base coat before applying an oil glaze. (For more on the compatibility of primers and base coats, see Preparing to Paint, Chapter Three.)

Which paint system should you select? That depends on such factors as the finish you want (see charts accompanying the technique in Part II for recommendations) and your surface (see Preparing to Paint, Chapter Three). In addition, you should review the advantages and disadvantages:

Oils are the traditional medium for decorative painting. Some techniques, such as marbling and wood graining, are particularly suited to them. For beginners, oils are easier because they offer a longer drying time, which gives you more time to work and to correct any mistakes. On the other hand, this longer drying time means you must wait before recoating a surface. In addition, oils give off fumes and make cleaning up a chore. And care must be taken because oils are flammable.

Water-based paints are virtually odourless and need only water for thinning and cleanup instead of the white spirit or turpentine that oils require. They dry faster, which is a plus when you are applying several layers of paint—you wait less time between coats.

The main disadvantage of water-based paints is that they dry quickly and thus demand more skill. It is possible to slow the drying time, however; see the suggestions under "Drying Times" later in this chapter. Still, you must consider that water-based paints may put advanced techniques (and even less challenging ones you want to apply to a large surface) out of your reach. Note also that though they are easily cleaned with water when wet, emulsion and acrylic paints are permanent and water resistant once they have dried. Drips and splashes are hard to wipe up. Remove them by rubbing lightly with methylated spirit.

Once you have chosen your paint system, the following sections will guide you in selecting paints you'll need. (For information on which colours to choose, see Mixing Paints, Chapter Four.)

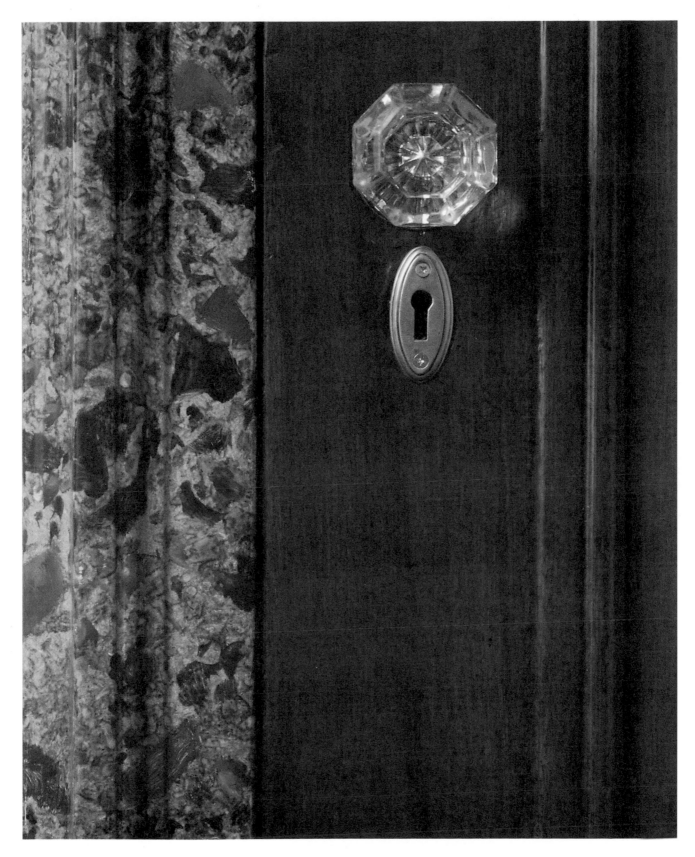

The longer drying time of oil-based paints makes them ideal for marbling and wood graining, but these techniques can also be executed in water-based paints.

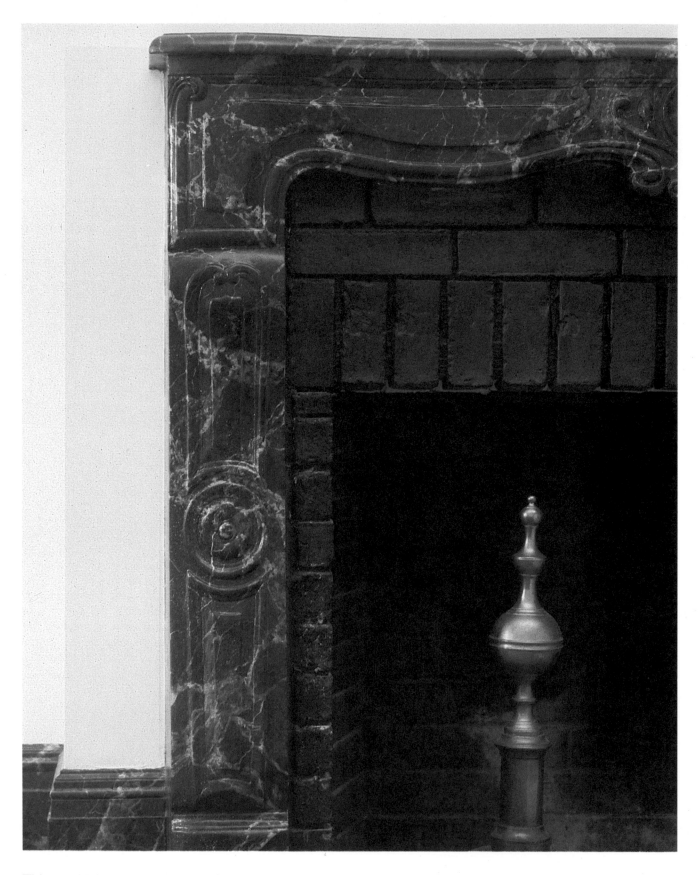

This marbleized fireplace was executed using a combination of water- and oil-based paint systems.

• WATER SYSTEM •

BASE COAT. Use emulsion paint as your base coat. Emulsion comes in two finishes, one dull, one shiny: vinyl matt and vinyl silk. Silk is recommended because it is less absorbent than a matt finish. This is especially important for "subtractive" finishes such as ragging off, in which you first apply a glaze and then remove it.

Tint your base coats with artist's acrylics, available in tubes and jars at art shops. Tubes are easier to control when adding paint; you can squeeze out a few drops at a time. 225 ml tubes are usually economical. For large jobs, however, or if you must make a big change in colour, liquid universal stainers are more cost effective. A tool of professionals, stainers are concentrated and thus less expensive to use for, say, several rooms or many large projects. But note that their colour range is not as extensive as that of acrylics, and because they contain no dryer, they should not constitute more than 5–10 percent of your paint.

GLAZE. Water-based glaze is part water, part colour—in the form of artist's acrylics—and part acrylic medium, a transparent gel-like substance. Sold in art stores and craft shops, acrylic medium comes in matt, and gloss finishes. Which finish you choose depends on the look you desire.

About 60 to 80 percent of your glaze will be water. The amount of water will determine the sheen of your finish. The more water you add, the flatter the finish will be. Adding more water also makes the glaze thinner and weaker and thus more easily scratched.

Although artist's acrylics are the most satisfactory colouring agent, you can also colour glazes with universal tints. Tempera paint can be used as well; it dries flat and opaque but is less permanent than acrylics.

For thinning water-based paints and for cleaning brushes, use water. Directions for mixing a glaze appear in Mixing Paints, Chapter Four. Glaze recipes for each technique are on the charts in Part II.

BASE COAT. Today's oil-based interior house paints are alkyd paints, which are composed of a mix of oil and resin that dries faster and contains no lead. Oil-based paint comes in flat, eggshell, satin, and gloss finishes. Satin is most often recommended as a base coat for decorative painting. Oil-based is best thinned with paint thinner.

To tint your base coat, use artist's oils, or universal tints. Artist's oils, sold in tubes, are found in craft shops and art stores.

GLAZE. Available in some paint and art stores (see source list), transparent oil glaze (also known as scumble glaze) comes ready-mixed in cans. Although it can be used straight from its container, it is best thinned with white spirit. Do not add more

than 10 percent spirit however, or the glaze will run. When glaze gets old, a skin forms on top of it. Remove the skin by straining the glaze through cheesecloth or a disposable sieve.

If you can't find ready-mixed oil glaze, you can make your own with ingredients found in most art supply stores. The resulting glaze, however, will take longer to dry and will have a stronger smell. To make a glaze, mix 3 parts pure turpentine to 1 part boiled linseed oil and add a few drops of terebine liquid dryer. (Linseed oil comes either raw or boiled; boiled is thicker and dries faster.)

You can colour oil glaze with universal stainers (see Water-Based Glaze, above), or artist's oils. Directions for mixing a glaze are in Mixing Paints, Chapter Four. Recipes for glazes appear on the charts for each technique in Part II.

• METALLIC PAINT •

Gilding is a favorite decorative technique that takes years to master. Often seen on ornaments and picture frames, it requires costly materials such as gold leaf. (Copper leaf is more affordable but still challenging to apply.) There are books that explain the gilding process, but training and experience are a must for professional results.

Your best alternative is gold paint. There are several kinds, none of which actually contain gold. Always apply these paints over an ochre-colored base coat for best effect.

One kind of gold paint is composed of bronze powdered pigment in a lacquer-based medium. Bronze powder is just one of many metallic powders available, including silver and copper. You can buy the powder and blend the paint yourself or buy the paint ready-mixed. The more powder there is in the paint, the more opaque the paint.

Because gold paint is lacquer-based, it dries rapidly, which makes it hard to apply smoothly. On small surfaces, use a long-haired brush; clean the brush with lacquer thinner. A disposable roller is best for large surfaces. The paint gives off fumes, so wear a mask. Note, too, that gold paint sometimes rubs off.

Another option combines oil-based liquid bronzing varnish with bronze pigment. This paint dries more slowly but still shows brush and roller marks.

A third choice is gold acrylic paint. This is considered the most durable and easiest to apply, but it doesn't cover well—it may need four or five coats to create a metallic shine.

• VARNISH •

Varnish is a final transparent layer that protects your decorative finish and makes it last longer. It also determines the sheen of your finish.

Varnishing is optional—some finishes may be sturdy enough without it. (See the charts for each technique in Part II for recommendations.) Sponging needs varnishing only in high-traffic areas like stairways or children's rooms. Finishes such as marbling and wood graining always need varnish—it gives them protection, depth, and an even sheen. In general, you should varnish all areas that get hard use—skirtings, chair rails, tabletops, doors, floors—no matter which technique.

A drawback of varnish, however, is that it usually yellows over time, especially in a room that gets no sunlight. Some finishes may have colours too delicate to be varnished. You'll have to weigh the advantages and disadvantages.

To prevent finishes from cracking, you should apply varnish only to surfaces that have fully dried. You can roll it on or paint it with special varnishing brushes made to hold large quantities of varnish. Keep these brushes just for varnishing. They are very difficult to clean, and if you leave even a bit of paint in their bristles, you might get a smear of colour on your surface the next time you use the brushes for varnishing. In addition, they hold too much paint for most regular jobs.

Like paint, varnish is best applied in several thin coats. For good protection, do three coats. Thin the first by about 20 percent and the second by about 10 percent. Rub down lightly after the second with 600- or 800-grade wet or dry paper. Then apply the final coat full strength. Unfortunately, the more coats you apply, the more yellowing will occur; for some projects you'll have to balance protection and appearance.

There are many kinds of varnishes. They come in both oil and water base. Some are available in a full range of finishes—matt, eggshell, satin, semi-gloss, gloss, and high-gloss.

Which finish you settle on will strongly affect your project because the sheen of its top layer will dictate the look. For example, if you apply flat glaze, perhaps to hide the condition of a less than perfect wall, and then top it with a gloss varnish, your surface will be shiny—which will underscore every defect in the wall's surface.

The varnishes used most frequently for interior work are listed below. Some kinds, and even some brands within each kind, yellow much less than others and thus would be a choice for subtly hued work. Ask your paint dealer for recommendations. Drying times and amount of varnish vary; read manufacturers' labels for specifics.

OIL VARNISH. This varnish can be used over oil- or water-based paints as long as the finish is fully cured—that is, completely dry. Thin oil varnish with white spirit. It dries to the touch in about three hours and dries completely in twelve to twenty-four hours. The higher its gloss, the more oil it contains and the slower it dries. Oil varnish, especially marine varnish, yellows; avoid using it over light colours.

POLYURETHANE. This is good over all oil- and water-based paints except artist's oils. It is especially good over freehand painting, which might peel if left unprotected. Thin polyurethane with paint thinner. Polyurethane yellows less than some varnishes, but it is not the best choice for use over pale shades. Wait at least twelve hours between coats.

ACRYLIC VARNISH. This varnish is compatible only with water-based paints. It is acrylic medium (used for water-based glazes) thinned with water. It dries fast and is best rolled on so that it doesn't leave marks. It yellows only slightly.

WATER POLYURETHANE. Stronger than acrylic varnish, water polyurethane takes longer to dry and should be rolled on. Thin it with water, if necessary. Yellowing is minimal.

WHITE REFINED BEESWAX. Rub beeswax on the surface with a cotton or linen cloth. Let it set; then buff it with a clean cloth. This clear finish does not turn yellow. In addition, if it gets dirty, you can remove it without disturbing the paint below. It does however, need to be re-applied often, as needed.

• HOW MUCH PAINT? •

Always buy and mix more than enough paint for base coats and glazes. Don't skimp here. Running out in the middle of a wall will probably mean redoing the whole thing; the change in color with a new batch may be noticeable, and a dark line will show where you left off. Besides, you'll need extra paint for touch-ups. And you may want to include the same paint colors in other rooms at a later date to create a coordinated look for your home.

First determine the square footage of your project. Then, to estimate the amount of paint you will need for your two base coats, read the label on the paint can to see how many square feet a can covers. Generally, a gallon of paint will cover about 300 square feet when applied with a roller or brush; a quart of paint covers about 75 square feet. To be safe, however, subtract about 20 percent from the estimate given on the can.

For the glaze, figure on about half the amount of paint you used for the base coat. (If you're having a house painter apply the base coats, ask him or her how much paint was used.) The glaze is usually a single coat and requires a thinner application, so you should have some left over for touch-ups.

· DRYING TIMES ·

Take drying times seriously—the success of your project will depend on the dryness of the surface. This is especially true for oil paints, but even emulsion paints don't dry immediately. Follow recommendations on paint cans.

Keep in mind that there are two kinds of dry: dry to the touch and dry to the core, or cured. Paint dries from the top down; even if it feels dry on the surface it might still be wet underneath. One layer must be cured before you add another. If a layer hasn't cured and you recoat it, the second layer might bubble, peel, or crack. Or, especially when actively distressing a glaze, as in rag-rolling, you might break through the base coat beneath, destroying your finish.

Estimating drying times is difficult because many factors come into play. Paint dries by oxidation: When combined with air and light, it is transformed from a liquid to a solid. So the amount of light and the type of weather are important; paint won't dry as fast in the dark or in a humid atmosphere. The sheen of the paint also counts: Matt paint dries quicker than satin or silk. How absorbent your surface is and how thickly you apply paint also matter. If acrylic paint is thinned with water, it dries faster; if oil-based paint is coloured with artist's oils, it dries more slowly.

Here are some averages to give you an idea how much time to set aside for your projects. An oil-based under coat dries to the touch in three to four hours but is best left overnight before recoating—and even then it is not fully cured. An emulsion base coat, depending on its sheen, takes about twenty minutes to dry to the touch and about two hours to be fully cured.

For some techniques, you may want to slow drying time so that you will have longer to work. For other techniques, you may want to speed it so that you can recoat a surface sooner. To speed drying of either oil- or water-based paint, use a fan in the room. For a sample or other small surface, use a blow dryer.

To slow drying of an oil base coat or glaze, add a little linseed oil, but note that the more oil you add, the glossier the finish will be. To speed drying, add terebine liquid dryer—but not more than 5 percent or the paint might crack.

With water-based glaze, slowing drying time is a challenge. A good technique is to wet down the walls with a sponge before you start painting. Working on a humid day or turning on a humidifier will make the glaze stay wet longer, as will blocking out direct sunlight. You can also add a bit more water to the glaze, but be careful that the glaze doesn't run. And you might try adding an acrylic gel retarder (available in art stores), but it should equal less than 10 percent of the total glaze solution or it will weaken the paint.

· STORING PAINT ·

Seal leftover paint in containers and label them well. Don't store paints in direct sunlight or next to a boiler, heater or stove. All paints will dry up in those conditions, and oil paints might explode.

When you're done painting for the day, pour dirty paint thinner into an empty paint can containing a little water, and put a lid on it. When you complete your project, discard the sealed can. Check with your local council to see if they offer disposal facilities for solvents. Don't throw it down the sink; it can clog the drain.

· CLEANING TIPS ·

When you are using water-based paints, keep a bucket of clean water, a sponge, and some rags beside you, and wipe up as you go. If paint gets on carpeting, upholstery, or clothes, try to pick it up with an almost-dry sponge. Dab it, don't rub it.

For drips on moulding or other surfaces that have dried for a day or two, rub lightly with methylated spirit so that you don't remove the paint underneath. For dry paint on fabric, try stain remover.

When using oil-based paints, keep a small container of white spirit and some soft, clean rags handy. If drips are still wet, just wipe them up with a dry rag. If they are a day or two old, use a soft rag dipped in spirit. Stubborn drips may require a coarser rag or, as a last resort, a cotton swab dipped in acetone. Acetone is very strong and could remove paint beneath. Wipe over it with paint thinner to stop its action.

On clothing, use a rag barely dampened with thinner. Dab the paint, turning the rag as you go so that you don't put paint back on the fabric. Don't rub the spot until you've almost removed the stain.

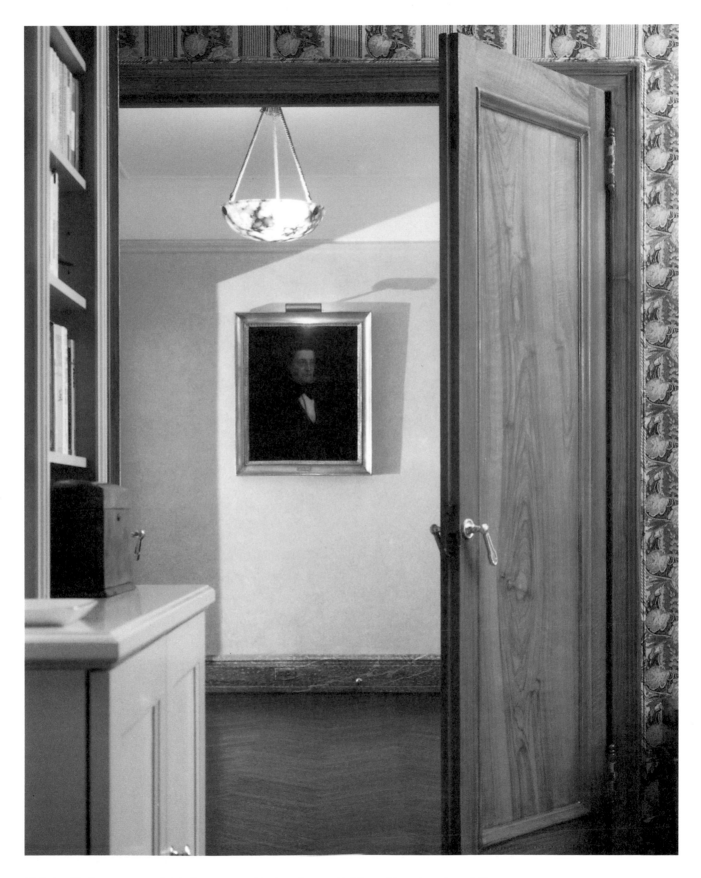

Paint will dry more quickly in a room that gets sunlight and has low humidity.

• SAFETY MEASURES •

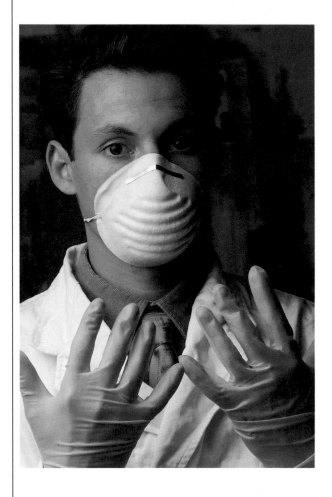

- Make sure the work area is well ventilated.

- When opening a can of paint, wear goggles to prevent paint from splashing into your eyes.

- When working with oil- or alcohol-based paints, wear a mask to guard against fumes.

- Wear rubber gloves to protect your hands from solvents; surgical gloves are recommended.

- Keep a bucket of water and perhaps a fire extinguisher nearby when using turpentine, shellac, and other flammable substances.

- Don't throw wet rags soaked in oil and thinner in the garbage. Spread them out to dry outside or in a well-ventilated room.

Protect your hands from solvents and wear a mask to guard against particles and mild fumes.

A chef might have a favorite saucepan: a decorative painter will have a favorite brush. The tools for painting finishes—especially those that help you achieve wonderful results—are easy to fall in love with.

Invest in good quality tools and care for them. In this section, you'll learn which tools to buy and how to make your own substitutes for costly or hard-to-locate tools. In addition, you'll find instructions on cleaning and storing your equipment for longer life. (For a look at the major tools and equipment, see the photos at the end of this chapter.)

Today, because painted finishes are more popular than ever, the tools that produce them are easier to obtain. You'll see even some of the more unusual tools in paint stores, home centres, art shops, and craft stores. Or you can order tools by mail (see source list).

Decorative-painting tools fall into three categories: preparation tools, basic tools, and speciality tools. Most speciality tools will be introduced in the chapter covering the technique to which they apply. Stencilling tools, for instance, are discussed in Chapter Eleven.

Preparation tools for painting a room include:

- dust sheets or plastic sheeting to cover furniture and newspaper to protect floors

- a three-step ladder, lightweight and in good condition, and a scaffold for large projects and ceilings

- soft absorbent cotton rags for cleaning up

TOOLS

- wet or dry paper (in several grades) and a sanding block

- 'tacky cloth,' chamois leather, or artist's dusting brush

- vacuum cleaner or broom and dustpan

- flexible filling knife and fine grade filler compound

- steel ruler, metal straightedge, T-square, chalkline, pencils, craft knife, and masking tape for measuring and laying out designs

- paint roller and roller cover for priming and painting base coats over large areas

Note that the pile of the roller cover must be suited for the job: For example, short pile is for smooth surfaces. Medium pile works for most surfaces, but check with your local paint store.

The purpose of both the basic and the specialty tools is to "distress" the paint, forming patterns in either of two ways—by applying glaze to the base coat, using additive methods such as sponging on (Chapter Five) or by removing glaze while it is still wet, using subtractive methods such as sponging off (Chapter Five). Tools for distressing include brushes, sponges, rags, and combs.

For mixing and painting, you will need clean rags, a paint roller for large surfaces, plastic containers with lids for storing paints, paper cups for mixing paint samples, paint stirrer (many professionals use old long-handled round brushes for this purpose), several one-gallon plastic buckets for water, and a roller tray to hold paint as you work.

· BRUSHES ·

Most of your painting tools will be brushes. As with all painting tools, you need the right type, size and quality for each job. This is especially important in decorative painting—sometimes the brush determines the success of the technique.

Good-quality brushes are hand-crafted from various materials. Natural-hair brushes, from least to most expensive, are made from pig, ox, squirrel, horse, or sable hair.

In some cases, an expensive brush might be worth the investment. A stippling brush, for example, can cost around £50, but no other tool gives as soft and subtle an effect.

Another expensive implement is a badger softener, which costs about £30–£45. Its long, soft bristles allow you to smooth a glaze. You can substitute a more affordable brush for the badger, however. Choose a brush with very soft and long white bristles (it will cost around £10) and work with a light touch.

Gear the size of your brush to the job. To speed priming and base-coating of large, flat areas, get the widest brush possible (but not one that overlaps the surface), making sure you are comfortable with it. Or use a roller.

Brushes come in several shapes. For priming and base coating large surfaces, you'll want a straightedged brush; for trim, use a chisel-edged brush. To smooth a glaze just after it has been applied, many professionals use an oval sash.

Look for quality when choosing brushes. A good brush is thick and has bristles of various lengths, which allows it to hold more paint. The bristles should also be springy, not stiff.

· CLEANING BRUSHES ·

Take care of your brushes at the end of each day of painting. How you clean them depends on whether you used oil- or water-based paint.

OIL-BASED PAINT. Into two containers, pour enough white spirit or brush cleaner to cover the bristles of the brush you are cleaning. Wearing rubber gloves, dip the brush into the first container, stir it around; then with your fingers work the paint out of the bristles and squeeze out the spirit. Rinse the brush in the second container of spirit and work out any remaining paint. If the bristles are still clogged with paint, rub them a few times against a wire brush. Then hold the paintbrush inside a bucket while you twirl its han-

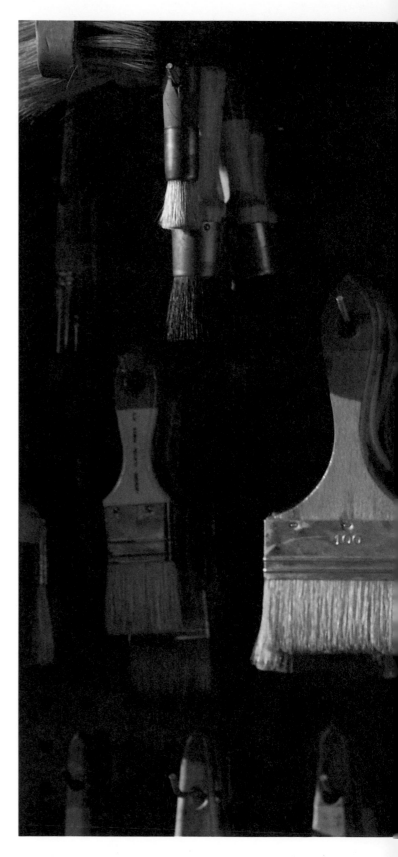

Take care of your brushes; after cleaning, let brushes dry hanging from a hook.

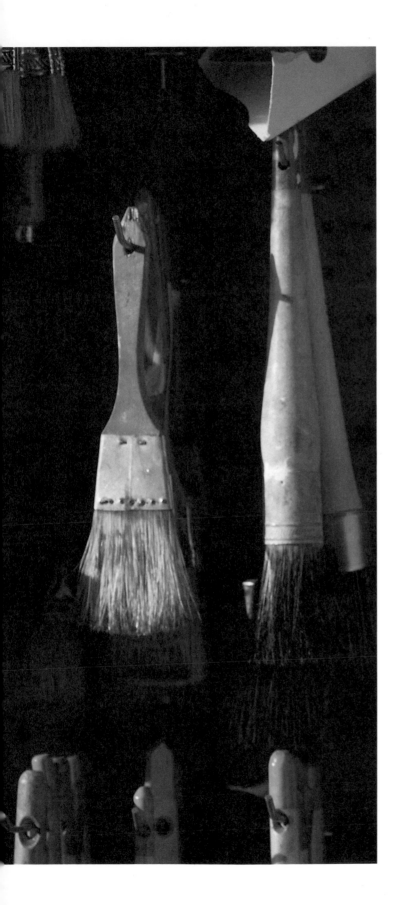

dle between your palms to get out rest of thinner. If you don't plan to use the brush again soon, wash it with soap and rinse it well with water.

Repeat the process with the next brush; for economy, when the second container of thinner gets dirty, use it as your first container and pour fresh thinner into the second container.

WATER-BASED PAINT. Rinse the brush under running water, soap it up, and work the paint out, working from the heel (the part nearest the handle) to the tips of the bristles. Don't bend the bristles or work against their natural direction. Then rinse soap from the brush and press the water out of the bristles.

Soft badger-hair brushes need special care. When washing, don't get them too wet: Hold their bristles and just wash the tips to prevent bristles from falling out. You may need to dip the tips in alcohol if they become caked with acrylic binder.

• DRYING BRUSHES •

Never leave any brush with its bristles resting in a bucket or container; this will ruin the bristles. Instead, if the brush has a hole in its handle, let it dry hanging from a hook.

If, occasionally, you don't have time to clean your brushes at the end of a day, you can put them in a container of paint thinner or water, depending on the kind of paint with which they were used. Tape the brushes to the side of the container so that their bristles don't touch the bottom.

There is one kind of brush that doesn't need to be cleaned all the time: a varnishing brush. Used specifically for oil varnishing, this thick-haired oval brush is especially hard to clean; it requires several washes with thinner. Because it is expensive, you don't want to take the chance of damaging it in the process, so only clean it when you won't be using it for a long time. In the meantime, suspend it in thinner: Pour thinner into a large jar, make a hole in the lid of the jar for the handle of the brush, and tape the handle in place so that the bristles don't touch the bottom of the jar when the lid is on. Replenish the thinner periodically.

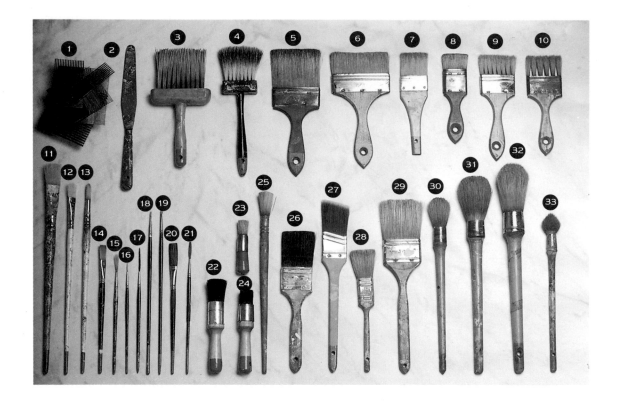

This photo displays the wide array of tools used in decorative painting:

1. set of steel combs for dragging or wood graining

2. palette knife for mixing artist's acrylics or oils

3. dragging brush, or flogger, used in dragging and graining techniques

4. badger softener of medium size for smoothing oil glaze

5. long-haired spalter (size 80) for smoothing oil glaze

6. short-haired spalter (size 100) wide enough for applying oil glaze and for smoothing it after it is applied

7, 8. mottlers, used in wood graining to smooth areas of oil glaze

9, 10. pencil draggers, specialty oil-paint brushes employed in wood graining

11, 12. fitches for marbling, touch-ups, and freehand painting in acrylics

13. fitch for touch-ups and thicker veining in marbling techniques with acrylics

14. flat long-haired brush for marbling and fine detail in acrylics

15. long-haired brush for marbling with acrylics

16. small pointed brush for fine veining when marbling with acrylics

17. long-haired ox-hair brush for marbling, wood graining, and freehand script and ornamentation (makes lines of varying thickness); best with oils

18, 19. flat white-bristle brushes for marbling, wood graining, and corner touch-ups with oil- or water-based paints

20. flat long-haired badger lettering brush, for marbling or freehand painting in oils

21. ox-hair sign painter's brush with long hair cut flat at end for marbling or freehand painting (makes clean edges) in oils or acrylics

22, 23, 24. stencil brushes—two with black bristles, one with white (slightly softer)—for stencilling in oil or acrylic

25. round thick brush for spattering

26. flat brush for painting emulsion base coat and acrylic glaze

27. angled brush—with white tip indicating a better-quality brush "preused" in factory so it will leave fewer marks—for emulsion painting or cutting in lines

28. small flat long-haired white-bristle brush for oil paints

29. flat 2½-inch white-bristle brush for oil base coating

30, 31, 32. domed sash brushes for oil glazing

33. well-worn round brush for stirring paints

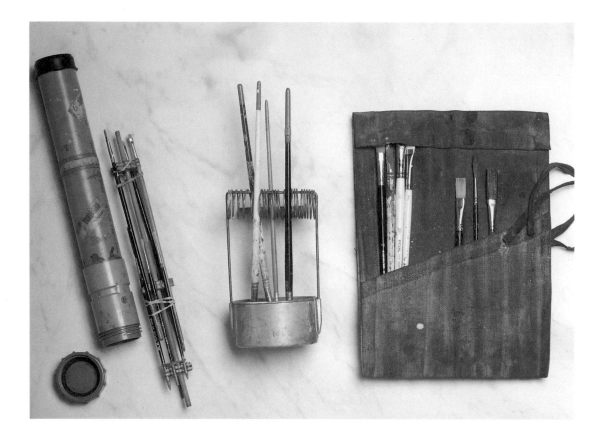

Keeping brushes in good condition means cleaning and storing them properly. You can find many items for safeguarding brushes in paint or art stores, or you can make these items yourself. The homemade case, at right, provides compartments for several brushes. It can be made of sturdy fabric such as hessian or denim. Slipped into one end is a wooden stick; at the other are fabric ties. Roll the case up from the stick end and secure it with the ties. You can buy the brush holder, at centre, in paint and art stores. It keeps brushes upright so that paint drips off, and it prevents the bristles from being damaged by resting on the bottom of the container. You can get the PVC tube and fittings that close its ends, at left, in plumbing-supply stores and then create the inside piece (shown beside tube) to hold your brushes. The piece is composed of a thin wooden dowel and three wooden circles notched around their edges; the brushes rest in the notches. Fit the dowel into the centre hole in each circle; place circles at the top, middle, and bottom of the dowel. Rest the brushes against the notches, secure them with rubber bands, and insert the device in the tube.

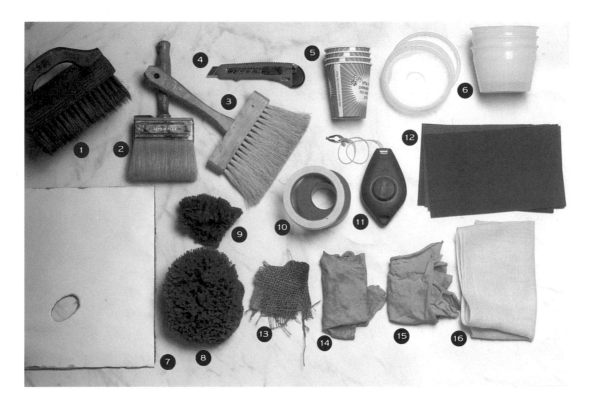

Additional tools you will need:

1. large stippling brush for walls and other surfaces

2. block brush, less costly alternative to stippling brush

3. dusting brush for dusting surfaces

4. craft knife for cutting stencils

5. paper cups in which to mix paints for samples

6. containers with lids for storing paints

7. disposable palette on which to mix artist's oils or acrylics

8. large sea sponge for sponging techniques

9. cut piece of sea sponge for marbling techniques and for dabbing excess paint from corners of rooms

10. low tack tape and masking tape to cover edges of areas not to be painted

11. snap line to aid in laying out straight guidelines for borders, paneling, stonework, and fade-aways

12. wet or dry paper, available in many grades from coarse to fine, for use in preparation and varnishing of surfaces.

13. hessian for cloth-distressing techniques

14. chamois-leather

15. cotton rag for cloth-distressing techniques and cleanup

16. cheesecloth for removing glaze in cheeseclothing technique

CHAPTER THREE

·

PREPARING TO PAINT

PREPARATION WORK IS NO MINOR PART OF YOUR DECORATIVE-PAINT-ing project. About 25 percent of the time set aside for the project should be spent on this vital stage. And with good reason: In decorative painting, each step builds on the previous step to create the final effect. Preparation work is your base. So, for pleasing results, be as clean and neat in this early stage as possible. Poor preparation can result in major problems. Besides marring the appearance of your finish, it might even cause the finish to peel soon after completion.

How much prep time you'll need will depend on the size and nature of your project. Readying an entire room, for instance, takes several days. Some tasks, like scraping and sanding, are painstaking. Others, such as skim-coating (explained later in this chapter) demand advanced skills. So, depending on your budget, the time you have, and how handy you are, you may want to do what many professional decorative painters do: Hire an interior house painter to complete this crucial stage. This is particularly recommended if the surfaces you want to paint are in rather poor condition.

In making your decision, keep in mind that the time it takes you to do the prep work yourself might not be worth the money you save. Your local painter does jobs like wallpaper stripping regularly and has both the skills and the equipment required. What he or she can do in a few days might take an inexperienced do-it-yourselfer more than a week. Consider whether your time might be better spent on the decorative painting itself.

But even if you hire a professional, you can still use the information in this chapter to determine what must be done, how long it will take, and how to communicate your needs to the painter. You can diagnose the condition of your surfaces, develop an effective treatment, and then compare it to the painter's estimate to ensure you get the quality preparation your project demands. Give weight, however, to your painter's advice. In preparation, practice counts more than theory. Each job is different, and sometimes past experience is the best guide.

Several factors will influence the type of preparation you will choose:

- the surface on which you'll work (new or old, painted or unpainted, porous or nonporous)

- the paint you'll use (oil- or water-based)

- the decorative finish you've selected (one that hides imperfections, like ragging, or one that requires a supersmooth surface, like marbling).

Preparation generally involves several steps—cleaning, filling, skim-coating, sanding, priming, and base-coating. Depending on your surface and intended finish, you may skip some steps or touch on them only slightly. New walls, for instance, require no cleaning except a light dusting and little or no filling.

In addition, the order in which you perform several of the steps—priming, sanding, filling, and skim-coating—varies for different surfaces. For example, unpainted wood, unpainted brickwork, and unpainted plaster must be primed before sanding to seal them and keep them from getting scratched. But painted wood, painted brickwork,

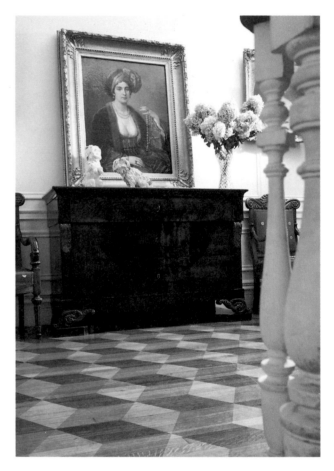

Floors require lots of preparation: stripping, sanding, and "screening" before painting or staining.

and painted plaster must first be filled and then sanded to roughen the old paint so that primer will adhere to it. Refer to the chart at the end of this chapter for the order in which to perform preparation steps for various surfaces. The following sections explain the preparation steps.

• STRIPPING FURNITURE AND WOODWORK •

For painted furniture and woodwork in good condition, you can skip stripping and start with sanding (see next section). For pieces in poor condition, however, you must often remove varnish and paint before you can create a surface suitable for decorative painting. You then prime, fill, and sand it as you would raw wood.

Before you strip a piece of furniture, make sure it is structurally sound. Move it from side to side, lean on it, check its legs and drawers, and repair it if necessary. And be certain the piece fits comfortably somewhere inside your house.

There are several ways to strip wood: You can have it done professionally, perhaps by the dipping process in which removable pieces are placed in a tank of chemical stripper; you can do it yourself with a scraper and one of the many chemical strippers available at DIY centres and paint stores today; or you can use a scraper and a hot-air gun.

Although a hot-air gun can be time-saving, you must practice the technique to avoid scorching surfaces. Be sure to check home-repair guides for instructions and safety measures.

When using a chemical stripper, read the manufacturer's instructions carefully before opening the can. Many strippers contain strong solvents, so heed all safety precautions: work in a well-ventilated area; wear goggles to protect your eyes from flying paint chips and splashing solvent; wear a mask to guard against toxic fumes; and wear chemical-grade rubber gloves, *not* surgical gloves (strippers will dissolve them) to protect your hands from chemicals.

Strippers soften paint and varnish so that they can be scraped off easily. Liquid gel stripper, which comes in cans, is particularly effective. Dip an old brush into the can and make a stroke about 6 inches long on the surface. Apply another 6-inch stroke beside the first and continue in this manner. Use the widest brush that will fit in the can. Don't paint back and forth with the brush or you'll reduce the effectiveness of the stripper.

See the manufacturer's instructions for the amount of time the stripper takes to work once it has been applied. Test a small patch to see if paint comes off easily. If it does, scrape it all off with a wide filling knife, wiping the knife after each pass. Stubborn finishes may require a second application.

Depending on the piece, you may need scrapers of various sizes. For small carved areas, try clay-modelling tools, old toothbrushes, toothpicks, or a wooden stick sharpened to a flat edge.

When you finish, wash the piece with a sponge and water to remove any remaining solvent. Some strippers today don't require rinsing, but you may want to rinse your surface anyway, as a precaution. Make sure the piece is completely dry before you paint it; wait three days in hot sunny weather, longer under cooler or damp conditions.

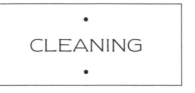

• CLEANING •

Cleaning is vital: It removes dirt from a surface so that the paint can bond to it. Whether your surface is painted or unpainted, new or old, will determine how to clean it. For example, if you have new walls, just dust them, wipe them with a soft cloth, or use the soft-brush attachment of a vacuum cleaner. For older painted walls and other surfaces in fairly good condition—a little peeling, a few small holes—it is a good idea to wash off any grease, smoke, or dust that has accumulated. But because this is a tough and messy job, you may want to limit it to particularly susceptible areas such as kitchen walls and furniture. Often, a good priming (explained later in this chapter) can replace washing.

How strong a cleaner you'll need depends on your goal. In most cases, it won't matter if the base coat rubs off during cleaning because you'll be repainting it later. You can use a strong powdered detergent, but test it on a small spot before applying it to the whole surface. In any case, choose a cleaner that has caustic powder but isn't too foamy, or you'll be rinsing for hours.

Professionals wash walls with a large round brush, but you can also use a large thick sponge, preferably one with a plastic scouring pad on one side. Before you start, cover the floor with plastic. Always wash walls from the bottom up; if you start from the top, dirty water will run down onto the dry wall below and stain it. Then rinse twice with clear water from the top down.

Drying is crucial after the cleaning process. Be safe, not sorry; let surfaces dry for about a day—two days if you're working with plaster or unfinished wood. If you paint before surfaces are completely dry, you'll seal water into them that might later cause the paint to bubble.

• SCRAPING •

Never remove paint from a surface unless it is absolutely necessary; the job is difficult and time-consuming. But for old surfaces in poor condition—peeling, chips, large holes—you'll begin the cleaning process by scraping paint from them instead of washing them.

Hold a stripping knife at a 45 degree angle, or a triangular shavehook (see diagram on right) with blade perpendicular to surface, and drag along the surface. Apply firm pressure and keep scraping until you hit a spot where the paint holds well. Skip this area and move to the next. You can use the same technique—but pressing lightly instead of firmly—to smooth new plaster walls.

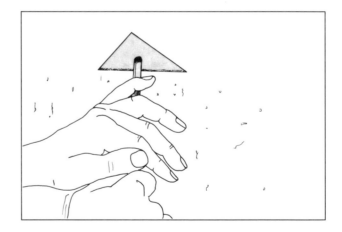

• STRIPPING WALLPAPER •

Even if the quality of the walls underneath is particularly poor, always remove wallpaper rather than paint over it. If you don't it could eventually peel off and ruin your finish. Occasionally, paper can be stripped off dry.

To begin, soak walls thoroughly using a large brush and hot water. This may take several applications. You can add a commercial wallpaper stripper to the water for extra power. Then, with a scraper, strip the paper off, working across rather than down the wall.

To remove several layers of paper, rent a steam stripper. This machine boils water and produces steam that softens wallpaper paste quickly. Starting at the bottom of the wall, soften a strip and then scrape it off with a wide stripping knife.

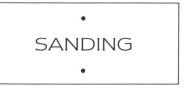

SANDING

Sanding evens surfaces so that they are smooth to the touch. It also helps paint bond with a surface. There are many grades of abrasive papers for a wide range of jobs—00 glass grade paper for sanding floors, 600 grade wet or dry for smoothing varnish, and up to 1200 grade for very fine work. You can check with your local paint or hardware shop to find out what grade paper your surface requires.

To get an even sanding, use a sanding block. You can buy one, usually a wooden or rubber block with a handle. Sometimes it comes on a long pole, which makes big jobs like walls much less tiring. You can also make a sanding block by taping sandpaper to a piece of two-by-four or a child's brick. Electric sanders are available, but they require a very careful touch. They can quickly make a surface uneven and are mainly recommended for small horizontal areas like dresser or tabletops. There are special sanders for floors, too, that you can rent by the day. The firm you rent from will advise you on how to use the sander, what kind of sandpaper to choose, and how much paper you will need per square foot.

Sand in a circular motion. How much to sand depends on the condition of your surfaces, the decorative finish you choose, and the sheen of the paint you'll use.

If your walls exhibit the orange-peel effect—many layers of paint rolled on in the same direction instead of crisscrossed and without sanding between layers—it will be nearly impossible to make them smooth. Instead, sand surfaces to a dull finish so that they will offer a good bond with paint, and pick a textured finish such as sponging, ragging, or spattering. In addition, select a paint with a flat finish: A glossy surface will reveal all imperfections, especially in a brightly lit room.

Wood trim is often painted in a glossy finish. This must be sanded before a new coat of paint can adhere to it. Fold sandpaper in half to get into hard-to-reach corners.

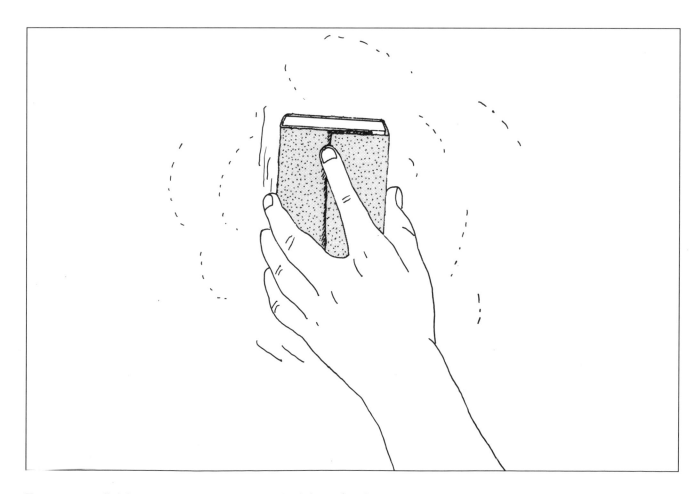

For an even finish, work with a sanding block in a circular motion.

PRIMING

Primer seals surfaces from dirt, fungus, and humidity. It saturates them with paint so that they can take on colours. And it makes them nonporous so you'll need fewer coats of paint to get the colour you want.

There is a primer for almost every surface, from laminate to glass to brick. Some primers are fire retardant. Others, designed for exterior work, help combat the effects of adverse weather. There are metal primers that prevent rust and help paint adhere to shiny surfaces. (See the chart at the end of this chapter for recommended primers for various surfaces.) If you want to apply decorative painting to an unusual surface, ask your home centre or paint shop which primer to use.

Primer comes in three types: water, oil, or alcohol base. This makes priming a good stage at which to decide the particular paint system—water or oil—to work with (see Paints and Tools, Chapter Two). Your choice depends very much on the decorative-painting technique you select. Turn to the technique in Part II that you want to execute, and see whether its chart recommends oil- or water-based paints.

If you haven't picked a technique yet but must continue prep work now, remember that you can put both oil- and water-based paints over alcohol- or water-based primers but only oil paints over oil primer. So play it safe and start with either a water- or an alcohol-based primer. Also make sure your surface is compatible with these primers—consult the chart at the end of this chapter.

Primer is usually white, which is fine in most cases. In general, the lighter your undercoats, the nicer your finish. Pale undercoats bring more light into a colour and make it richer, while dark undercoats can dull it. The Renaissance masters knew this well; they used light washes of colour over white to give their paintings a glow.

But if you're planning a dark base coat, you may want to darken your primer with artist's oils or acrylics, depending on the type of primer—oils for oil, acrylics for water-based—to make coverage easier. For instance, red paints don't always cover well; by tinting your primer light pink, you are closer to the colour you desire for a base coat and may even need one less layer of base coat to achieve it. You can also have your primer tinted at a paint store.

Most primers come in both interior and exterior grade. In almost all cases, you'll want interior grade (refer to the chart at the end of this chapter to see if your surface is an exception).

One primer—shellac—comes only in interior grade. It is alcohol-based and available in two colours: white, which dries transparent; and blond, which has an orange tint.

It is one of the best primers to use in decorative painting because it dries to the touch in about fifteen minutes and can be recoated in about a half-hour. Check the label of the product you buy for precise drying times. Because it dries so fast, however, you may have difficulty smoothing out brush or roller marks when you apply it. Also, it can't easily be sanded down. So put it on with a very fine roller and do not go back over it. Small disposable rollers are best because shellac is hard to clean. If you must clean tools or wipe up spills, use methylated spirits. Wear a mask when working with shellac so that you don't inhale its fumes.

Shellac is particularly good for sealing plaster. It dries quickly, cutting down on lost time between coats. If, for instance, you used an oil-based primer, you'd have to wait up to twelve hours between coats and apply three or four coats, because the plaster would absorb so much primer. But with shellac, you'd need only two coats.

Shellac is also one of the best sealers for unpainted wood and is excellent for sealing knots. This is an important step because it prevents resin from seeping through; paint won't take over resin. Apply shellac directly to knots with a disposable brush. You can buy other knot-sealing products at your local home centre or paint store.

Use shellac on furniture when you don't know what kind of wood it is. Tropical woods, for instance, have an oily resin that might repel paint; shellacking the entire piece will prevent this.

Shellac can also be used as a varnish, the final protective coat. But applying shellac as a varnish is an art in itself—one best left to professionals.

A word about metal primers: There are rusting and nonrusting metals, and each has its own primer. For example, iron, which rusts, either comes factory primed or needs a rustproofing primer-sealer, which is usually orange or grey. In addition to preventing rust, this primer dries fast and provides a surface to which paint can easily adhere. Aluminum, on the other hand, doesn't rust; but it does need a primer that helps paint bind to its surface. Both primers give off fumes that are extremely toxic, so wear a mask when using them.

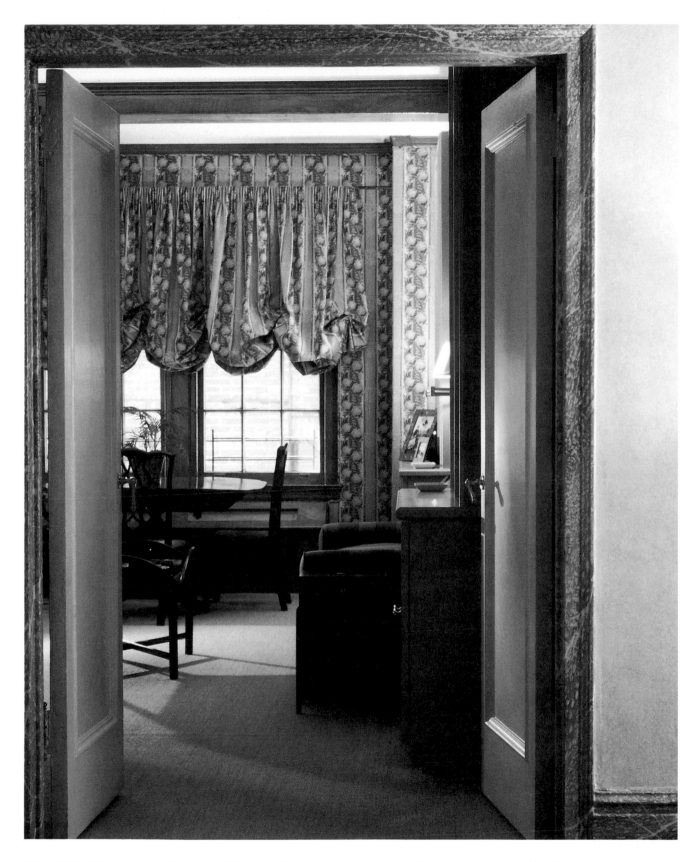

The walls, trim, door, ceiling, and beams of a room may have surfaces in various condition and may require different preparation. See the chart on pages 66–69 for the appropriate preparation for each surface.

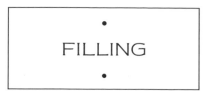

FILLING

Many surfaces need filling. The process involves filling holes, cracks, and nicks with a fine-grade filler, plaster of paris, or a mix of the two. There are many ready-mixed fillers on the market today; they usually come in cans, tubes, or tubs. For best results, ask your paint store what professional painters use.

When dealing with a crack in an old wall, you must fill it properly so that it won't soon reappear in your freshly painted surface. First, insert a triangular shavehook into one end of the crack; then run the scraper along the crack, enlarging it evenly to about ⅛-inch deep. Wipe the crack with a damp sponge. Apply filler in two or three coats, letting it dry between applications so that the compound will hold better.

Because the compound shrinks as it dries, over-fill the crack. If the compound forms a bump, you can sand it smooth after it dries, then dust the surface with a soft brush. Apply primer over any areas you have filled. (Shellac primer is recommended for this because it dries fast.) The primer will prevent filled holes and cracks from appearing as dull spots in your painted finish.

After you finish filling and sanding, dust the surfaces and vacuum the floor so that dust doesn't get into your paint. You can also sprinkle water on the floor to trap the dust, then sweep it up with a broom. To dust walls thoroughly, painters use a dusting brush. For furniture, they sometimes use a 'tacky rag', a slightly sticky cloth sold in specialist paint stores. (Use it gently, or it may leave a waxy film on surfaces.)

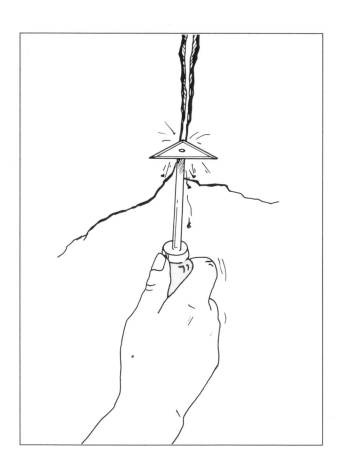

To fill a crack, first enlarge it using a triangular shavehook. Cut a dovetail-shaped groove so that the compound will fill it securely.

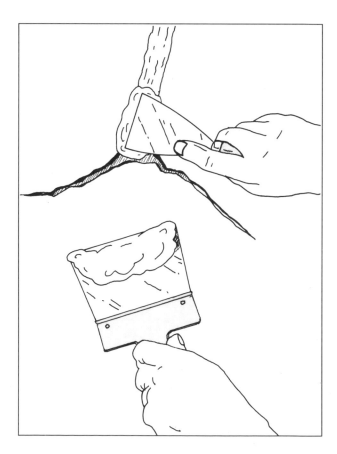

Before filling a crack, wipe it with a damp sponge or mist it with a spray bottle. Then, scoop some compound from the container onto a large filling knife, scrape a bit of the compound at a time onto a smaller knife, and fill the crack.

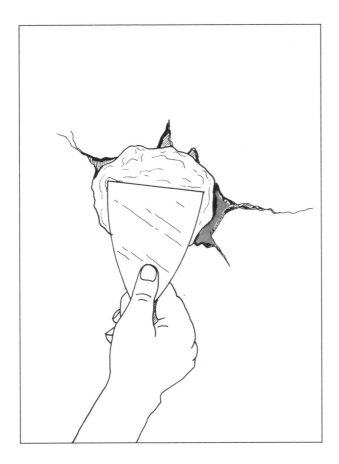

For a round crack, push the compound into the center to fill it.

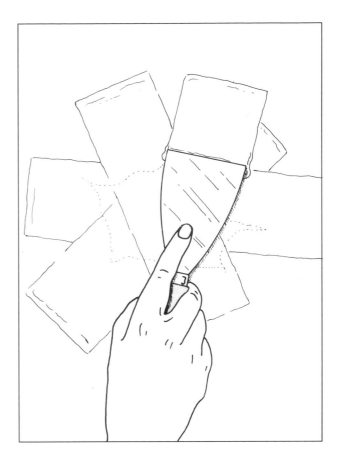

Work out to the edges. Let the compound dry, then sand it flush with the surface.

After your surfaces are filled and primed, step back and examine them. Now that they're all one colour, you can see what you have to work with. Keep in mind that their condition will strongly influence how your decorative finish will look. Hold a light up to a surface, and its imperfections will become apparent.

For some finishes, especially a gloss or high-gloss finish like Chinese lacquer or a realistic marbling, the surface may not be smooth enough. In that case, you can skim-coat it. This process is difficult and time-consuming—and thus best professionally done—but it will give you a very smooth surface.

Skim coating is done over the primer (see drawings below and right). Because it is a thin coat of filler, you probably won't have to reprime afterward unless you've applied several skim coats to obtain a smooth surface. This isn't advisable, however. The more skim coats you apply, the weaker your surface becomes and the more likely it is to crack.

SKIM COATING

You skim-coat with fine-grade surface filler. Hold a large filling knife flat, and run it lightly over the walls, filling in any gaps and dents with filler. Working in 3-foot sections, apply the compound in a long sweep. Then clean off the knife and drag the clean blade back over the surface; the filler will remain.

Skim coating is frequently used for flat surfaces like walls, tabletops, and wood furniture. Say you strip, prime, and sand a piece to prepare it for marbling, but its wood grain shows through too strongly. You can skim-coat the piece with filler, following the length of its grain and dragging the knife over the surface at a slight angle so that you fill in only the grain. Then sand again, and apply a second skim coat, if needed. If you apply more than two skim coats, however, you will have to reprime the surface.

Another way to get a very smooth surface, albeit an expensive one, is to have your walls canvased. Canvas is applied like wallpaper, then skim-coated and sanded smooth.

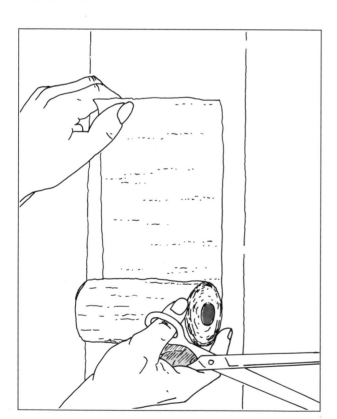

Even a carefully filled crack can reappear over time. For extra protection, "tape" it after filling it. Once the filled crack is dry, cover a thin coat of compound with gauze, flattening it to set it.

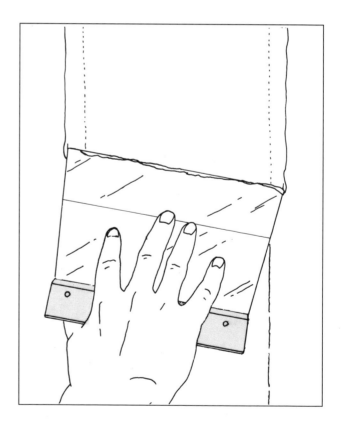

After sanding smooth, skim-coat with a wide compounding knife over the gauze to cover it.

Skim-coat any patches with a wide filling knife for an even finish.

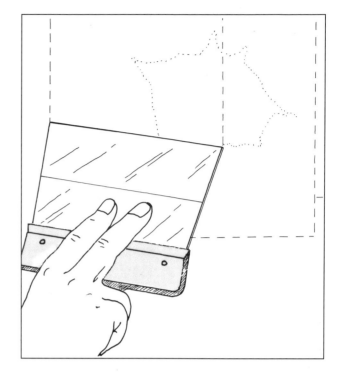

The diagram below illustrates how to skim-coat a wall. Work in sections about 2½ feet × 2 feet, starting in the top left-hand corner if you are right handed or the top right-hand corner if you are left handed. Move down the wall in vertical rows.

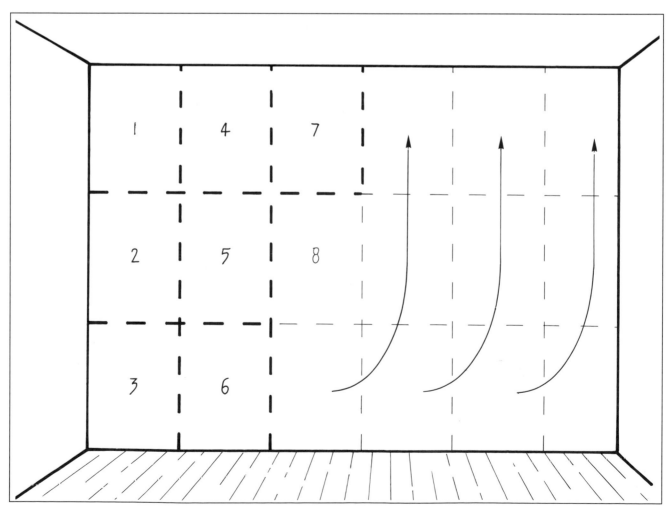

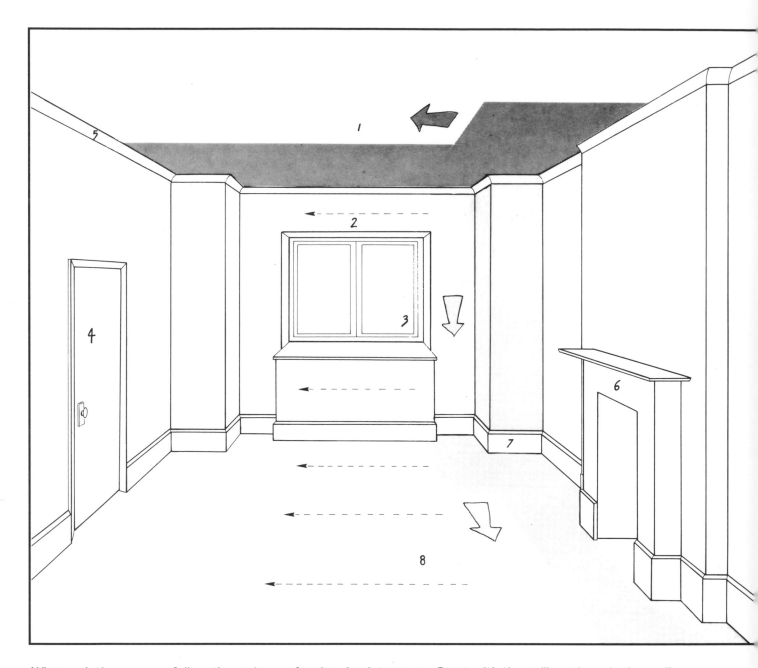

When painting a room, follow the order professional painters use: Start with the ceiling, then do the walls, windows, doors and architrave, cornice mouldings, fireplace, skirtings, and floor. When doing the floor, work out to the door so you don't paint yourself into a corner.

This crucial step will only look as good as the steps that preceded it. Compared to the previous tasks, this is finer work. Before you start, make the room as dust-free as possible. It's much easier to paint if your work area is clear; stow away all equipment and materials from earlier stages. Dust the walls and baseboards, vacuum the floor, and put down clean paper.

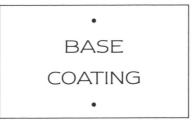

BASE COATING

At this point, you must select from Part II the technique you want to execute. Look at the chart for that technique to determine whether your base coat should be oil- or water-based. You must also decide on your base coat and glaze colours. Then, following the directions in Mixing Paints, Chapter Four, blend your colours, make samples of them using the technique you've chosen, and study them in various lights. After adjusting the colours as needed, you are ready to apply your base coat—which in all cases will consist of at least two coats of paint.

If you are painting an entire room, follow the practical order that professionals employ. Start with the ceiling, then do walls, window and door trim, doors, cornice, skirtings, and floor. (See diagram, left.)

For surfaces larger than a set of double doors, apply the base coats with a roller. For small surfaces, use a brush.

Apply base coats in crisscross fashion. In particular, paint strokes on flat surfaces like panels, doors, and tables should be crisscrossed. Paint down first, then across, then down again with a brush that is almost free of paint. (Note: Don't paint the top and bottom edges of wood doors;

this allows the wood to breath and prevents warping.)

Crisscrossing is easy with a brush, but not always possible with a roller. When you are using water-based paints—which, because they dry faster, tend to leave brush or roller marks— work in 4-foot sections and go over the second layer in the same direction with a dry roller while the paint is still wet.

Before starting a large project that requires several gallons of paint, pour the paint from all of the 1-gallon cans into a 5-gallon bucket (available at paint and hardware stores) or a plastic garbage can. Mix thoroughly, then pour it back into the 1-gallon cans until it is needed. This extra effort helps ensure satisfying results: Despite colour differences among paint batches, you'll get exactly the same hue throughout your project.

Paint taken directly from the can is too thick to work with. Although it covers well, it also drips, leaves marks, and dries slowly. For a smoother finish and a shorter drying time between coats, thin your first coat 10 to 15 percent with the appropriate solvent (water for emulsion, white spirit for oil). Add solvent a bit at a time so that paint doesn't get too thin. (If it does, leave it out uncovered until the solvent evaporates.) Stir the paint well and test its consistency with a brush.

Thin your second coat so that it is almost as thin as your first—but never thinner or the paint will crack when it dries. Wait until the first coat is completely dry before applying the second. Give yourself plenty of time in which to complete your project. Whenever possible, let each coat dry before applying the next one.

Here is one of many possible ways to divide a fireplace wall into panels. Note that a variation of this design might better suit your particular wall. Draw your design to scale on paper first. Start drawing from the centre of the wall and work out. Then transfer your design to the wall using a chalkline to "snap" first the vertical lines and then the horizontals.

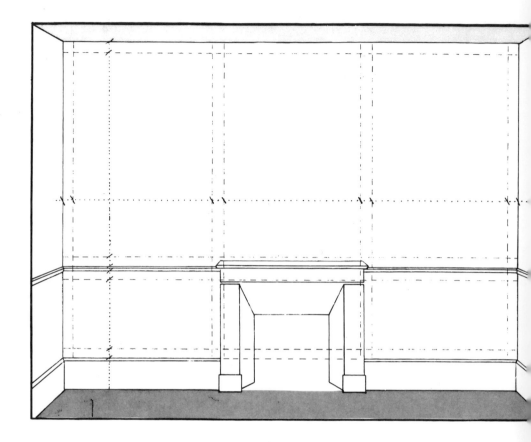

This illustration shows the finished drawing on the wall. Walls divided into panels are most often wood-grained, usually in more than one wood type for an inlaid look. Try figured graining for the panels and straight graining for the frame.

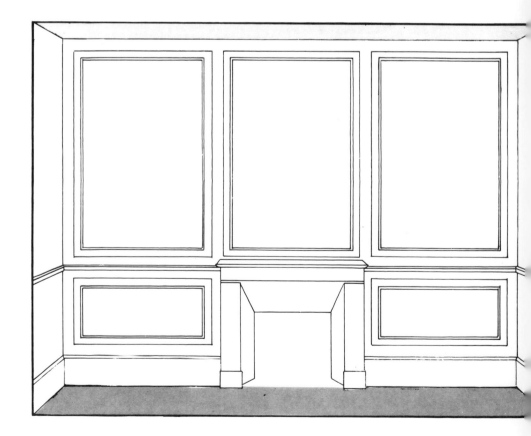

• LOADING AND HOLDING BRUSHES AND ROLLERS •

BRUSHES. Pour paint from the large storage container into a smaller bucket. This lets you keep most of your paint covered so that it doesn't dry or form a skin on top. In addition, if debris falls into your open paint bucket, the rest of the batch will still be uncontaminated. Dip your brush into the bucket so that about two-thirds of the bristles are covered with paint. Then wipe the brush on the *inside* edge of your bucket to prevent drips. Don't wipe the brush on the outside edge; you might drag foreign material into your paint.

For priming and base coating, hold your brush at a slight angle, and apply moderate, even pressure.

Grasp the brush low on the handle near the bristles for a firm grip. Avoid using excessive pressure, even in corners and other hard-to-reach places; this could damage the bristles of your brush.

ROLLERS. Fill a roller tray so that no more than half its ribbed bottom is covered with paint. Dip the roller into the paint at the shallow end of the tray, and work it back and forth a few times above the paint line to remove excess paint and prevent drips. Place the roller against the wall and roll it over the surface in long, even strokes.

• APPLYING A BASE COAT •

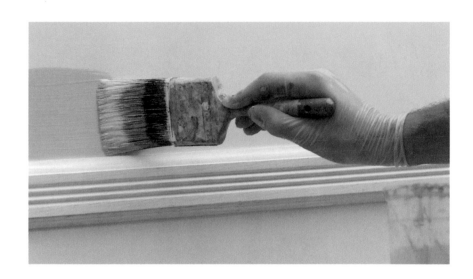

1 Before using a roller to apply base coat to a primed wall, paint the edge of the wall next to the moulding with a brush. (The one used here is a 2-inch household paint brush.) Rolling evenly up to the mouldings would be impossible; cutting a line gives you a straight line from which to work.

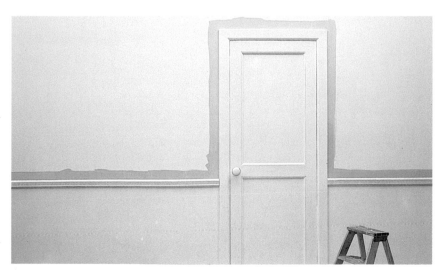

2 Because the areas above and below the chair rail will be different colours, only the area above the wall has been edged at this point. (Note that you always work from the top of a wall down to avoid dripping paint on a freshly coated surface.) Once the trim is edged, as shown, you can fill in the rest of the wall using a roller.

3 For ease of application, get an extension pole for your roller. Roller handles come hollow and threaded so that you can attach whatever size pole you need for a particular job. There are adjustable poles as well as those that come in standard lengths of 6 inches, 1 foot, and 2 feet.

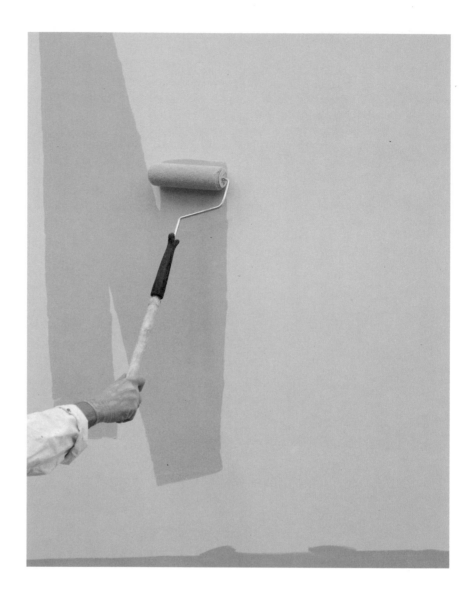

4 After edging the trim of the area below the chair rail, apply the second base coat colour to it. (Note: This area is called the dado.)

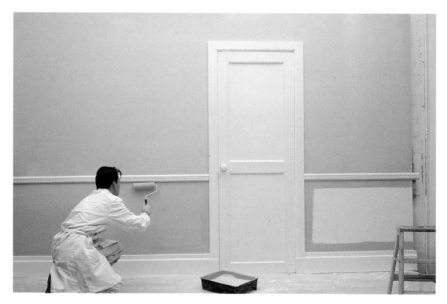

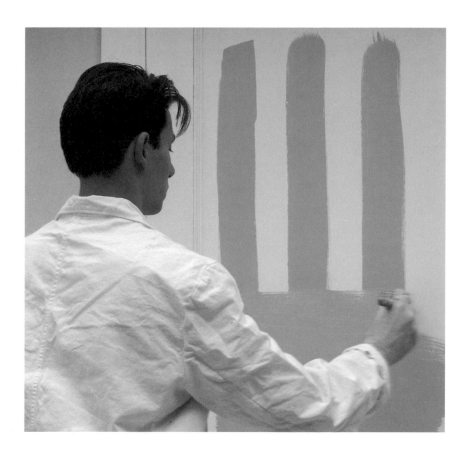

5 To base-coat a door, start with the panels. Dip your brush into paint, coating it well. Discharge brush by painting three vertical strokes on the top panel. Next, without redipping brush, work first from left to right, then top to bottom, and left to right again in crisscross fashion to smooth paint and prevent colour variations.

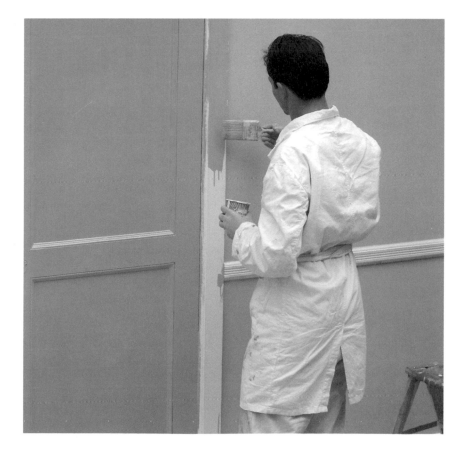

6 Do the lower panel of the door in the same manner; then paint the horizontal, then the vertical members, and, finally, the door frame.

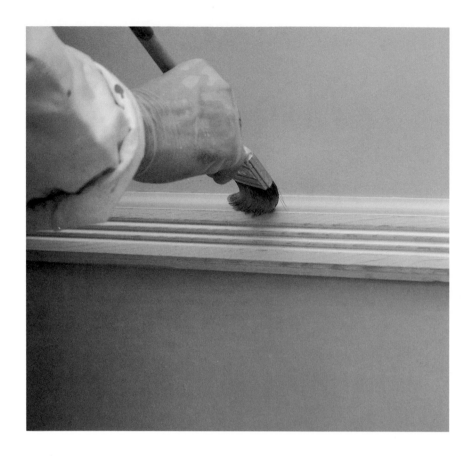

7 Next, with a slanted 2-inch brush, tackle the chair rail. As with any surface, paint mouldings from the top part down to prevent dripping on just-coated areas. After the chair rail, do the skirting.

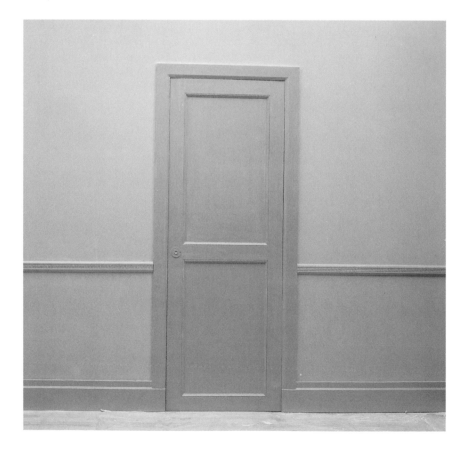

8 This photo depicts the wall with base coating completed. Three different colours—in the classic arrangement of trim, dado, and wall—are the average number used in a room.

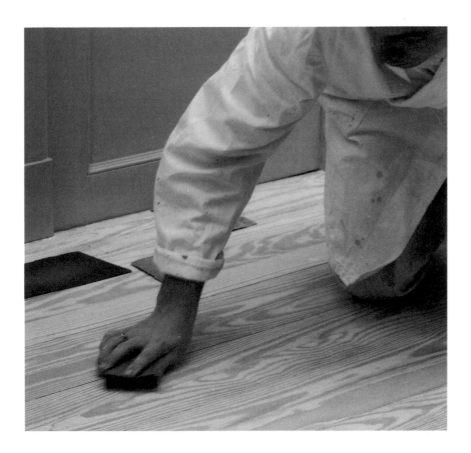

9 Preparation work for the floor is in progress. The surface has been smoothed with a floor sander, then its imperfections filled with wood filler. Here, the filler is sanded lightly by hand with a block.

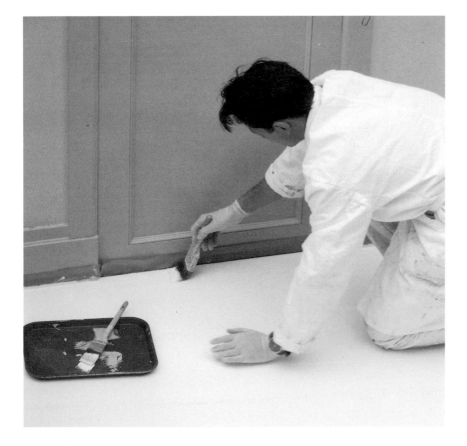

10 Once skirtings were dry, they were taped, and the floor was primed with oil-based primer. Now, the base coat is being carefully applied to the edge of the floor by the skirting.

• PREPARATION OF SURFACES •

MATERIAL	CLEANING	PRIMING, SANDING, FILLING, AND SKIM-COATING	BASE COAT
Raw wood (old furniture, stripped; new furniture and mouldings, unpainted; doors, panelling, cabinetry)	Dust lightly with hand broom or soft-brush attachment on vacuum cleaner.	1. Seal knots in wood with shellac or patent knotting. 2. Prime surface to harden pores and seal wood. Use an oil-based wood primer for softwoods; use an oil-based aluminum wood primer for hardwoods. 3. Sand primer, dust surfaces, and sweep area. 4. Fill and skim-coat, if needed, with filler. 5. Sand surfaces lightly, dust surfaces, and sweep area.	Oil-based paint is recommended for wood.
Painted wood (furniture, doors, panelling, moulding, etc.)	1. Wash with industrial-strength detergent if very dirty. 2. Let dry about a day. *Note:* Test detergent on small area first to see how it affects painted surface. 3. Scrape if needed.	1. Fill areas of painted surface in poor condition. 2. Skim-coat, if necessary. 3. Touch up filled and skim-coated areas with primer to seal them. Prime any areas where raw wood has been exposed. (You need not prime over painted wood in good condition.)	Use oil-based paint. Choose finish depending on technique you've chosen.
Unpainted brickwork (walls)	Dust lightly with hand broom or soft-brush attachment on vacuum cleaner.	1. Fill and skim-coat, if you want a very smooth finish. (If you apply more than two skim coats, reprime.)	Masonry or emulsion paint.

MATERIAL	CLEANING	PRIMING, SANDING, FILLING, AND SKIM-COATING	BASE COAT
Painted brickwork.	1. Wash with industrial-strength detergent if very dirty. 2. Let dry about a day. Note: Test on small area first to see how detergent affects painted surface.	1. Fill, if necessary, to fill holes and cracks. Touch up filled areas with primer. 2. Skim-coat if you want a very smooth finish.	Masonry or emulsion paint, depending on primer you've used and technique you've chosen.
Unpainted plaster (new walls [rare today], architectural details, ornaments, sconces, pedestals, capitals, etc.)	Dust new plaster lightly with soft-bristle brush. Dust old plaster with hard-bristle brush. Sand flat surfaces lightly, only if necessary, taking care not to scratch surface. Then dust with soft-bristle brush.	1. Fill, if necessary. 2. Prime with plaster primer or a coat of thinned emulsion.	Emulsion, though oil-based paint can be used as long as the plastering is over 12 months.
Painted plaster (old walls, architectural details, ornaments, sconces, pedestals, capitals, etc.)	1. Wash with industrial-strength detergent if very dirty. Wash around spots of exposed raw plaster. 2. Let dry at least two days, especially if paint is chipped and water seeps into plaster.	1. Fill, if necessary, to fill holes and cracks. Touch up areas with plaster primer or thinned emulsion. 2. Skim-coat if you want a very smooth finish; then prime. 3. Depending on surface condition and if you're painting a light color over a dark one, you may want to seal whole area with coat of primer. (See Painted Wood, PRIMING, for kind to use.)	Emulsion, though oil-based paint can be used as long as the plastering is over 12 months.

MATERIAL	CLEANING	PRIMING, SANDING, FILLING, AND SKIM-COATING	BASE COAT
Laminates, plastics, and resins (kitchen cabinets and counters, appliances, tabletops, pedestals and capitals, light fixtures, etc.)	Wipe down with methylated spirit. Then wash with industrial-strength detergent, rinse well, and let dry. *Note:* Wash new pieces well; many have waxy factory finish.	1. Roughen surface by sanding with 150-grade wet or dry paper. 2. Apply "surface duller" such as acetone. (Wear gloves, goggles, and mask and take safety precautions with these flammable solvents.) 3. Prime with plastic-grade primer.	Oil-based paint recommended for durability and compatibility with oil-based primer.
Closely-woven canvas	(None)	1. For large floorcloth, you can stretch canvas by stapling it to wall, but will need scaffold to work on it. Place inexpensive fabric and plastic sheet behind canvas to cushion canvas and create smooth surface for sanding. 2. Sand canvas lightly. 3. Prime canvas with synthetic gesso or acrylic primer, available in art supply shops, or 5 parts emulsion to 2 parts PVA. PVA is available in art shops. Apply two coats.	Apply two base coats of 5 parts emulsion to 2 parts PVA.
Other fabrics (T-shirts, curtains, etc.)	Wash, iron, and press, if necessary.	(None)	Textile paint using special brushes with stiff, short hair, available in art supply shops.
Paper (posterboard for samples—hot-press with semigloss finish recommended)	Dust lightly, if needed.	1. Prime with oil-based primer. (Do not use water-based primer.) 2. Sand lightly.	Two coats of oil- or latex-based paint, whichever you used for your technique. *Note:* In making samples, you can put water over oil—paper will absorb most of the oil and the results don't need to be durable.
Papier-mâché, papers for making your own wall-paper, gift-wrap, etc.	Dust lightly if needed.	1. Prime with oil-based primer.	Use oil-based paints.

MATERIAL	CLEANING	PRIMING, SANDING, FILLING, AND SKIM-COATING	BASE COAT
Metal, rusting—iron (furniture, accessories, stair rails)	Go over entire surface with wire brush to remove rust, if necessary. Wash new factory-primed surfaces with detergent.	1. Use rustproofing primer.	Check manufacturer's labels to see which oil-based paints are compatible with primer.
Metal, non-rusting—aluminum (appliances, cabinets, etc.)	Remove protective grease finish from new and *unprimed* surfaces with acetone. *Note:* Acetone is flammable and toxic. Take safety precautions; wear mask, goggles, and gloves.	1. Use primer for non-rusting metals to help paint adhere to surface.	Oil-based paint.
Ceramic (tubs, sinks, tiles, old appliances with baked-on ceramic finishes, etc.)	Wash with industrial-strength detergent.	1. To roughen surface, sand with heavy-grade paper in circular motion.	Ask your hardware or paint store for ceramic-grade spray paint. Do a sample on tile to test paint for adherence and durability. *Caution:* Because ceramic is nonporous, finishes will be less durable than on other surfaces.
Glass (tabletops)	Clean with spray window cleaner to dissolve grease. For difficult jobs, cover surface with layer of powdered cleanser; then wipe off with damp cotton rag to absorb dirt and grease.	(None)	Use gloss (no undercoat) or special glass paints. Paint on underside of glass. *Caution:* Test paint on glass for durability: Finish can scratch off. Glass is nonporous and thus less durable than, say, wood or brickwork.

PART II

·

THE RECIPES

CHAPTER FOUR

•

MIXING PAINTS

MIXING A BASE COAT
MIXING A GLAZE
GLOSSARY OF TERMS
BEFORE YOU BEGIN

CREATING YOUR OWN PAINT COLOURS IS ONE OF THE MOST EXCITING aspects of decorative painting. It lets you match the colour of your surfaces to anything from the jewel-toned antique rug in your entry hall to the shade of the sky outside your window after a rainstorm.

There are certain steps to follow in creating colours, as the instructions in this chapter make clear. But mixing base coats and glazes in the hues of your choice is, above all, something that must be learned by doing. The more you practice, the more familiar you'll become with what colours look like when combined in varying proportions. You'll get a feel for how much of each colour is needed to create the hue you desire as well as how much of that hue will tint your base-coat paint or transparent glazing medium to the intensity you want.

• THE DECORATIVE PAINTER'S PALETTE •

Here is a list of colours for all kinds of decorative painting. (Colour names are standard for both oil and acrylic paints.) Combinations of these colours will produce almost any hue you'll need for base coats and glazes, but you may want to buy additional colours as your projects evolve. Choose the medium tones of colours; they require the smallest amount of paint to lighten or darken.

Ivory black (or lamp black)

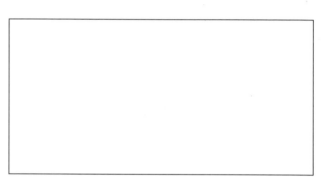

Titanium white (or zinc white)

Burnt umber

Raw umber

Burnt sienna

Raw sienna

Yellow ochre (or oxide)

Chrome yellow medium

Red ochre (or oxide)

Chrome orange (or cadmium orange)

Alizarin crimson

Vermillion red (or cadmium red)

Ultramarine blue

Chrome green medium

The paint colours used for the decorative finishes in this book are given in the recipes accompanying the techniques. The colours are listed so that those used in largest quantity appear first. Just as in cooking, you'll need only a dash of some colours.

To learn about mixing paints (and to be able to apply what you've learned to future projects), determine how much of each colour to use the way professional painters do—with your eye. Don't worry about exact amounts—you're working with paints, not chemicals. You don't have to measure precisely. Just start with a light tone and add it *drop by drop*, seeing how the colour develops. Increase the colour very slowly—it's easier and requires much less paint to darken a colour than to lighten it. Adjust the colour till it pleases you. Over time, you'll become familiar with how much of a colour gives you the results you want, and you'll add the paint all at once, thus speeding the job.

As you work, be sure to keep a log book or charts of how many drops make up the colour you're mixing so that you can produce more of it later. Also, label all paint containers and any samples you do. You may later want to use the same hues in other rooms to create a unified colour scheme. You may need extra paint for touch-ups.

To make recording colours easier, you can abbreviate their names. Use "BU" for burnt umber, "RS" for raw sienna, and so forth. Be sure to keep your abbreviations consistent.

The more you practice, the more you'll get a feel for how colours respond when combined. You'll find that there are differences between colours of the same name in various brands. You'll also see that while it takes only a little of some colours (like blue) to create deep hues, it takes a lot of others (like yellow). Several drops of blue tint would alter a white base coat much more than would the same amount of a yellow tint.

If a colour comes out too bright, don't add black to it; this dulls it. Instead, tone it down with its complementary, the hue opposite it on the colour wheel. (You will find a colour wheel and details on colour relationships in Chapter One.) If it's too pink, try adding some green; too blue, use a little orange. Also experiment with one of its split complementaries, the hues that flank its complementary on the colour wheel.

For base coats, a rule of thumb is that you should add no more than 10 to 20 percent colouring (tints or artist's colours) to a white or off-white base-coat paint. If you have to add more than 20 percent, it is more economical to buy a ready-mixed paint in the colour closest to the one you're trying to create and then adjust it slightly. For instance, using the 10 to 20 percent rule, you won't be able to mix a deep red or yellow. To get one of those colours, buy a ready-mixed red or yellow base coat and then adjust its colouring to the hue you desire.

One of the most popular colours for base coats is grey, and you can create many shades of it. Just mixing black and white produces a dull hue; instead, try ultramarine blue, raw umber, white, and a bit of black to darken the colour, if necessary. For a cooler grey, add a dash more blue. For a warmer grey, substitute raw umber for burnt umber and add a little red and/or yellow.

DULL GREY: mixed from black and white

DARK GREY: mixed from ultramarine blue, raw umber, white, and a bit of black

COOL GREY: same as DARK GREY and add more blue

WARM GREY: mixed from ultramarine blue, burnt umber, white, a bit of black, and a little red and/or yellow

PEACH: used in sponging on: three colours; see page 98

BEIGE: used in sponging on; see page 94

PALE BLUE: used in dragging with a hard-bristle brush; see page 184

WARM BROWN: used in ma-hogany wood graining; see page 236

YELLOW: used in the rag-rolling techniques; see pages 120—123

GREEN-BLUE: used in brush washing in two tones; see page 154

Some common base coat colours, above. For large surfaces, mix your own sample base coats and buy the ready-mixed paint that's closest in colour, tinting it until it's what you want.

For glazes, keep in mind that their special quality is their transparency. You'll find that you need very little colouring (stains or artist's colours) to create them. In general, you should add less than one part colour to a transparent glaze, depending on the degree of translucence you want. Some techniques, such as colour washing, call for a very transparent glaze; you might need only a few drops of colour to create it.

You can also learn about blending hues by using a colour mixing chart (see source list). Charts and accompanying guides, sold in art supply stores, will help you visualize relationships between colours and find colours you'd like to buy or create. In addition, these charts supply information on permanency, translucence, and cost of colours. Permanency ratings indicate how light affects a colour—red, for example, fades in sunlight. Translucence ratings tell which colours combine well with glaze for a see-through effect. Cost is related to the quality of paints, which come in several grades. Because paints are a small part of a project's total expense, it is usually worth your while to buy the best quality. Note, too, that some colours in the same grade cost more than others. The charts indicate less expensive but effective alternatives, such as chrome yellow for cadmium yellow.

Mixing your own colours has advantages. Instead of standing in the store and getting overwhelmed by row upon row of paint cans or lots of charts, you can create and/or adjust hues with your source of colour inspiration right beside you, in the same light in which the hues will be seen.

Try to mix your colours in daylight, which is "true" light, instead of, say, in your basement under a 40-watt bulb. Then make samples of your colours, and make sure you like the way they look under all light conditions to which they will be exposed: pale early-morning light, midday sun, twilight, fluorescent and incandescent lights.

• EXPERIMENTING WITH SAMPLES •

Paint your samples on double-ply hot-press illustration (or bristol) board. Use boards about 15 by 20 inches so that you can get a good preview of your finished effect. Prime the boards so that they won't bubble and will absorb paint in the same way as your surface. Use the type of primer (oil, emulsion, or shellac) that is compatible with your base coat. (See the chart in Preparing to Paint, Chapter Three.) Then base-coat the boards twice so that your colours will look the same.

• MIXING A BASE COAT •

This example shows an emulsion base coat being mixed, but the steps below apply for both emulsion and oil-based paints. Here, just enough paint for several samples is being prepared. But you can use the same steps to mix as much paint as you need. (See Paints and Tools, Chapter Two, for help in estimating amounts.)

It is always a good idea to start with a small batch before tinting, say, a gallon container. Write down colours and quantities as you tint so that you can reproduce it for larger batches.

If you just need enough paint for a tabletop or skirtings, mixing your own paints is the best alternative. But mixing enough paint to base-coat large areas such as walls can be expensive and time-consuming. Try this method instead: Buy a small amount of white paint, and tint it to the colour you want. Make samples with it to be sure, then find the paint colour closest to your samples on a commercial paint chart. Buy however many gallons you need in the ready-mixed colour and pour them all into one large container. Then, with artist's colours, adjust the hue slightly, if necessary, to match your sample.

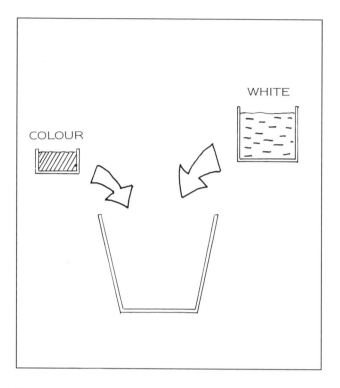

COLOUR

WHITE

Base coats are most often light in hue and, thus, usually about one-half to two-thirds white paint and the rest whatever colour paint you choose. If you want a deep colour, it is much more economical to buy it ready-mixed.

TYPE OF PAINT	TINT WITH:
Emulsion base coat or acrylic glaze	artist's acrylics universal stainers (use less than 5–10%)
Oil-based under-coat or oil glaze	japan colors artist's oils universal stainers (use less than 5–10%)

1   Pour the paint into a plastic container, filling it just halfway so that paint doesn't splash out when you stir. For emulsion paint, use either artist's acrylics or universal stainers. (Tints contain no dryer; so never add more than 10 percent of total volume to paint.) For oil-based paint, use artist's oils or universal stainers. With tints, add drops of colour directly into the paint; with artist's oils or acrylics, dab the colour on the end of a well-worn brush and stir it into the paint to disperse it more easily.

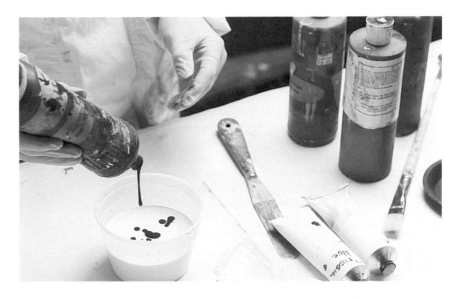

2   Mix tints with a palette knife as shown or stir in dabs of artist's colours with an old brush. Then cover the container and shake it. Mix in stages. Add a bit of paint, make a sample, then adjust the colour as needed.

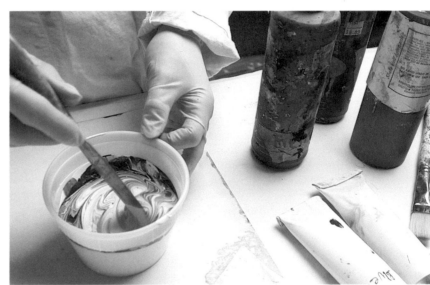

3   Sample on primed bristol board and label the board as shown. Emulsion paint dries darker, so dry emulsion samples with hair dryer to see what the colours will actually look like. Oil-based paints look about the same wet or dry. When you are satisfied with the colour, label the container. On a chart or in a log book, list the colours and quantities you used.

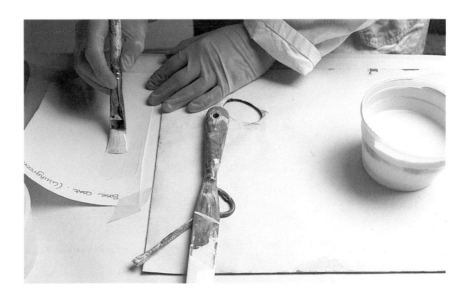

• MIXING A GLAZE •

After preparing your base coat and painting several samples with it, mix your glaze. (The next two sections tell you how to mix acrylic and oil glazes.)

To mix glazes for the decorative finishes in this book, first consult the recipe chart accompanying the technique you plan to execute. Look under "Glaze" to learn whether you need a water- or oil-based glaze, what elements you need to mix it, and how much of each element to add. This will give you a *transparent* glaze. (For the amount of glaze to prepare for a project, see Paints and Tools, Chapter Two.)

Then turn to the heading "Colours: glaze" in the recipe chart. There you will find the paint or tint colours used for the glaze in that technique. The colours are listed in order of the amount used, from most to least.

Just as in cooking, recipes for glazes are general guides. In cooking, you follow the steps, taking into account variations in, say, cooking times because of individual oven temperatures and consistency of food being prepared. Mixing a glaze also depends on various factors, including what kind of opacity and consistency you need for a particular technique or surface. Some techniques demand a very translucent glaze. Some surfaces need a thick glaze that won't run.

Always read the introductory section and the entire recipe for the technique you've chosen before mixing your glaze. They often offer tips on the glaze consistency and translucence.

Always test a glaze over a base coat and evaluate whether its consistency and translucence are appropriate to your surface and technique. Sometimes, however, even after you've tested a glaze, you might find it doesn't cover your surface well and needs to be thinned or thickened.

Don't panic. First, wipe the glaze off with a clean cloth. Then, only if necessary, wipe the surface with a cloth dampened with thinner (white spirit for oil glaze, water for water-based glaze).

To thin a glaze, mix in more diluent (white spirit for oil-based, water for water-based). But add the diluent a little at a time so that the glaze doesn't get runny, and make new samples before applying glaze to your surface.

Thickening a glaze that you've thinned too much isn't as easy. If you discover a small amount of glaze mixed for a sample is too runny, it's probably best to mix a new batch. For a large amount of glaze, you can let it stand open to the air for about twelve hours until most of its diluent evaporates. A skin may form on top of the glaze as it thickens, but you can strain the glaze through cheesecloth to remove the skin.

Another challenge in glaze mixing is translucence. You need only a small amount of paint or tint to colour a glaze. The less colour you add, the more transparent the glaze will be. If your glaze comes out too opaque, you can adjust it in several ways, depending on how much it must be altered:

- For a very slight change, add more thinner—as long as the glaze doesn't get too runny.

- For a bigger change, add more transparent medium as well as more thinner in the same ratio as the original glaze.

- To redo, pour one-third of the glaze into a container and fill it two-thirds full with medium plus thinner in the same ratio as the original glaze. Set aside the rest of the original glaze for later projects.

- Or make new batch of glaze, adding less colour.

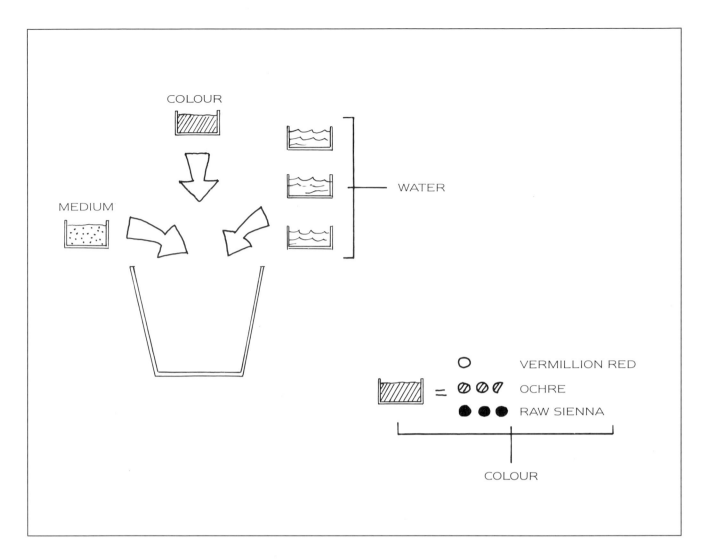

The diagram shows proportions of water, acrylic medium, and paint or tint colour frequently used in creating an acrylic glaze. Note that the colour portion of the mix usually comprises varying amounts of several hues. Here, vermillion, ochre, and raw sienna combine to form a warm terracotta.

• WORKING WITH A PALETTE •

When mixing glazes—as well as when spattering, marbling, and wood graining—you will sometimes need to arrange your artist's colours on a palette. (See step one in the Acrylic Glaze section, which follows.) First, take paint from tubes or jars and place it on the palette using a palette knife. Put colours around the outer edge of the palette from left to right if you are right-handed, right to left if you are left-handed. Arrange them so that the colour you will probably need most of is on the left (if you are right-handed; on the right if you are left-handed), the colour you'll need second most is next to it, and so on. Leave the centre of the palette free for mixing paints. If you are right-handed, hold the palette in your left hand; if left-handed, hold it in your right.

· ACRYLIC GLAZE ·

You can blend a small amount of acrylic glaze by combining artist's acrylics with transparent medium on a palette, then transferring this mix to a container and adding water to get the desired consistency. This gives you more control over colour and helps prevent mistakes. For larger batches, however, save time by adding acrylics or tints directly to a container of medium; thin it with water as needed. In either case, proceed slowly, adding a little colour at a time, then testing results.

1 Set up the palette: squeeze artist's acrylics around edges and put transparent medium in the centre.

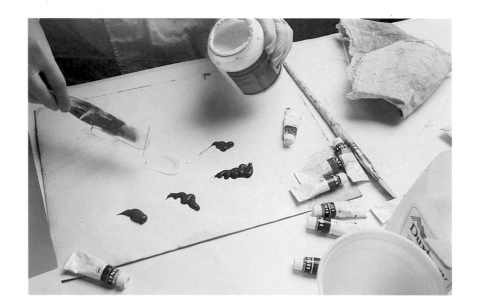

2 Spread the acrylics toward the medium, mixing to achieve the colour you want. Make the colour a little darker than you think it should be: colours lighten considerably when they are thinned with water.

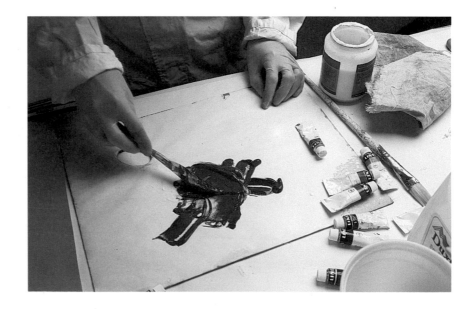

3 Scrape the colour from your palette into a container, add some water, and stir well. Then cover and shake. Test your glaze on base-coat sample with the implement you will be using for the technique. If you are satisfied, cover the glaze and label it. On a chart or in a log, note the colours and quantities used.

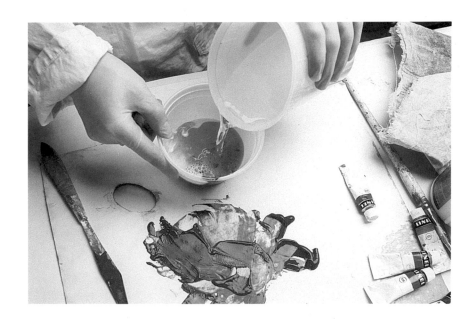

• OIL GLAZE •

Pour some ready-mixed transparent oil glaze into a paper cup. To get the desired hue, squeeze drops of tints into the glaze and blend the mixture with a palette knife or stir in dabs of artist's oils on the end of a well-worn brush. Make the colour darker than you think it should be: It will lighten considerably when the colour is added to the full amount of transparent glaze required for the project.

Pour colour from the paper cup into a container of transparent glaze. Stir well to dissolve any streaks or blobs of colour, which would make dark spots in your finish. Glaze cans are filled to the rim; if you want to tint a whole can, you must transfer it to a larger container with room for mixing without splashing over.

If you wish, you can make your own glaze from linseed oil and turpentine and then colour it in the same way (see Paints and Tools, Chapter Two).

Now add diluent to get the desired consistency. For most of the decorative finishes that require an oil glaze, you'll need a standard mix of about one part thinner to six parts glaze. Consult the chart accompanying the finish you've chosen to see what mix you need.

The kind of diluent you use will affect the consistency and drying time of your glaze:

- Use one of the following more readily available diluents, depending on your technique and the condition of your surface.

- White spirit makes glazes dry faster because it evaporates quickly.

- Turpentine causes glazes to dry more slowly than white spirit does, giving you more time to work on a technique.

• GLOSSARY OF TERMS •

Acrylic gel retarder: Chemical added to water-based glaze to slow drying time.

Acrylic medium: Synthetic resin in transparent gel form. The base of all acrylic paints. Colour it with artist's acrylics or tints to form water-based glazes.

Additive techniques: One-person techniques in which you make impressions with glaze on a base coat using various tools such as sponges, rags, and brushes. Among these techniques are sponging on and ragging on.

Alkyd paint: Interior or exterior house paint that comprises a mix of alkyd resin and oil. Used today instead of purely oil-based paint because it dries faster and contains no lead.

Artist's acrylics: Paints made from ground pigment bound with acrylic medium. They dry quickly to a waterproof finish and can be thinned with water. Decorative painters use them for such techniques as marbling and trompe l'oeil, and to tint emulsion base coats and water-based glazes.

Artist's oils: Paints made of ground pigment bound with linseed oil. They dry slowly to a waterproof finish. Decorative painters use them for such techniques as marbling and trompe l'oeil, and to tint oil-based under-coats and oil glazes.

Base coat or Undercoat: Opaque layers of emulsion or oil-based paint that dry to a durable finish. In decorative painting, glaze is applied over the base coat.

Blending: Toning down imprints left in a glaze by an implement such as a sponge, brush, or cloth to achieve a softer effect or to combine different coloured glazes on a surface. Done by brushing over the surface with a light feathering motion.

Cloth distressing: The use of materials such as cheesecloth or cotton rags to apply or remove glaze. Material may be bunched up, as in cheeseclothing or ragging, or rolled into a tube, as in rag-rolling.

Colour washing: Techniques in which thin layers of very transparent glazes are applied with a roller or brush, then worked over with a sponge, cloth, or brush, and finally smoothed and blended to varying degrees with a soft-haired brush.

Combing: Drawing a toothed instrument such as a graining comb through wet glaze to produce effects such as basketweave and naive wood graining.

Crisscrossing: Method of applying base coat and glaze smoothly and evenly to a surface. Should always be employed when applying glaze with brush so as to minimize brush marks; optional when applying glaze with roller. Begin by applying glaze from top to bottom, then, without picking up more paint, go over glaze from side to side and, finally, lightly from top to bottom until you eliminate all brush marks.

Cutting: Thinning pure paint or glazing medium with diluent to give it a workable consistency.

Dabbing: Touching a surface lightly and repeatedly with an implement in quick motions, creating smooth, even marks. You dab with a sponge in sponging and marbling techniques, with a brush in stippling and stencilling techniques.

Diluents: Solvents or thinners that dilute paint to workable consistency (e.g., white spirit for oil-based paints, water for water-based paints).

Dryer: A chemical found in ready-mixed oil-based paints that speeds drying time. Add dryer a few drops at a time to oil-based paint if you want to accelerate drying.

Dragging: Two-person technique in which one person applies glaze with a brush or roller and the other person removes some of the glaze by sweeping over it with a dry brush, metal comb, steel wool, or other implement.

Dryer: A chemical found in ready-mixed oil-based paints that speeds drying time. Add dryer a few drops at a time to oil-based paint if you want to accelerate drying.

Emulsion: Water-based interior house paint similar to acrylic. It dries quickly, has little odour, and is available in finishes from flat to silk.

Fade-away: An effect featuring a gradual progression of a glaze colour from dark to light, from light to dark, or from one colour to another. Favorite fade-away techniques include fade-away stippling, colour washing, and stencilling.

Glaze: Oil- or water-based paint that is transparent because it contains much more diluent than pigment. When applied over a base coat, its transparency allows the base coat colour to show through.

Marbling: Advanced decorative-painting technique for replicating the look of marble on a non-marble surface.

Oil-based paint: Interior or exterior house paint that comprises a mix of resin and oil.

Palette: A thin oval or rectangular board or a tablet of disposable sheets on which an artist mixes paints. The palette has a hole in the middle through which you stick your thumb to hold it.

Pigment: Powder ground from natural or synthetic material that gives paint its colour.

Primer: Sealant that goes under the base coat to protect the raw surface, make it nonporous, and prevent humidity and dirt from seeping in. There are many primers—which kind you use depends on your surface material.

Sample: A surface on which to practice techniques, experiment with colours, and preview your final effects—primed 15- by 20-inch double-ply, hot-press illustration boards are recommended.

Shellac: Alcohol-based varnish and sealant made from natural resin that dries fast. Depending on the kind you use, it will dry to a clear or amber.

Smoothing out: Getting rid of brush marks or softening painted lines on a still-wet painted or glazed surface. Move brush over surface in soft, feathery motion. Use badger-hair brush for water-based paints; any long, soft-haired brush except badger for oils.

Spattering: Creating a fine array of coloured dots on a base coat by various methods including flicking paint from a brush and spraying paint from an air gun with a special nozzle.

Sponging: Applying or removing glaze by dabbing a sea sponge on the surface. Used in sponging, colour washing, and marbling. Also useful in removing excess paint from corners.

Stencil: Design cut out of cardboard, acetate, Mylar, or stencil paper. You can buy stencils or make your own.

Stencilling: Placing a cutout design on a surface and applying paint through it, using a sponge or a stencilling brush.

Stippling: Creating a fine texture of dots by dabbing a brush repeatedly over a surface. A rectangular stippling brush is the best tool for this technique.

Subtexture: A textured glazed surface over which you execute your final finish. Used in techniques such as marbling and spattering. After applying glaze in a criss-cross fashion, you sponge it off, dab it with a stencil brush, or stipple the entire surface with a large brush to create a subtexture that brings surface closer to the look of your final finish and enhances the illusion of depth.

Subtractive techniques: Two-step techniques in which glaze is first applied to surface with brush or roller, then partly removed or moved with implements such as rags, sponges, and brushes.

Universal stainers: Highly concentrated liquid pigments for colouring oil- or water-based paints, used by professional house painters and decorative painters. Tints contain no dryer and so should never equal more than 5–10 percent of the total volume of your paint (or else paint may not dry fully).

Varnish: Final transparent coating that protects decorative painting, extends its life, and determines its sheen. Comes in finishes ranging from flat to high gloss and is available in water, oil, and alcohol base.

Veining: Reproducing the linear pattern of marble using a paintbrush or sea sponge with ragged edges.

Wiping off: Painting a glaze over a highly carved surface, then wiping it off the surface with a cloth while it is still wet. Glaze remains in crevices, giving surfaces an aged look.

Wood graining: Advanced technique for imitating the appearance of wood using a range of tools such as steel combs and artist's brushes.

Working dry: Applying a thin layer of glaze, just enough to cover a surface; or applying a bit of pure paint (or paint to which just a little thinner or glazing medium has been added) and working it across surface with a brush.

Working wet: Applying a lot of glaze so that it is almost dripping down the wall. Used in techniques such as colour washing.

• BEFORE YOU BEGIN •

Here are some pointers to review before starting your decorative-painting project:

• Before you begin, read the entire recipe for a technique as well as the introduction to the chapter that technique is in. As in cooking, try to have everything you need on hand. Set aside enough time to complete the recipe, and practice any challenging aspects of the technique.

• To create painted finishes you can use additive techniques, like sponging or ragging *on*; subtractive techniques, like sponging or ragging *off*; or techniques in which you manipulate the glaze, like stippling.

   For additive techniques, you apply glaze directly to your base coat with a tool such as a sponge, cloth, or brush. These techniques can usually be executed by just one person.

   Because subtractive techniques require glaze to be brushed on and then removed with a tool while still wet, they are best executed by two people. The first person applies the glaze, and the second person follows close behind, removing it. This method also works best for techniques in which you manipulate glaze. You can do some subtractive and manipulative techniques by yourself, however, if your surface is small enough, if you are skilled in the technique, and if you can work quickly.

• When doing subtractive techniques on surfaces smaller than a set of double doors, apply the glaze with a brush in crisscross fashion. Dip the brush into the glaze and paint from top to bottom. Then, without redipping the brush, go over the surface from side to side and, finally,
from top to bottom. This helps minimize brush marks and coat surface evenly.

   For some techniques, such as marbling, you will next either rag, cheesecloth, or stipple over the crisscrossed glaze to create a textured surface and eliminate any remaining brush marks.

• For subtractive techniques on surfaces larger than a set of double doors, apply glaze with a roller. As long as the roller is well coated with paint, you probably won't need to crisscross the glaze or create a subtexture. For extra smoothness, however, you can roll the glaze on in sections, going over each section with a dry roller while the glaze is still wet.

• One of your biggest challenges in applying glaze will be the corners of rooms. Excess glaze tends to gather in corners. You can dab some of it out with a household, stippling, or small flat brush or with a piece of sponge cut to fit. Dab each spot once, and wipe the tool on a clean cloth every few times.

   But your best bet is to paint opposite walls one day, and let them dry overnight. Tape their edges the next day and do the two remaining walls (see diagram, page 89).

• Before applying glaze, always make sure your base coat is fully dry. The chart accompanying your technique will tell you what kind of base coat to use. (For directions on how to prepare a base coat, see the section earlier in this chapter. Instructions on how to apply it are in Preparing to Paint, Chapter Three.)

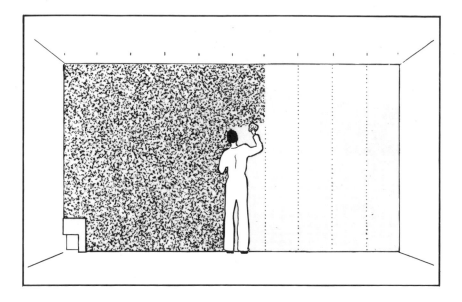

The diagram shows you how to apply glaze to a wall using an additive technique. Start in a top corner—the left one if you are right-handed, the right if you are left-handed, so that your arm doesn't accidentally touch completed work. Work down the wall in a 2- to 3-foot-wide strip; then move to the top of the wall and begin a new strip next to it. Try to overlap the strips just enough to avoid leaving a space where the base coat shows through but not enough to form a dark line between rows. Step back from your work frequently to examine the pattern you are producing.

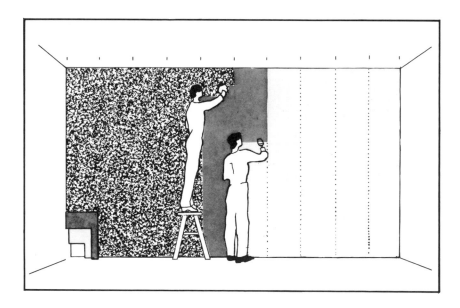

The diagram shows how to glaze a wall using a subtractive or manipulative technique. Work in pairs: one person begins rolling on glaze from a top corner (left for right-handed, right for left-handed), working in a 2- to 3-foot-wide strip. After reaching the bottom of the wall, this person returns to the top of the wall and begins glazing a strip next to it while the other person manipulates the wet glaze on the first strip.

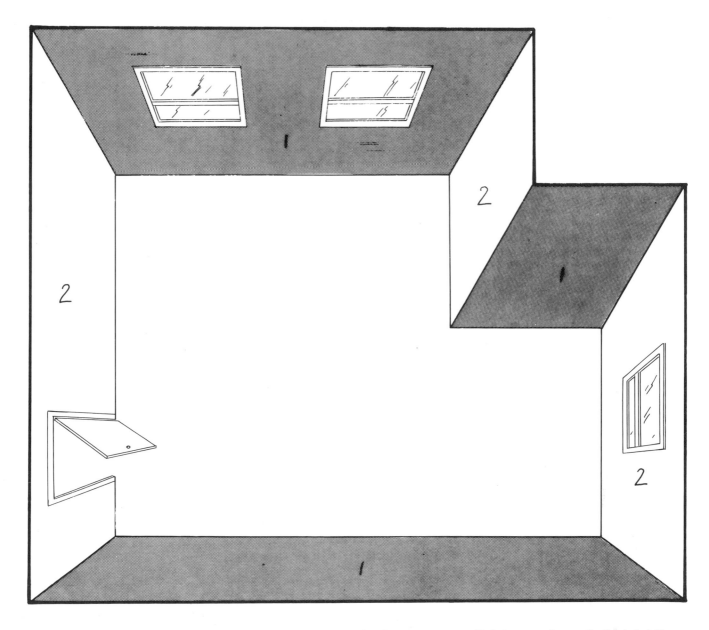

The diagram illustrates the most effective way to apply glaze to a room. Paint opposite walls first, let them dry, and then paint the remaining walls. This method gives you neatly painted corners.

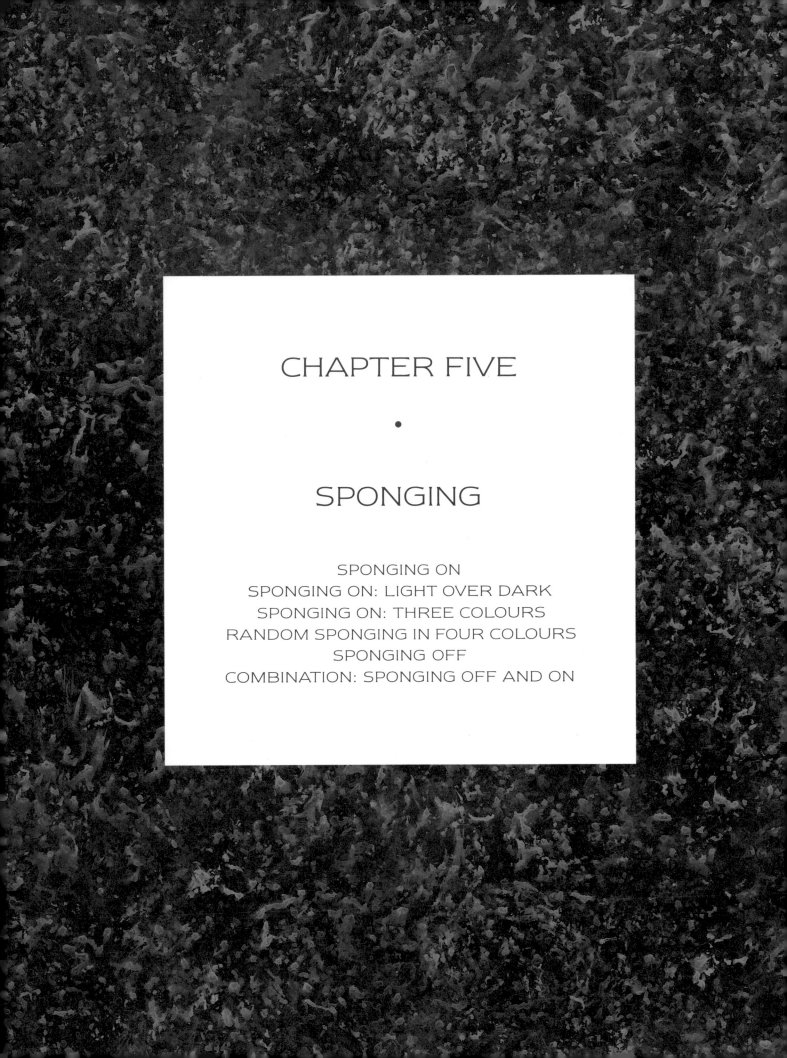

CHAPTER FIVE

•

SPONGING

AMONG THE SIMPLEST AND MOST VERSATILE FINISHES, SPONGING

can achieve effects from subtle to powerful. Many variations are possible, depending on the colours you select for your base coat and glaze; whether your glaze is glossy or flat; how translucent your glaze is; and how lightly or heavily you apply it.

Pastels and bright hues over a pale base will give you a fresh effect; but be sure you can live with the contrast—big differences in colours can be overwhelming. Tones from the same colour family for both base and glaze will provide a rich surface with a lot of depth.

The technique derives its name from the basic tool—a sponge—and its character from the kind of sponge you use—a sea sponge. The irregular shape and surface of the sea sponge help you create a mottled texture rather than a regular series of clearly defined marks. As with the other techniques in this book, your goal in sponging is *not* to be able to count how many imprints you've made on a surface.

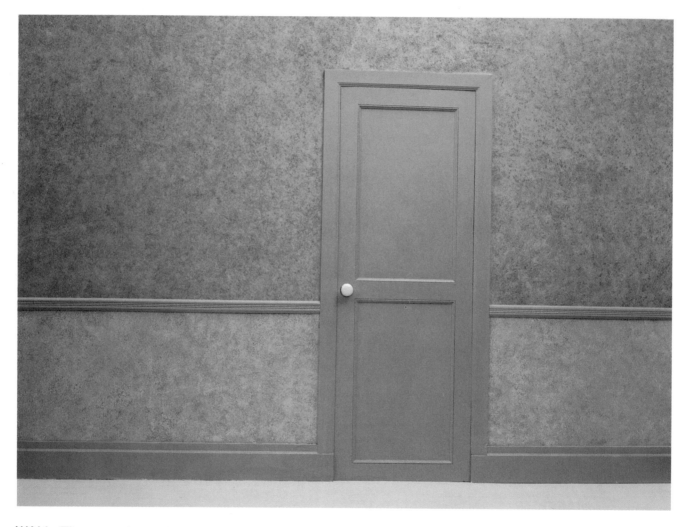

WALL: The area above the chair rail displays sponging on and off in soft tones of beige, shown in detail, opposite page, left. DADO: Below the chair rail is a five-colour random sponging that combines shades of red, pink, and white, shown in detail, opposite page, right. DOOR & ARCHITRAVE: The warm, light brown hue of the door and architrave blends well with the beige and rose colours on the wall. This same hue serves as the background colour for the burr wood graining technique on page 240.

Thanks to increased interest in decorative finishes, you can often find sea sponges in paint shops today. Or you can order them by mail (see source list). They are also available in the cosmetics sections of chemists and health food shops, but they usually cost a bit more when obtained from these sources.

Sea sponges are either flat or round. For best results, pick a large flat one. If only round ones are available, however, you can cut them in half to get a flat surface. If you can't get a sea sponge, try converting a household sponge: When it's dry, cut random bits out of it with a craft knife to approximate the irregular texture of a sea sponge.

For the techniques in this chapter, strive to show off the sponge pattern and to let the background come through. Sponging produces highly textured finishes that offer special bonuses: The finishes are particularly effective for camouflaging walls in poor condition. And sponged finishes are durable enough for high-traffic areas such as hallways and hard-use spaces such as children's bedrooms and playrooms.

Sponged finishes can be executed quickly and thus are well suited to emulsion paint, which dries much faster than oil paint. Because emulsion dries so quickly, however, correct any mistakes immediately with a clean sponge and water. If you're working on a hot dry day and executing either sponging off or another "subtractive" technique (one in which glaze is painted on, then removed with a sponge), sponge your surfaces with water beforehand to slow the drying process. Note that the glaze coat used in sponging requires less paint than most finishes because so much of the background remains visible.

To avoid repeating the same pattern over and over, vary your movements as you apply the sponge to the surface. Turn your hand slightly from side to side before each touch, and occasionally change the position of the sponge.

Step-by-step instructions for each technique begin with the glaze coat. Before you start, your base coat should be dry and cured. (Information on mixing a base coat is found in Chapter Four; details on applying it are in Chapter Three.)

Detail of wall, as shown opposite page.

Detail of dado, as shown opposite page.

• SPONGING ON •

The technique of sponging on is a great introduction to decorative painting. It lets you get a feel for the process, master the basics of mixing paints, and practice applying them evenly to a surface. Sponging on is one of the easiest techniques because it is *additive*—it requires only that you apply glaze, not remove it, too.

The effect shown here uses a glaze of acrylic medium, water, and artist's acrylics. For a more opaque look, you can sponge on emulsion paint thinned with a little water.

Before you begin, pour the glaze from the container into a roller tray, then reseal the container and put it away to prevent accidents. Next, dip your sponge into a bucket of water to soften it; then wring it out well. Now proceed to step one.

• R E C I P E •

SPONGING ON

LEVEL OF EXPERTISE:

RECOMMENDED ON: walls, floors, ceilings, large and small flat surfaces, furniture with minimal carving

NOT RECOMMENDED ON: small areas with extensive carving such as ornate mouldings

NUMBER OF PEOPLE: 1

TOOLS: containers for paint, 2 sea sponges, roller tray, gallon bucket of water, clean rags for wiping mistakes, gloves

BASE COAT: satin emulsion paint

GLAZE: 2 parts acrylic medium to 1 part water

COLOURS: sample base coat—$2/3$ white emulsion plus $2/9$ burnt umber acrylic, $1/9$ yellow ochre acrylic, and dash of red acrylic

glaze—$1/3$ white, $1/3$ burnt umber, and $1/3$ ultramarine blue acrylic

VARNISH: optional

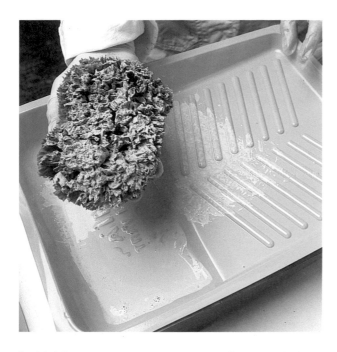

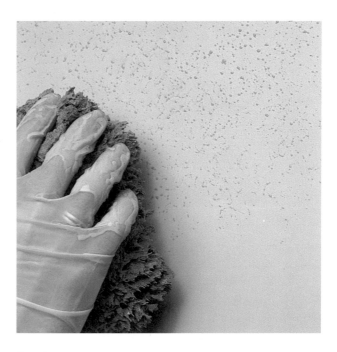

1 Holding a dampened sponge flat, dip it into glaze, then slide sponge toward top of tray and move it in a circle. Check that glaze coats sponge evenly. Don't overload sponge, or your first imprint will be muddy and drippy. Until you feel confident, test your first imprint on paper after loading and reloading the sponge.

2 Keeping sponge flat, dab surface quickly. Hold sponge lightly—squeezing it will change its shape. Work from the wrist, not the elbow, for a light touch. To vary the pattern, turn the sponge slightly as you lift it—not when it's on the surface, or you'll make sliding marks.

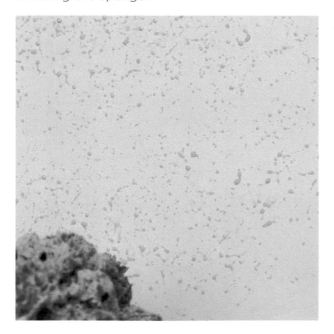

3 Apply glaze so that individual sponge marks don't show. To get an even finish, increase pressure on the sponge as it runs low on paint.

4 Dark and light areas create depth on the finished surface. Note that you can't tell how many sponge imprints were made. This finish derives its translucence from its thin, transparent glaze. For a variation, use opaque emulsion paint thinned to medium consistency in place of glaze.

• SPONGING ON: LIGHT OVER DARK •

Simple sponging on can take on sophistication and imbue a room with dramatic flair when you execute it in light and dark hues like the ones shown. Make an extra effort to ensure that you sponge on in a random manner: Any repetitive pattern that forms will be particularly noticeable because of the great contrast in colours. Step back and examine your surface frequently.

• R E C I P E •

SPONGING ON: LIGHT OVER DARK

LEVEL OF EXPERTISE:

RECOMMENDED ON: walls, ceilings, floors, large or small flat surfaces, furniture with minimal carving

NOT RECOMMENDED ON: small areas with extensive carving such as ornate mouldings

NUMBER OF PEOPLE: 1

TOOLS: containers for paint, sea sponges, roller tray, gallon bucket of water, clean rags for wiping mistakes, gloves

BASE COAT: satin emulsion paint

GLAZE: light glaze—2 parts medium to 1 part water
transparent blue glaze—1 part medium to 3 parts water

COLOURS: sample base coat—½ Mars violet acrylic plus ¼ black latex and ¼ Prussian blue acrylic

light glaze—¾ ultramarine blue and ¼ white plus a little burnt umber and black acrylic

transparent blue glaze—ultramarine blue acrylic

VARNISH: optional

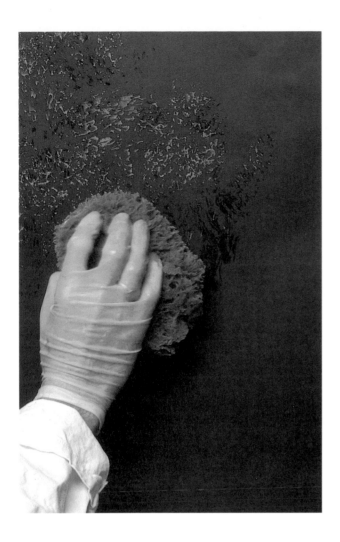

1 Sponge on light glaze over dark base coat. Cover surface evenly but not thickly so that base coat shows through in places. Let glaze dry.

2 When light glaze dries, sponge on transparent blue glaze. Work with sponge, touching lightly in spots. In other places slide the sponge along surface a bit to tone down white glaze but not cover it completely—thus infusing the final effect with a subtle glow.

• SPONGING ON: THREE COLOURS •

When mixing the three glazes for this technique, first prepare a big container of the darkest colour. Pour two-thirds of that into another container, and add some white acrylic to get your medium colour. Add the white a little at a time, testing in between until you get the hue you desire. Finally, pour half of the medium colour into another container, and add enough white to produce your lightest shade. Make this shade whiter than you might want because it will dry transparent and look darker.

A good way to give extra depth to a sponged finish is by employing several tones of the same hue. You can create the tones by adding various amounts of white to whichever colour you choose. A maximum of four tones is recommended, however, because with more than four colours the finish can turn blotchy. No matter how many tones you include, you'll get the most appealing results by allowing the base coat to show through and placing the lightest-toned glaze on top.

• R E C I P E •

SPONGING ON: THREE COLOURS

LEVEL OF EXPERTISE:

RECOMMENDED ON: walls, floors, large or small flat surfaces, furniture with minimal carving

NOT RECOMMENDED ON: ceilings and small areas with extensive carving such as ornate mouldings

NUMBER OF PEOPLE: 1

TOOLS: containers for paint, sea sponges, roller tray, gallon bucket of water, clean rags for wiping mistakes, gloves

BASE COAT: satin emulsion paint

GLAZE: 2 parts acrylic medium to 1 part water

COLOURS: sample base coat—$\frac{2}{3}$ white emulsion plus $\frac{1}{6}$ vermillion red and $\frac{1}{6}$ chrome orange acrylic

dark glaze—$\frac{1}{3}$ deep red, $\frac{1}{3}$ vermillion red, and $\frac{1}{3}$ chrome orange acrylic

medium glaze—the above-mentioned glaze colours plus a dash of white

light glaze—the above-mentioned glaze colours with still more white

VARNISH: optional

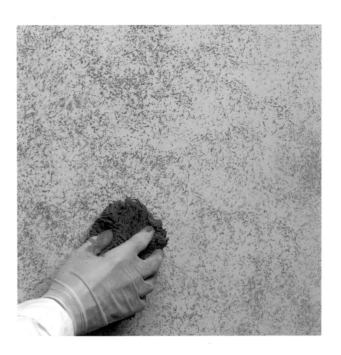

1 Pour medium-toned glaze into roller tray. Dip sponge in water to soften, and wring well. Begin sponging on medium glaze. Cover entire surface, from top to bottom, working in 2-foot-wide vertical strips. Allow glaze to dry. Rinse out sponges and roller and refill bucket with fresh water.

2 Fill tray with darkest glaze. Soften sponge in water. Apply glaze to entire surface in 2-foot-wide strips, but this time create horizontal strips from top to bottom. Let glaze dry. Clean sponges and tray, and change water in bucket.

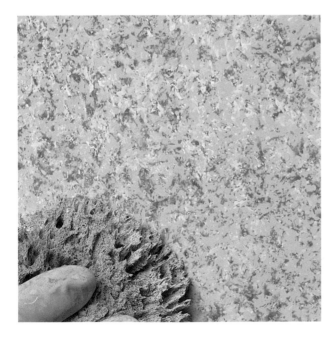

3 Finally, repeat process with lightest glaze. Put it on in 2-foot-wide vertical strips, working from top to bottom.

4 Stand back from your surface and check your final effect for evenness—you shouldn't be able to count the number of times the sponge has marked the surface. Touch up the surface with lightest tone as needed.

· RANDOM SPONGING IN FOUR COLOURS ·

You always want your sponged effects to look "random"—that is, they should appear even from a distance, and you shouldn't be able to count the number of separate sponge marks. But in the name of this technique, "random" applies to the loose arrangement of shapes you create in sponging on the darkest of the four glazes, thus giving the effect a painterly quality.

· R E C I P E ·

RANDOM SPONGING IN FOUR COLOURS

LEVEL OF EXPERTISE:

RECOMMENDED FOR: walls, floors, large and small flat surfaces, furniture with minimal carving

NOT RECOMMENDED ON: ceilings and small areas with extensive carving such as ornate mouldings

NUMBER OF PEOPLE: 1

TOOLS: containers for paint, sea sponges, roller tray, gallon bucket of water, clean rags for wiping mistakes, gloves

BASE COAT: satin emulsion paint

GLAZE: 2 parts acrylic medium to 1 part water

COLOURS: sample base coat—$\frac{2}{3}$ white latex plus $\frac{1}{6}$ ultramarine blue, $\frac{1}{12}$ burnt umber, and $\frac{1}{12}$ chromium oxide acrylic

medium green glaze—$\frac{1}{3}$ white, $\frac{1}{3}$ chromium oxide, $\frac{1}{3}$ ultramarine blue acrylic

dark green glaze—same as above, but more green and less white acrylic

light green glaze—same as medium green glaze plus yellow ochre and more white acrylic

pale pink glaze—$\frac{2}{3}$ white, $\frac{1}{3}$ vermillion red acrylic

VARNISH: optional

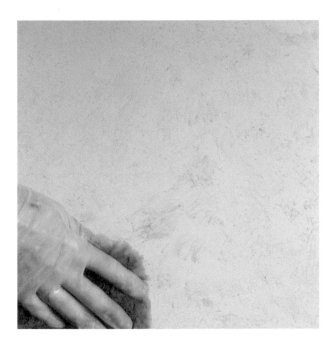

1 Sponge on medium green glaze over entire surface. Occasionally, as you touch sponge to surface, shift it slightly to get dragging effect shown. Allow glaze to dry.

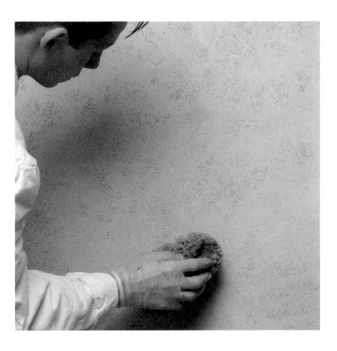

2 Apply dark green glaze in random patches to form a pattern that allows areas of the medium green glaze to remain untouched. Let glaze dry.

3 With light green glaze, mainly fill in areas left untouched by dark glaze. But, for variety, leave some medium green areas uncovered and sponge over a few dark areas as well.

4 Using a lighter touch, apply pale pink glaze to soften the finish. Stand back and examine your surface frequently as you work. Overlap and fill in with pale pink glaze as needed.

• SPONGING OFF •

One of the *subtractive* techniques, sponging off produces a finish that is more subtle and thus perhaps even more pleasing than sponging on. Like all subtractive techniques, this is easiest as a two-person project: One paints on the glaze with a brush; the other follows close behind, removing it with a sponge.

Timing is important here. Don't let the painter get too far ahead of the sponger or the glaze will dry before the sponger reaches it. But don't sponge the glaze off immediately after it's been applied, either, because the glaze might run. Experiment to see what works best.

The project pictured here is done in emulsion paints. On large surfaces like walls, however, sponging off is more easily executed in oil paint, which has a slower drying time. This holds true for all the two-step techniques.

• R E C I P E •

SPONGING OFF

LEVEL OF EXPERTISE:

RECOMMENDED ON: flat surfaces (but use oil instead of water-based paint for large surfaces like walls)

NOT RECOMMENDED ON: ceilings and small areas with extensive carving such as ornate mouldings

NUMBER OF PEOPLE: 2

TOOLS: containers for paint, household brush for applying glaze, sea sponges for removing glaze, roller tray, 2 buckets of water to rinse sponges, gloves

BASE COAT: silk emulsion paint

GLAZE: 3½ parts water to ½ part acrylic medium plus retarder to slow drying time (for amount, follow instructions on label)

COLOURS: sample base coat—⅔ white emulsion plus ⅙ oxide of chrome, ⅙ burnt umber, and a dash of ultramarine blue

acrylic glaze—⅓ ultramarine blue, ⅓ raw umber, ⅙ green oxide, ⅙ black, and a dash of white acrylic

VARNISH: optional

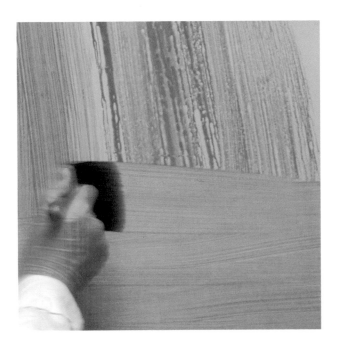

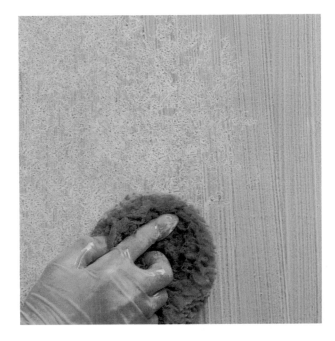

1 For smooth and even coverage on a small surface, first person applies glaze in a crisscross fashion with fully loaded brush. First, paint it on from top to bottom; then run brush over it from side to side; finally, move from top to bottom again. Reload brush as needed. (For large surfaces, apply glaze with a roller. If you load roller well with glaze, you may not have to crisscross your glaze; it may look even enough on the first pass.) Work in 2-foot-wide strips so that glaze doesn't dry too quickly to be sponged off. Glaze should be very wet, almost runny. Second person immerses sea sponge in bucket of water, then wrings sponge thoroughly. (Rinse sponge often and wring well during the process. When water in first bucket darkens, use second bucket. For best results, switch to a clean sponge when you're halfway through the project.)

2 Then, before glaze dries, second person repeatedly pats sponge lightly against wall, turning it slightly in air to avoid creating the same pattern each time. For large surfaces, second person must follow first person closely, working in 2-foot-wide vertical strips. Make sure edges of strips meet but don't overlap and form dark edges.

3 When completed, surface should be dry enough to hold its pattern. If glaze is still runny, go over surface quickly with fresh sponge. Note, however, that this will lighten finish. As with all subtractive techniques, the more glaze you remove, the lighter your finish.

COMBINATION:
• SPONGING OFF AND ON •

This technique offers a more delicate alternative to the multi-toned method for achieving depth. For best effect, it should be executed with two glazes of the same color and tone, but the glaze used for sponging off should be a thinned-down version of the glaze used for sponging on.

The process starts with sponging off, explained on page 102 and recapped here. Follow this effect with sponging on, discussed on page 94.

• R E C I P E •

COMBINATION: SPONGING OFF AND ON

LEVEL OF EXPERTISE:

RECOMMENDED ON: walls, floors, large and small flat surfaces, furniture with minimal carving

NOT RECOMMENDED ON: ceilings and small areas with extensive carving such as ornate mouldings

NUMBER OF PEOPLE: 2

TOOLS: containers for paint, sea sponges, 2 gallon buckets of water, roller or household brush for applying glaze, clean rags for wiping mistakes, gloves

BASE COAT: silk emulsion paint

GLAZE: thin glaze—3 parts water to 1 part acrylic medium (for sponging off)

thick glaze—1 part water to 2 parts acrylic medium (for sponging on)

COLOURS: sample base coat—⅔ white latex plus ⅙ burnt umber and ⅙ ultramarine blue acrylic

glazes—⅓ white, a little more than ⅓ burnt umber, a little less than ⅓ ultramarine blue, a dash of black acrylic

VARNISH: optional

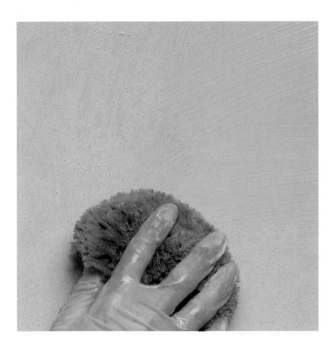

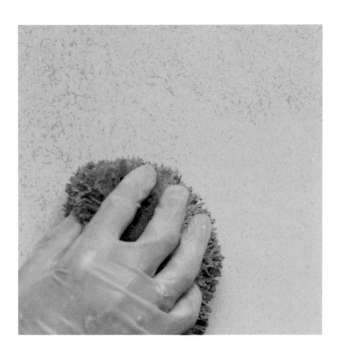

1 First person begins by crisscrossing layers of thin glaze with brush or roller—apply glaze first from top to bottom, then go over it from side to side and, finally, top to bottom. (Use brush for small surfaces, roller for large ones.) Second person follows quickly, removing glaze with fresh dampened sponge. Allow surface to dry before proceeding to step 2.

2 Sponge thick glaze on over entire surface. (Only one person is needed for sponging on.)

3 The finished effect exhibits subtlety and depth, thanks to the blending of two techniques.

CHAPTER SIX

•

CLOTH DISTRESSING

RAGGING ON
TWO-TONE RAGGING ON
RAGGING OFF
CHEESECLOTHING
RAG-ROLLING ON
RAG-ROLLING OFF

COMBINATION:
RAGGING OFF AND CHEESECLOTHING

COMBINATION:
RAGGING OFF AND
CHEESECLOTHING IN TWO COLOURS

RAGGING OFF AND CHEESECLOTHING:
LIGHT OVER DARK

ONE OF THE MOST POPULAR FINISHES TODAY, CLOTH DISTRESSING IS
both quick and easy to execute. As its name indicates, it "distresses" a surface by using cloth to apply or
remove paint. Although often considered a delicate finish, it is great at hiding imperfections in surfaces. For
cloth distressing, however, good preparation is a must—especially on surfaces with cracks. The techniques
require a thin glaze, which can easily seep into cracks and make them appear darker. (See Preparing to Paint,
Chapter Three, for advice.)

Cloth distressing is one of the more versatile finishes. Its look changes depending on the colours and the
kind of cloth you use. More refined than sponging, it offers effects from homey to sophisticated. Done in
deep, rich colours, a cloth-distressed surface can even look like leather.

In producing these techniques, you will frequently dip rags into oil glaze and turpentine; so wear rubber
gloves to protect your hands and a mask to guard against fumes. Work in a well-ventilated area, but don't

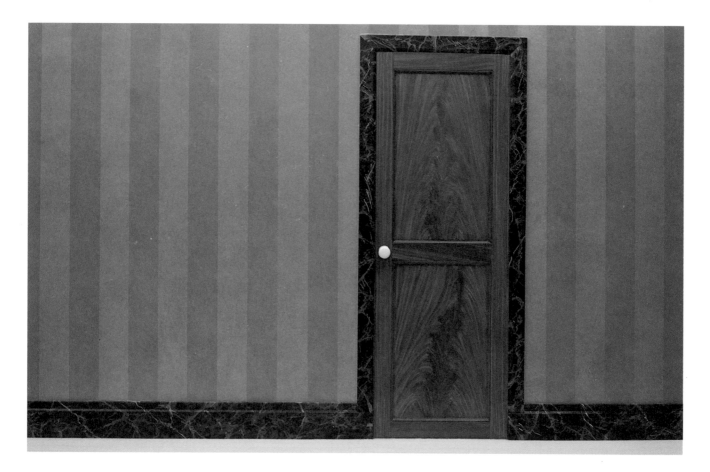

WALL: The entire base-coated surface, above and below the chair rail, was divided into 5-inch strips. Then
every other strip was taped to create clean edges. The untaped strips were cheeseclothed first in a warm
red tone. When the paint dried, the tape was carefully removed, and the entire surface was then cheese-
clothed in a similar value. WOODWORK: The skirting displays a sea green marble, executed in acrylics.
DOOR: A rich feathered mahogany enhances the panelled door.

create a draught because dust might get stirred up and stick to wet paint. Never leave rags soaked in paint or turpentine in a confined area—they can catch fire. Instead, spread them out to dry before discarding them.

If you like, you can substitute semigloss emulsion paint for the oil-based under-coat listed in the charts. Emulsion is more absorbent than oil-based but can still be topped with oil glaze to fine effect. Since cloth distressing can be executed quickly, you might even try some of these techniques on small surfaces with faster-drying water-based glaze—once you have gained some experience.

As with all finishes, the final appearance depends greatly on the colours of your glaze and base coats, on the glossiness and translucence of your glaze, and on how lightly or firmly you dab your tool (cloth) on the surface when applying or removing glaze. The harder you touch the surface, the more glaze you will apply with additive techniques and remove with subtractive techniques. In addition, the subtractive methods, such as ragging *off*, give smoother and more sophisticated looks than the additive techniques like ragging *on*. But keep in mind that subtractive techniques usually require two people—one to paint or roll on the glaze and the other to remove the glaze before it dries. For small objects, however, one person can probably handle both parts of the process.

Take care that your glaze isn't too runny. A glaze that is too thin will be hard to work with. Mix a small batch first, and test it on a sample and then on an inconspicuous spot on your surface. If the glaze runs, wipe it off your surface with a clean cloth, and mix a new batch using less thinner.

Stand back at intervals as you work to see that you are applying glaze evenly. As glaze dries, its appearance changes and looks more even.

Use good-quality rags. Cotton or linen is best (linen is more expensive). Old T-shirts and sheets are great choices. Wash them just before painting to remove lint, and cut them into 2-foot squares with scissors so that no fibres from frayed edges get into the paint.

You can buy cheesecloth or muttoncloth for the cheeseclothing techniques in packages at specialist paint shops. It should be ready to use when removed from the package, but if the edges are frayed, you should trim them.

The subtle quality of cloth distressing can be made more exuberant by employing bright, contrasting hues such as a red glaze over a yellow base coat. You can also alter the look of this finish by experimenting with various materials. In addition to distressing with cotton and cheesecloth, try paper, lace netting, plastic bags, carpet padding, thin canvas, hessian (as long as it doesn't have a lot of loose ends), and anything else that doesn't give off lint.

Make samples to see which materials please you most. For each project, however, use only one material to keep the texture the same throughout. And have enough of the material on hand so that you don't run out in the middle of your project. (During the cloth-distressing process, pieces of material become so saturated that they must be discarded.) Less porous fabrics, like canvas, will produce stronger finishes. For nonporous materials such as plastic, have plenty of newspaper to blot glaze buildup.

• RAGGING ON •

This recipe presents the quick and simple additive technique of ragging on. You apply glaze directly to your base coat with a rag or other material (see preceding suggestions). Start by pouring some glaze from its container into a roller tray, then resealing the container and storing it.

• R E C I P E •

RAGGING ON

LEVEL OF EXPERTISE:

RECOMMENDED ON: flat surfaces—walls, doors, panelling, furniture, small objects

NOT RECOMMENDED ON: ceilings and small highly carved elements such as ornate mouldings

NUMBER OF PEOPLE: 1

TOOLS: cotton rags, container of white spirit for cleanup, roller tray, gloves

BASE COAT: eggshell or satin oil-based paint

GLAZE: about 6 parts ready-mixed oil glaze to 1 part thinner (see Mixing Paints, Chapter Four)

COLOURS: sample base coat—½ white oil-based paint, ¼ raw umber, a little less than ¼ ultramarine blue, and a dash of yellow ochre artist's oils

glaze—⅔ raw umber, ⅓ ultramarine blue, plus a dash of white and a dash of yellow ochre artist's oils

VARNISH: optional

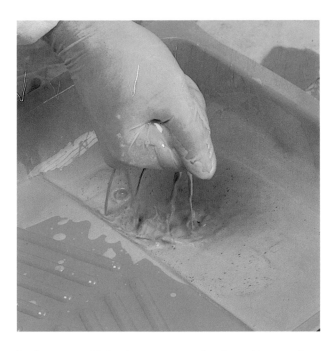

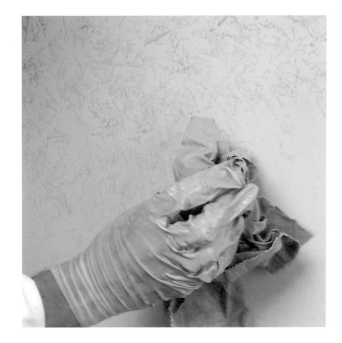

1   Immerse 2-foot-square rag in glaze, then wring.

2   Bunch rag and tuck in ends so that you have as many ridges as possible. (To grasp rag, first hold it high in one hand, then let it fall into a soft pile in your "painting" hand—the one with which you would hold a brush.) Hold rag lightly, using just enough pressure to retain its shape and keep it from falling out of your hand.

3   Touch rag lightly to wall—don't squeeze. When rag is off surface, move your wrist, and sometimes your whole arm, to shift rag from side to side, thereby avoiding a repeat pattern. Rearrange the rag in your hand often. (You shouldn't be able to count how many marks the rag has left on the wall.) Work in 2-foot strips, moving from top of wall to bottom. In the final effect, the opposition of the light base coat and the dark glaze creates depth. Also contributing to depth is the variation in tone of the imprints, caused by the rag's losing paint as you work, then being replenished, and coming back darker. Stand back and review your work. The farther away you stand, the more even the effect will look. You can fix errors, drips, and imbalances by touching up lightly with a rag barely dampened with paint.

• TWO-TONE RAGGING ON •

This technique begins where the preceding recipe—ragging on—leaves off. Note that in this technique you can include another glaze layer in a third tone, if desired. But always be sure to let some of the base coat show—it contributes to the contrast of the finished effect.

• R E C I P E •

TWO-TONE RAGGING ON

LEVEL OF EXPERTISE:

RECOMMENDED ON: flat surfaces—walls, doors, panelling, furniture, accessories

NOT RECOMMENDED ON: ceilings, small highly carved elements such as ornate mouldings

NUMBER OF PEOPLE: 1

TOOLS: cotton rags, container of white spirit, roller tray, gloves

BASE COAT: eggshell or satin oil-based paint

GLAZE: about 6 parts ready-mixed oil glaze to 1 part thinner (see Mixing Paints, Chapter Four)

COLOURS: sample base coat—½ white oil-based paint plus ¼ raw umber, a little less than ¼ ultramarine blue, and a dash of yellow ochre artist's oils

lighter glaze—⅔ raw umber, ⅓ ultramarine blue, and a dash of white and a dash of yellow ochre artist's oils

darker glaze—same as above with more raw umber added

VARNISH: optional

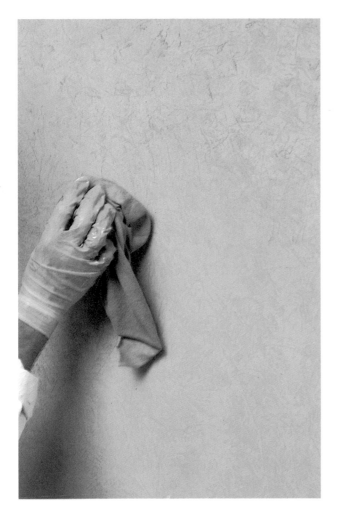

1   Apply pale glaze as instructed in the preceding recipe, ragging on, to get the finish shown in this photo. When the first glaze layer dries, rerag the entire surface with glaze in darker tone to create more depth.

2   Step back and view your end result. It should look random, yet overall should appear even when seen from a distance. You shouldn't be able to count how many times the rags touched your surface.

• RAGGING OFF •

A subtractive technique, ragging off requires one person to paint on the glaze and another to remove it with a bunched-up cloth (or other material, see beginning of this chapter). In exchange for this double duty, however, it offers a smoother and subtler finish than ragging on. To begin, pour some glaze from its container into a roller tray and store the rest of the glaze to prevent spills.

• R E C I P E •

RAGGING OFF

LEVEL OF EXPERTISE:

RECOMMENDED ON: flat surfaces—walls, doors, panelling, furniture, accessories

NOT RECOMMENDED ON: ceilings and small highly carved elements such as ornate mouldings

NUMBER OF PEOPLE: 2

TOOLS: roller or decorating brush, cotton rags, container of white spirit, roller tray, gloves

BASE COAT: satin oil-based paint

GLAZE: about 6 parts ready-mixed oil glaze to 1 part thinner (see Mixing Paints, Chapter Four)

COLOURS: sample base coat—¾ white oil-based paint plus ⅛ raw umber and ⅛ yellow ochre artist's oils

glaze—⅓ raw umber, ⅓ oxide of chrome, and ⅓ yellow ochre artist's oils

VARNISH: optional

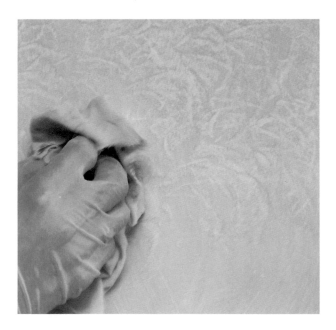

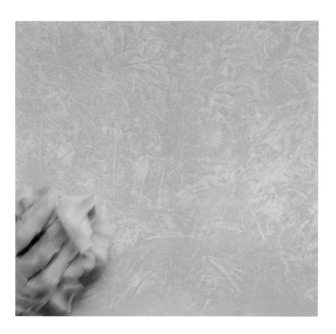

1 First person applies glaze in crisscross fashion—top to bottom, side to side, then top to bottom—with brush or roller, depending on size of surface. Next, if glaze has been applied with a brush, the same person breaks up linear brush marks and creates subtexture by reworking surface with short angled strokes of brush, made by flicking wrist. Form a pattern like the one shown. Second person dips rag into container of white spirit, wrings thoroughly, and bunches rag as described in ragging on (page 111, step 2). Touch surface lightly to remove paint. Shift hand and arm while rag is in air, and rearrange rag in hand at intervals to prevent repetitive pattern. When paint saturates rag (you can tell because rag puts paint back on surface instead of removing it), dip rag in thinner, and wring well. One 2-foot-square rag should last for a medium-sized wall. Try not to change or rinse rag when in the middle of a wall or large panel—this will create a light spot next to an already-glazed area. Wait until you reach a corner, or blot the first few impressions on paper.

2 Rag in 2-foot-wide columns from top to bottom. Avoid reworking completed sections—white spirit on rag may remove too much paint, making a reworked section much lighter than the rest. "Imperfections" may seem glaring during execution but often go unnoticed in a completed project. Ragged walls will "even out" once a room is filled with furniture, paintings, and accessories.

3 Here, similar tones for base coat and glaze give a finish that resembles suede. Note that no lines show where rows of ragging overlap.

• CHEESECLOTHING •

Thin, gauzelike cheesecloth, the material used here to remove glaze, produces the subtle texture of this subtractive finish, which offers a softer effect than ragging off. You can buy cheesecloth or muttoncloth in packages at home centers, hardware stores, and some supermarkets. You'll need about three packages for a medium-sized wall.

Work with large pieces measuring about 2 feet by 3 feet. You can cover more space with them and avoid getting finger marks on your surface.

Cut cloth carefully, and fold the pieces so that the outside edges are tucked in to keep loose threads from getting into paint.

To remove a lot of glaze and thus achieve a lighter effect, change your cloth often. Before applying a new cloth to your surface, however, "ink" the cloth by putting some glaze on a board or palette, and rolling the cloth in the glaze. This will stop the cloth from absorbing too much glaze and leaving an almost white mark on the surface.

• R E C I P E •

CHEESECLOTHING

LEVEL OF EXPERTISE:

RECOMMENDED ON: flat surfaces—walls, doors, panelling, furniture, accessories

NOT RECOMMENDED ON: ceilings, small highly carved elements like ornate mouldings

NUMBER OF PEOPLE: 2

TOOLS: glazing brush, cheesecloth (about 3 packages for medium-size wall), container of white spirit for cleanup, roller tray, board or palette, gloves

BASE COAT: satin oil-based paint

GLAZE: about 6 parts ready-mixed oil glaze to 1 part thinner (see Mixing Paints, Chapter Four)

COLOURS: sample base coat—⅔ white alkyd paint plus ⅙ raw sienna and ⅙ burnt umber and a dash of chrome yellow artist's oils

glaze—½ burnt umber plus ⅓ raw umber and ⅙ burnt sienna artist's oils

VARNISH: optional

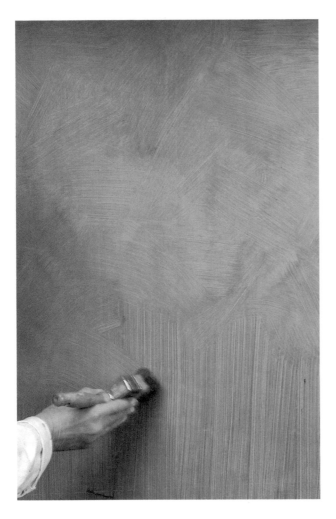 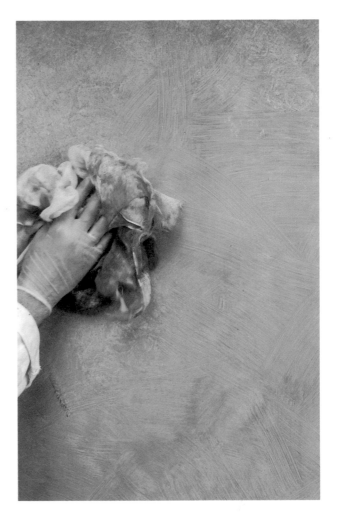

1 First person applies glaze in crisscross fashion—top to bottom, side to side, and top to bottom—with brush or roller, depending on size of surface. Next, if glaze has been applied with brush, break strié effect and create textured background with short, angled strokes of brush made by flicking wrist. Form pattern shown. (See diagram, page 88, for how to apply and remove glaze working in pairs.)

2 Second person "inks" cheesecloth as described in introduction to this technique, bunches cloth in hand, and dabs surface lightly, starting in a top corner and working down the surface in 2-foot-wide vertical strips. Overlap strips just slightly so that no line forms between them.

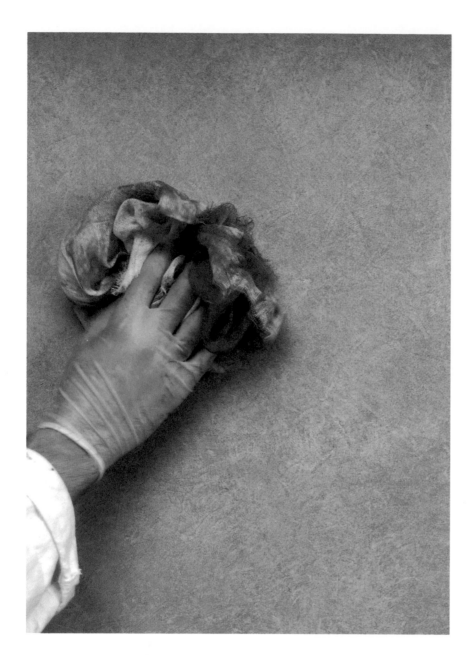

3 To avoid repetitive pattern, move wrist from side to side each time you lift cloth from surface. Rebunch cloth frequently to vary imprints.

4 For finer texture, rework the surface again lightly. The more you go over it, the subtler—and the paler—your texture will be.

• RAG-ROLLING ON •

The shape of the rag is the key to the distinctive look of this technique. Whether applying or removing glaze, you work with a roll of cloth that produces a rhythmic linear pattern in contrast to the random effect of the loosely bunched rag in the previous techniques. The challenge of rag-rolling is to move the rag evenly down the wall. For best results, practice first on a board or an inconspicuous area of your surface.

The technique looks especially rich when done with a light base coat and just slightly darker glaze over a large, flat surface. As for all techniques, the more contrast there is between base coat and glaze, the more pronounced the pattern.

• R E C I P E •

RAG-ROLLING ON

LEVEL OF EXPERTISE:

RECOMMENDED ON: flat surfaces—walls, doors, panelling, furniture

NOT RECOMMENDED ON: ceilings, rounded surfaces like the leg of a chair or small highly carved elements such as ornate mouldings

NUMBER OF PEOPLE: 1

TOOLS: cotton rags, container of white spirit for cleanup and touch-up, roller tray, gloves

BASE COAT: eggshell or satin oil-based paint

GLAZE: about 6 parts ready-mixed oil glaze to 1 part thinner (see Mixing Paints, Chapter Four)

COLOURS: sample base coat—$\frac{2}{3}$ chrome yellow artist's oils and $\frac{1}{3}$ white alkyd paint

glaze—$\frac{2}{3}$ chrome yellow plus $\frac{1}{3}$ raw sienna artist's oils

VARNISH: optional

1 Pour some glaze from its container into roller tray, and re-cover container to avoid spills. Saturate a 2-foot-square rag in glaze, then squeeze thoroughly so that it doesn't drip. Fold rag in half and roll it lengthwise into a loose cylinder, twisting slightly.

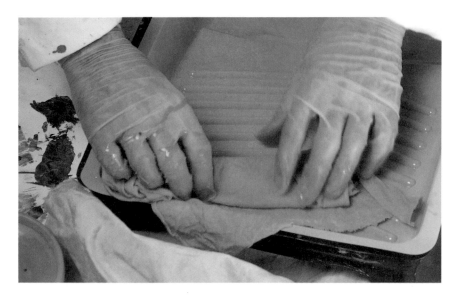

2 Place rag on surface. Work from top to bottom in vertical strips the width of the rag, each strip just touching the next. Roll rag from end with one hand while guiding rag with the other hand until rag starts to unroll (usually after about a foot). Concentrate on rolling rag evenly. When you reach the bottom of the strip, move to the top of the next strip, overlapping imprints slightly. Redip rag when imprint gets too light. Re-roll and test before continuing.

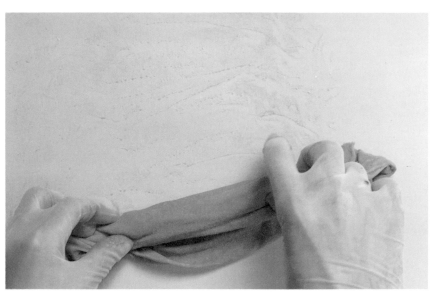

3 The completed effect features a more linear pattern than ragging, thanks to the shape of the cloth.

· RAG-ROLLING OFF ·

Like the previous technique, the subtractive version of rag-rolling looks especially good when executed in light colours, and large flat surfaces display it to best effect. The challenge—keeping your cloth moving evenly along your surface—remains the same, as does the solution: Practice beforehand on a board, paper, or inconspicuous area of your surface.

· R E C I P E ·

RAG-ROLLING OFF

LEVEL OF EXPERTISE:

RECOMMENDED ON: flat surfaces—especially walls, but also doors, panelling, furniture, accessories

NOT RECOMMENDED ON: ceilings, rounded surfaces like chair legs, small highly carved elements such as ornate mouldings

NUMBER OF PEOPLE: 2

TOOLS: glazing brush, cotton rags, container of white spirit, roller tray, gloves

BASE COAT: satin oil-based paint

GLAZE: about 6 parts ready-mixed oil glaze to 1 part thinner (see Mixing Paints, Chapter Four)

COLOURS: sample base coat—⅔ chrome yellow artist's oils and ⅓ white oil-based paint

glaze—⅔ chrome yellow plus ⅓ raw sienna artist's oils

VARNISH: optional

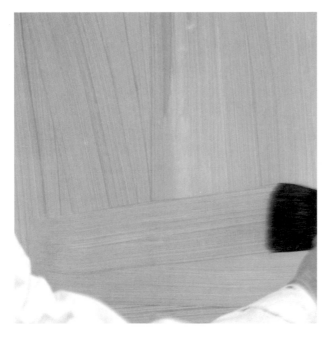

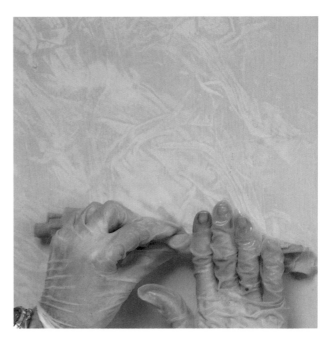

1 Apply glaze with brush or roller, depending on surface size, in crisscross fashion: top to bottom, side to side, then top to bottom. (See diagram, page 88, for advice on how to execute subtractive techniques on large surfaces working in pairs.) Dip 2-foot-square rag into container of white spirit. Squeeze rag thoroughly, until almost dry, to prevent drips. Then fold rag in half and roll it lengthwise into a cylinder, twisting slightly.

2 Place rag on surface, and begin working from top to bottom in vertical strips the width of the rag. Strips should just touch each other. As photo shows, roll rag from end with one hand while guiding it with fingers of other hand to lift glaze and let background show through. Work until rag starts to unroll (after about a foot), then reroll and continue.

3 Overlap the rows of rag-rolling slightly so that no line appears between them. Once you've completed a section, don't rework it—you might pick up too much glaze and leave a white spot. The finished surface should have an even, linear look.

COMBINATION:
• RAGGING OFF AND CHEESECLOTHING •

This recipe, like the two previous techniques, produces a soft, elegant effect. Start with ragging off because it provides more contrast. Then use cheeseclothing to tone down the effect. This technique works well with a base coat and glaze that have good contrast because you go over the surface twice, blending the colours thoroughly.

distinction between pale tones would blur too easily, and the finish would lose depth.

You must work fast on this technique because you have to go over the glaze twice before it dries. Work with a partner. The first person applies the glaze, the second person rags off, and then the first person does the cheeseclothing.

• R E C I P E •

COMBINATION: RAGGING OFF AND CHEESECLOTHING

LEVEL OF EXPERTISE:

RECOMMENDED ON: flat surfaces—especially walls but also doors, panels, tabletops

NOT RECOMMENDED ON: ceilings, rounded surfaces like chair legs, small highly carved elements such as ornate mouldings

NUMBER OF PEOPLE: 2

TOOLS: roller or household brush, cotton rags, cheesecloth, roller tray, container of white spirit (not needed if base coat and glaze are light coloured or you don't want a lot of contrast), gloves

BASE COAT: eggshell or satin oil-based paint

GLAZE: about 6 parts ready-mixed oil glaze to 1 part thinner (see Mixing Paints, Chapter Four)

COLOURS: sample base coat—⅔ white oil-based paint plus ⅙ burnt sienna and ⅙ yellow ochre artist's oils

glaze—⅓ red ochre plus ⅙ raw umber, ⅙ burnt umber, ⅙ vermillion red, and ⅙ ultramarine blue artist's oils

VARNISH: optional

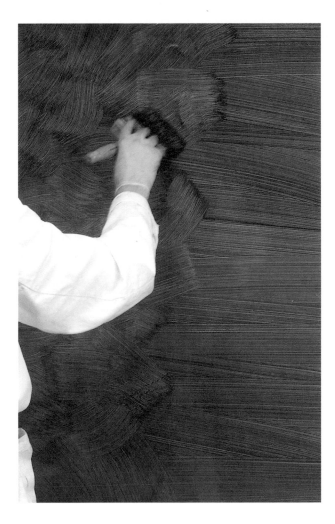

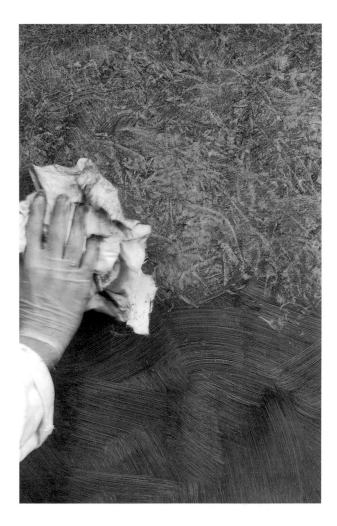

1 Apply glaze in crisscross manner—up and down, side to side, and up and down—with roller or brush, depending on size of surface. Next, if glaze has been applied with brush, break strié effect and add background texture by reworking surface with sharp angled strokes of brush, made by flicking wrist, to form pattern shown. (See diagram, page 88, for how to execute subtractive techniques on large surfaces by working in pairs.)

2 First, rag off over entire surface. Follow instructions for ragging off (page 114), with one exception: if using light glaze over even lighter background, as illustrated here, do not dip cloth into turpentine. A dry rag removes enough glaze to create depth and contrast. And don't be afraid to rag off vigorously—the next step will temper its effect.

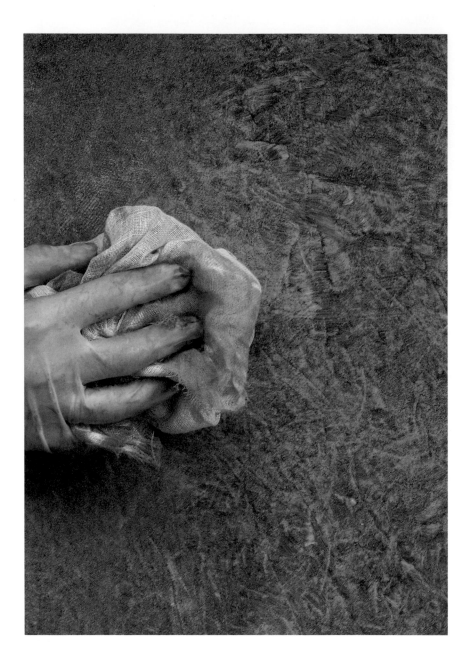

3 Cheesecloth—following instructions in cheeseclothing recipe, page 116—on top of ragging off to soften and smooth the finish.

4 The completed effect offers more depth than plain cheeseclothing and more subtlety than just ragging off. For a less textured look, fold cheesecloth into a flat pad instead of bunching it in your hand.

COMBINATION:

• RAGGING OFF AND CHEESECLOTHING IN TWO COLOURS •

Although similar to rag-rolling off, this version has a painterly quality to it. The job is a bit more challenging because it involves some painting composition. By standing back and studying your surface, you decide how much of two glaze colours to use and where to place them. Your goal is an effect that appears random yet has an overall evenness to it when viewed from a distance.

To begin, mix two batches of glaze. As this ex-ample depicts, two contrasting hues are best and one colour should be darker than the other. Here, ragging and cheeseclothing soften and blend the amber glaze with the grey yet leave enough con-trast for a finish with great depth.

Note: It is important to do several samples and view them in various lights to ensure that the colo-urs you've selected blend well together. Always use less of the darker colour in your design.

• R E C I P E •

COMBINATION: RAGGING OFF AND CHEESECLOTHING IN TWO COLOURS

LEVEL OF EXPERTISE:

RECOMMENDED ON: flat surfaces—walls, doors, panelling, furniture, accessories

NOT RECOMMENDED ON: ceilings, highly carved elements such as ornate mould-ings, very large rooms (because of exten-sive time required)

NUMBER OF PEOPLE: 2

TOOLS: 2 flat 1-inch-wide brushes, 2 con-tainers for glazes, cotton rags, cheese-cloth, container of white spirit, roller tray, gloves

BASE COAT: eggshell or satin oil-based paint

GLAZE: about 6 parts ready-mixed oil glaze to 1 part thinner (see Mixing Paints, Chapter Four)

COLOURS: sample base coat—⅔ white al-kyd paint plus 2/9 raw umber and 1/9 yellow ochre artist's oils

grey glaze—⅓ white oil-based paint plus ⅓ raw umber, ⅙ black, and ⅙ ultramarine blue artist's oils

amber glaze—½ chrome orange, ⅙ yellow ochre, ⅙ burnt sienna, and ⅙ vermillion red artist's oils

VARNISH: optional

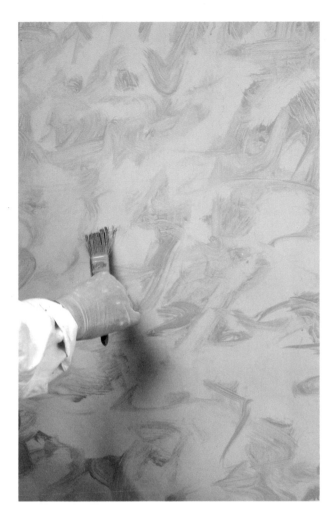 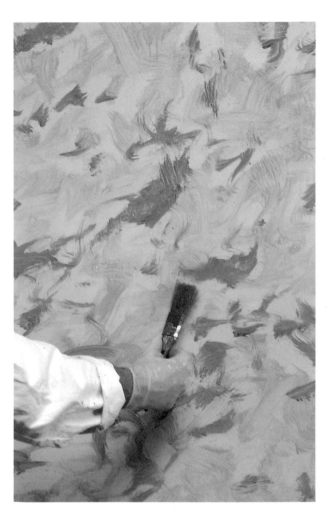

1 With a 1-inch-wide long-haired brush, apply grey glaze in random array of squiggly lines, as shown. Vary size, shape, and intensity (some light, some dark) of your strokes. Cover about 50 percent of your surface, taking care not to create highly defined sections or patterns.

2 With another 1-inch brush, fill some gaps in grey glaze with amber glaze. Base coat should be visible around all brush marks in both colours. As with grey glaze, make random strokes that vary in size, shape, and intensity. In some spots, leave the base coat showing; in a few others, let amber overlap grey glaze. Dip cotton cloth in white spirit, and start ragging off, following directions on page 114.

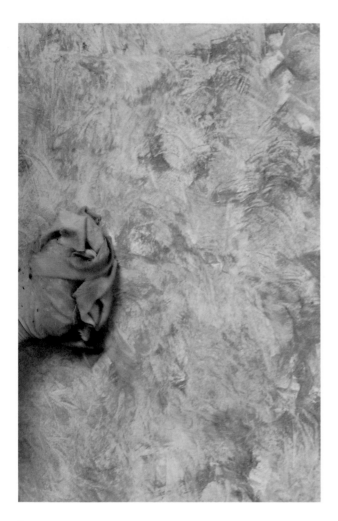

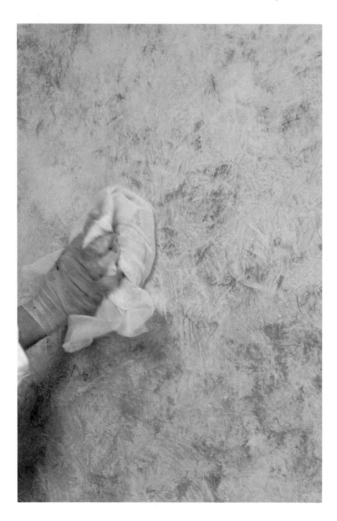

3 Rag off over entire surface, flattening brush strokes and combining colours.

4 Cheesecloth over entire surface to smooth finish, following instructions on page 116.

5 A close-up of the finished effect shows its resemblance to marble. In fact, the finish makes a good background over which to execute some of the marbling techniques in Chapter Twelve. Because it recalls marble, the finish adds weight to a surface visually and works well on the lower half of a wall. You might, perhaps, use it on a dado and do a stippled effect (see Chapter Seven) on the wall above.

• RAGGING OFF AND CHEESECLOTHING: LIGHT OVER DARK •

A subtle finish when executed in two similar tones, ragging off and cheeseclothing takes on a dramatic look when done in a dark base coat and light glaze. On accessories such as a small table, it conveys some of the richness of marble. Try it on columns or mouldings for a striking effect that might complement a high-tech setting in a home, a restaurant, a gallery, or a boutique.

• R E C I P E •

RAGGING OFF AND CHEESECLOTHING: LIGHT OVER DARK

LEVEL OF EXPERTISE:

RECOMMENDED ON: flat surfaces— walls, doors, panels, furniture, accessories

NOT RECOMMENDED ON: ceilings, highly carved elements such as ornate mouldings

NUMBER OF PEOPLE: 2

TOOLS: flat 1-inch-wide brush, container of white spirit, cotton rags, cheesecloth, gloves

BASE COAT: satin oil-based paint

GLAZE: about 6 parts ready-mixed oil glaze to 1 part thinner (see Mixing Paints, Chapter Four)

COLOURS: sample base coat—½ black oil-based paint plus ¼ emerald green plus ¼ chrome green artist's oils

glaze—½ titanium white, ½ oxide of chrome, and a dash of chrome yellow artist's oils

VARNISH: optional

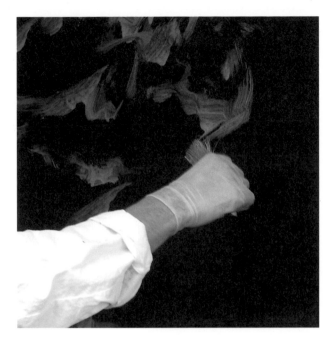

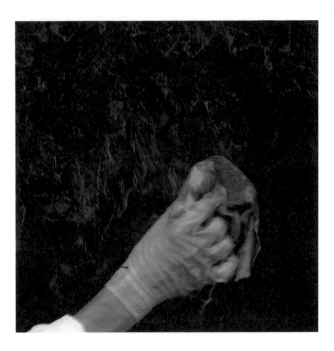

1 Over a dark base coat, apply pale glaze with a 1-inch-wide brush. As described in step 1 of preceding recipe, paint a random array of wavy strokes, covering about 50 percent of your surface. Vary size, shape, and intensity of your strokes.

2 Rag off over entire surface, following directions on page 114.

3 Cheesecloth over entire surface, following directions on page 116. The final effect offers a marblelike surface with great depth. Note: this finish serves as the background for the green marble finish in Chapter Twelve.

CHAPTER SEVEN

•

STIPPLING

STIPPLING
WIPING OFF
WIPING OFF IN THREE COLOURS
FADE-AWAY STIPPLING

FOR CLASSIC ELEGANCE, TURN TO THE STIPPLED FINISH. GREAT FOR

giving new surfaces an aged look, stippling has a fine texture and little depth. Because of its smoothness and evenness, however, it is best executed only on surfaces that are in excellent condition. While some techniques, like sponging and ragging, hide imperfections, stippling practically underscores them.

Stippling requires a more even, consistent touch in applying glaze than the techniques in preceding chapters. Decorative painters traditionally use special brushes to create its subtle texture. Stippling brushes have round wooden handles and long, soft bristles; they come in various sizes to suit a range of projects.

You'll find, however, that stippling brushes are expensive (at least £50 for a wall-sized 5- by 7-inch one) and cannot always be found in paint stores or art supply stores. (See source list for mail-order outlets.) Instead of a stippling brush, you can try a long, narrow white-bristled brush. Sometimes a shoe, clothes, or even scrub brush will work. And before you rule out a stippling brush on the basis of cost, consider that it's handy for

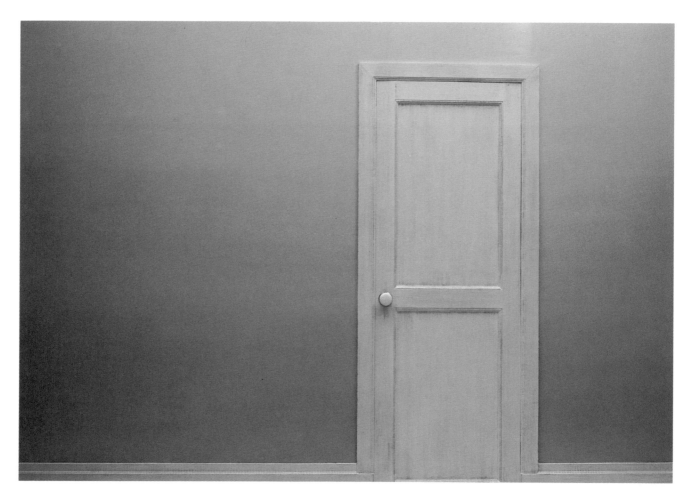

Arranging stippled bands from dark to light as shown here adds height to a room visually. The technique is more effective in, say, a large dining room, where you can view it from a distance, than in a narrow hall.

stippling out corners as well as developing a sub-texture and smoothing in other techniques.

In most decorative techniques, you either re-move or add glaze, but in stippling you just move the glaze. By dabbing it lightly and steadily with your brush, you transform the paint into a mass of tiny dots.

An oil-based base coat is a must in stippling, and oil glaze is highly recommended for all surfaces except very small ones—emulsion and acrylic paints dry too fast. If you can work quickly, you can apply the glaze and stipple it yourself; but for large surfaces, you'll probably prefer working with a partner.

Stippling complements other historical finishes such as dragging. It has an excellent softening effect on bright or dark colours, and although subtle, its texture is much richer than a rolled-on or brush-painted surface.

Try to keep stippled surfaces free of drips and splotches; fixing them can mean redoing an entire surface. The more you go over stippling, the lighter it gets, and in this delicate finish, white areas really stand out. So it is usually best to leave small imperfections. They'll fade into obscurity in a room filled with furniture.

Stippling usually requires two passes for even-ness. One person applies glaze, working from top to bottom of a surface in 2-foot-wide strips. The other person goes over the strips with a stippling brush while glaze is still wet. (See diagram, page 88, for how to work in pairs.)

Experiment with the timing of applying and stip-pling glaze to determine what works best. Stand back from your completed surface and check its evenness. If needed, have one person restipple it, starting in a top corner and moving *across* the surface in 2-foot-wide strips.

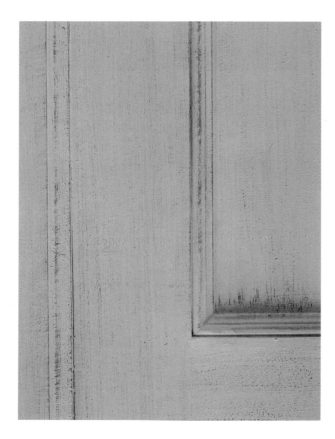

DOOR: The time-worn finish is obtained by apply-ing fine lines of grey paint over an off-white base coat with a flat wide white-bristle brush, using paint that is almost dry.

STIPPLING: The fine-grained texture of this finish helps emphasize the fade-away effect.

• STIPPLING •

The example shown here was small enough to be glazed with a brush (step 1). However, for best results in stippling a large surface—anything bigger than a set of double doors—apply glaze using a roller with a medium-fine cover. A roller speeds up the job, leaves fewer marks than a brush, and naturally forms a stippled-like subtexture, which lets you save more time by skipping the "prestippling" portion of step 1 below.

The technique is easiest with a partner. One person applies the glaze in 2-foot-wide strips and "prestipples" it, if needed. The other follows with a stippling brush.

• R E C I P E •

STIPPLING

LEVEL OF EXPERTISE:

RECOMMENDED ON: almost all surfaces—flat, curved, or high relief

NOT RECOMMENDED ON: porous surfaces like raw plaster or surfaces in poor condition

NUMBER OF PEOPLE: 2

TOOLS: roller or household brush, roller tray, stippling brush, gloves, goggles

BASE COAT: satin or oil-based paint

GLAZE: *either* about 6 parts ready-mixed glaze to 1 part thinner (see Mixing Paints, Chapter Four) *or* about 1 part linseed oil to 3 parts turpentine plus a few drops of terebine liquid dryer

COLOURS: sample base coat—deep red oil-based paint

glaze—¾ raw umber plus ¼ black artist's oils

VARNISH: optional

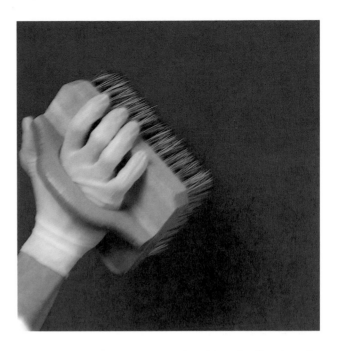

1 With large flat brush, apply glaze in crisscross manner—top to bottom, side to side, and top to bottom. To break up brush marks and texture background, stipple quickly over entire surface with brush.

2 Dab entire surface evenly with stippling brush. Hold brush as illustrated in photo. Touch surface lightly and quickly in bouncing motion. Work from wrist, not arm—it's less tiring and ensures a soft touch. Move wrist from side to side when brush is in air to vary imprints; overlap imprints slightly.

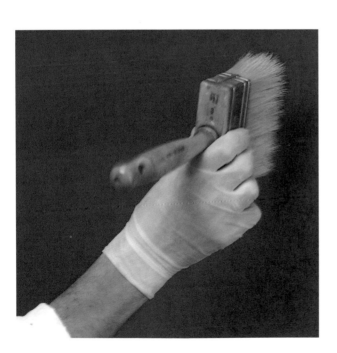

3 If you don't have a stippling brush, you can use a block brush. Hold it as shown here. Because it makes smaller imprints, however, work is slower and evenness harder to obtain.

4 Stippling here mellows a strong color while playing up its richness.

• WIPING OFF •

A wonderful way to add character to a room is to "age" its architectural elements with the technique of wiping off. A delicate and elegant finish, it enhances skirting, chair rails, cornice mouldings, and ceiling medallions without overemphasizing them and can bring out detail lost under layers of paint. Aptly nicknamed "the maid's technique," it imitates the look of mouldings dusted over and over again—wiped almost clean on the flat areas but not thoroughly cleaned of dust in the grooves.

Of course, as wiping off emphasizes details, it also pulls up any nicks and scratches. In most cases, however, this just embellishes the time-worn appearance.

Wiped-off moulding makes a fine complement to the subtlety of stippled walls. For optimum effect, select a light base coat and a slightly darker glaze. Mix a glaze that "looks like dust" by combining the main colour of your base coat with raw umber. If, for example, your base coat is salmon, create a soft, warm-toned glaze with raw umber and red.

One or two people can execute this technique. If working with a partner, one person applies the glaze and stipples it, and then the other wipes. Wiping can take time—don't let the first person get too far ahead of the second. Glaze should be wiped when fresh or it will be hard to remove.

• R E C I P E •

WIPING OFF

LEVEL OF EXPERTISE:

RECOMMENDED ON: only high-relief ornate surfaces such as mouldings and carved furniture

NOT RECOMMENDED ON: flat surfaces

NUMBER OF PEOPLE: 1 or 2

TOOLS: 1- or 2-inch-wide gloss brush, medium stippling or stainer's brush, small round brush, clean and soft cotton rags, small wooden block (optional), gloves, goggles

BASE COAT: satin oil-based paint

GLAZE: *either* about 6 parts ready-mixed oil glaze to 1 part thinner (see Mixing Paints, Chapter Four) or about 1 part linseed oil to 3 parts turpentine plus few drops terebine liquid dryer

COLOURS: sample base coat—⅔ white oil-based paint plus ⅙ raw umber, ⅙ yellow ochre, and a dash of burnt sienna artist's oils

glaze—½ raw umber and ½ burnt umber artist's oils

VARNISH: none

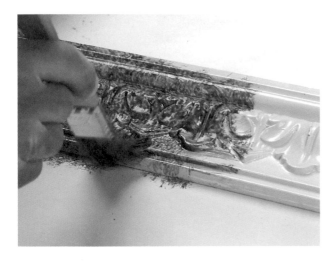

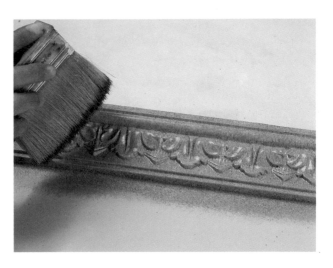

1 Apply glaze to moulding with a 1- or 2-inch-wide brush, depending on moulding size. Dab glaze into carving so that all areas are fully coated. Surface will look rough; glaze can overlap slightly onto wall.

2 Stipple moulding finely with stainer's brush. Make two passes—but not more or glaze will get too light.

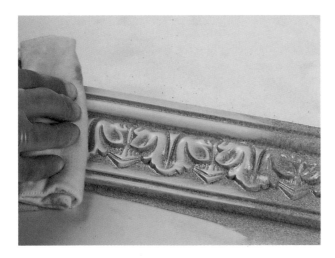

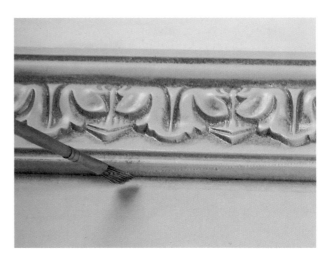

3 Form cotton cloth pad with some body to it by folding a 16-inch square into a 4-inch square, then folding it in half as shown. If needed, tuck small wood block into cloth so that cloth doesn't get into carvings. Wipe along moulding in short strokes. Keep turning cloth, wiping only with a clean section so that you don't put paint back on surface. Fold cloth pad around thumb and work on areas with fine detail. Rotate cloth so that clean section always touches surface.

4 Wipe edges of moulding with rag where it meets the wall. Then, for authenticity, stipple edges of moulding and fade onto wall with dry stippling brush. The refined finish adds visual interest by quietly drawing attention to details of moulding.

· WIPING OFF IN THREE COLOURS ·

A richer-looking version of wiping off (see preceding recipe), the three-colour technique works well with glazes that are close in colour. Shown here on a ceiling medallion, it subtly distinguishes the three sections of the piece.

In contrast to the preceding technique, this example features several harmonious colours—ochre, sienna, and burgundy—which create a look that is more decorative than aged. Because of the relationships between the colours—two are close in tone (sienna and burgundy) and two are from the same colour family (ochre and sienna)—they offer contrast without being jarring.

The process begins here with the largest carved section. Follow steps 1 through 3 of the wiping off recipe: apply one glaze colour with 1- to 2-inch brush, stipple glaze with stippling brush, then fold cloth into firm pad. Now proceed to step 1 below.

· R E C I P E ·

WIPING OFF IN THREE COLOURS

LEVEL OF EXPERTISE:

RECOMMENDED ON: only high-relief ornate surfaces such as mouldings and carved furniture

NOT RECOMMENDED ON: flat surfaces

NUMBER OF PEOPLE: 1 or 2

TOOLS: 1- or 2-inch-wide gloss brush, medium stippling brush, clean and soft cotton rags, small wooden block (optional), small round brush for stippling edges to blend, gloves, goggles

BASE COAT: satin oil-based paint

GLAZE: *either* about 1 part linseed oil to 3 parts turpentine plus few drops terebine liquid dryer *or* about 6 parts ready-mixed oil glaze to 1 part thinner (see Mixing Paints, Chapter Four)

COLOURS: sample base coat—½ white oil-based paint and ½ chrome yellow artist's oils

ochre glaze—⅓ yellow ochre, ⅓ chrome yellow, and ⅓ raw umber artist's oils

sienna glaze—½ raw umber and ½ yellow ochre artist's oils

burgundy glaze—⅓ raw umber, ⅓ alizarin crimson, ⅙ burnt umber, and ⅙ red ochre artist's oils

VARNISH: none

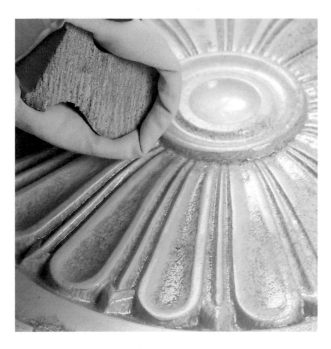

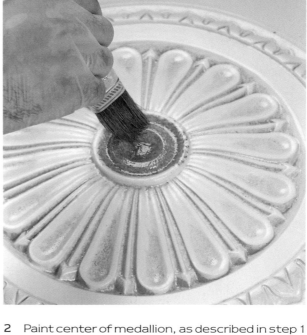

1 Fold cloth around piece of wood and wipe glazed section. (Refer to step 3 of the wiping off recipe for detailed instructions.)

2 Paint center of medallion, as described in step 1 of wiping off, using second glaze colour. Then follow steps 2 and 3 of wiping off (stippling and wiping off glaze) to complete this section. You don't have to wait until previous sections are dry as long as you work very carefully to prevent drips or overlapping onto completed areas.

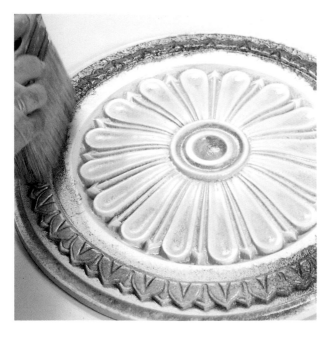

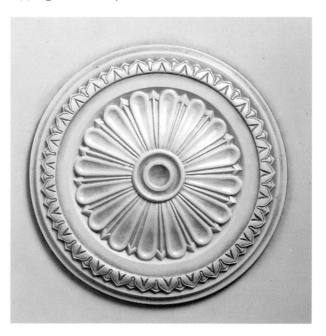

3 Glaze outside ring with third glaze colour (see step 1 of wiping off). Next stipple with stippling brush as shown. Then follow step 3 of wiping off.

4 As described in step 4 of wiping off, stipple edges of medallion and fade off onto ceiling with small round brush.

• FADE-AWAY STIPPLING •

Working fast and evenly with a large stippling brush is the key to success with this advanced technique. It is best displayed on the wall of a room large enough for you to step back and admire the skylike effect. For your glazes, select three tones of a colour—or more, depending on the size of your surface and the difference between your darkest and lightest tones. In this example, tones range from medium to light; three tones were enough to make a smooth transition. But if your tones run from dark to light, you may want two or three tones in between. Try several tones of orange for a sunset effect.

To get tones of glaze that will harmonize, mix them in the following way: Prepare a batch of your darkest tone. Pour one part into a clean container, and add two parts clear glaze to it to get medium tone. Next pour one part medium tone into a clean container, and add two more parts clear glaze to it to get lightest tone. Be sure to mix enough dark glaze so that you don't run out of the different colours in the middle of your project.

Start by taping around mouldings, windows, and doors. Divide your wall horizontally into three bands of equal width. Use a chalkline to mark lines on the wall, trace lines very lightly with a pencil, and dust off chalk. (For how to use a chalkline, see Chapter Nine, Stone-Block Effect.)

• R E C I P E •

FADE-AWAY STIPPLING

LEVEL OF EXPERTISE:

RECOMMENDED ON: flat surfaces only—effect best displayed on large vertical surfaces you can stand back from such as walls, floors, or ceilings, with darkest tone around edges and lightest tone in center

NOT RECOMMENDED ON: carved or rounded surfaces, flat areas less than 3 feet square

NUMBER OF PEOPLE: 2

TOOLS: chalkline, pencil, stepstool, large gloss brushes, large stippling brush, 2 soft flat 1- to 2-inch-wide bristle brushes, gloves, goggles

BASE COAT: semigloss oil-based paint

GLAZE: about 6 parts ready-mixed oil glaze to 1 part thinner (see Mixing Paints, Chapter Four)

COLOURS: sample base coat—½ white oil-based paint, ⅓ ultramarine blue, ⅙ raw umber, and ⅙ black artist's oils

glaze—darkest tone: ⅔ ultramarine blue and ⅓ raw umber plus a dash of titanium white artist's oils

VARNISH: optional

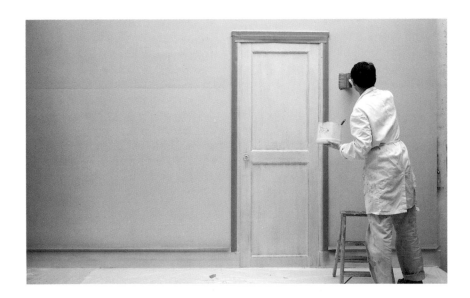

1 With a large gloss brush, paint top band in lightest tone. (By starting with lightest tone, you don't have to clean brush before painting other bands.)

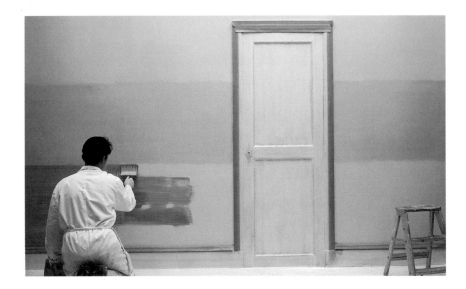

2 Paint next band in medium tone; then apply darkest tone to last band.

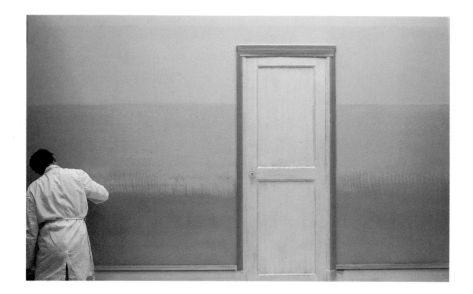

3 Using a dry 1- to 2-inch brush, smooth edges of bands and ease transition between tones. Start between darkest and medium tones: with zigzag motion, sweep some dark tone about 6 inches up into medium color, then some medium tone about 6 inches down into dark. With another brush, repeat process between medium and lightest tone.

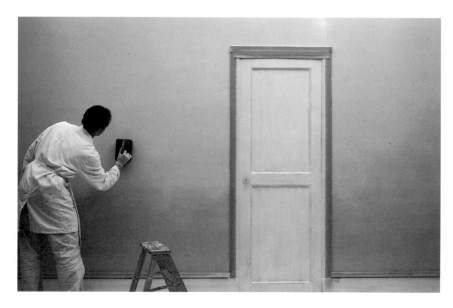

4 With a large stippling brush, start stippling at the bottom of wall and work across. Move up a row, and work across again. Never work in vertical rows—it would ruin the effect. Moving from dark to light brings one colour into the next and blurs bands. Do the whole wall without stopping and don't rework any areas or you'll get light spots, which often can be fixed only by redoing the whole wall.

5 When you reach the top, start down again in horizontal rows, bringing light tone into darker tones now. Don't clean brush at any time during the process.

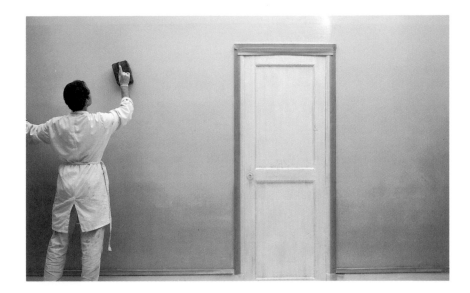

6 Step back and check surface for evenness. If you see any dark or light spots, restipple the surface from bottom to top. Or, using a light touch when surface is almost dry, you might be able to restipple the surface where spots appear.

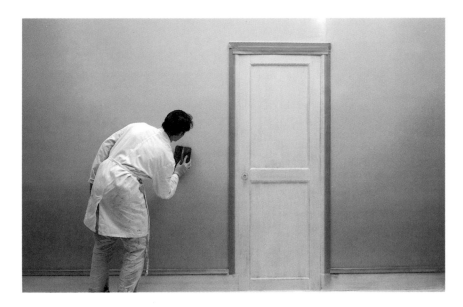

CHAPTER EIGHT

•

COLOUR WASHING

SPONGE WASHING
BRUSH WASHING IN TWO TONES
FADE-AWAY WASHING

COLOUR WASHING CAN IMBUE A ROOM WITH RUSTIC CHARM. SOFT YET with depth and texture, this free-form finish is especially noted for its warm glow, which comes from its thin, translucent glazing. A range of effects are possible, depending on the tool—sponge, brush, cloth—with which you move glaze and whether your glaze is oil or acrylic. Cloth leaves the fewest marks and thus produces the softest effect. An acrylic glaze makes the technique more challenging because it dries fast.

Colour washing suits walls in poor condition because its textured appearance hides imperfections, especially when base coat and glaze are close in colour. Pale glaze over a pale base coat is more informal than dark glaze over a base coat, which can lend a sophisticated air. Earth tones look great colour washed; surfaces appear naturally worn and unevenly faded by time. In most cases, the thinner your glaze, the better, as long as it doesn't run. If you do get drips, you can smooth them out with a dry brush. Work with a partner on these techniques—a thin glaze, whether acrylic or oil, dries fast.

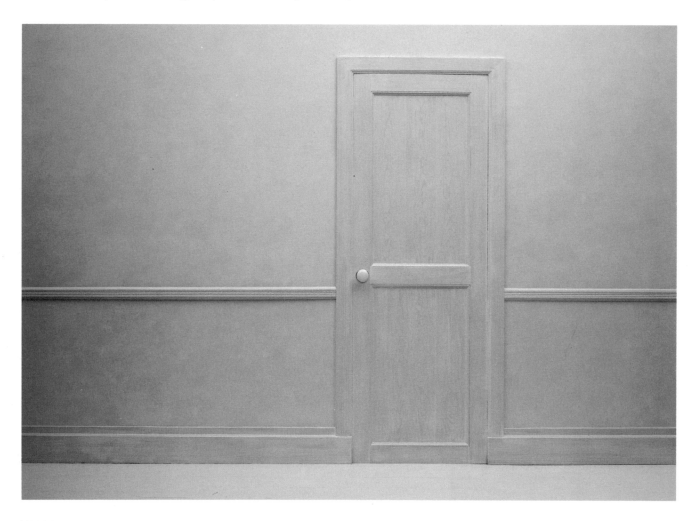

WALL: A brush washing technique embellishes the wall above the chair rail. To create it, work dry with emulsion paints in shades of gray and white over a yellow base coat. Paint with loose, crisscross strokes. DADO: White sponging over a deeper yellow base coat gives the effect that appears on the dado. DOOR & TRIM: After being decorated with pine graining, the door and trim were "aged." White paint was dry brushed over the graining to give the look of an old door that has been painted and sanded several times.

• SPONGE WASHING •

This example shows colour washing done in acrylic glaze with a sea sponge. The technique builds on one from a previous chapter—sponging off. Read the general introduction to Sponging (Chapter Five), and refer to the step-by-step directions for sponging off (page 102) for a detailed explanation of steps 1 and 2 below.

Because water-based glaze dries fast, you will have to work quickly. (You may find it easier to use oil-based paint for very large walls or floors.) This is at least a two-person project—one applies glaze, the other sponges off. A third person to smooth the sponging (step 3) would help.

Your glaze should be watery but not runny. If you're working on a hot day, sponge the surface with water beforehand. (See Paints and Tools, Chapter Two, for more hints on slowing drying time.) When painting a room, dab excess glaze from corners with a piece of sea sponge cut to size, if needed.

• R E C I P E •

SPONGE WASHING

LEVEL OF EXPERTISE:

RECOMMENDED ON: flat surfaces—walls, floors, tabletops

NOT RECOMMENDED ON: ceilings, small highly carved elements such as ornate mouldings

NUMBER OF PEOPLE: 2 or 3

TOOLS: emulsion brush or roller, sea sponges, roller tray, buckets of water, badger-hair brush or soft long-bristle brush for smoothing, gloves

BASE COAT: silk emulsion paint

GLAZE: 3½ parts water to ½ part acrylic medium plus acrylic-gel retarder to slow drying (for amount, follow instructions on label)

COLOURS: sample base coat—⅔ white emulsion paint plus ⅙ vermillion red and ⅙ yellow ochre with a dash of raw sienna artist's acrylics

glaze—½ burnt umber and ½ burnt sienna artist's acrylics

VARNISH: optional (matt finish only)

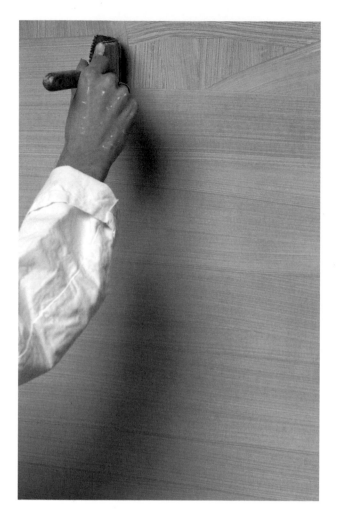 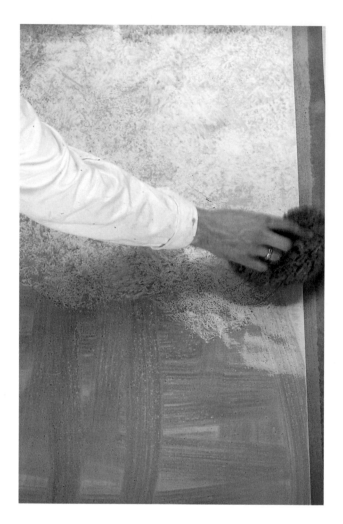

1 Apply watery glaze in crisscross fashion with roller or brush, depending on size of your project. Work in 2-foot-wide strips.

2 Dip clean sponge in water and wring well. Sponge off surface, dragging, rolling, and dabbing sponge in places. Rinse sponge as soon as it stops removing glaze well.

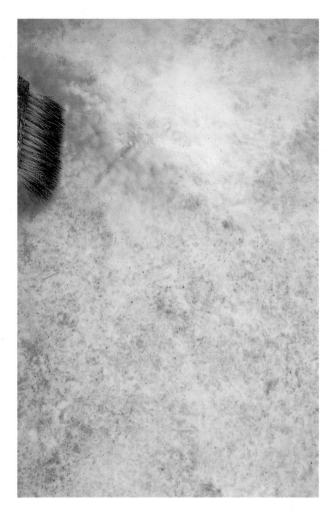

3 While glaze is still wet, smooth out with badger-hair brush. With wrist, make figure-eight motions, barely touching brush tip to surface to avoid brushmarks.

4 Continue blending lightly until glaze is just dry and brush starts to leave marks. Work as fast as possible; you want to finish the entire surface. (A third person could start smoothing before whole surface has been sponged off to ensure this.) Depth and softness characterize the effect.

· BRUSH WASHING IN TWO TONES ·

Because this example features oil glazes, which dry slower than acrylic, more time is available for blending and smoothing. Choosing base-coat and glaze colours like those shown will give you a gentle cloudlike effect. The first glaze is a medium blue-green; the second, a slightly darker version.

· R E C I P E ·

BRUSH WASHING IN TWO TONES

LEVEL OF EXPERTISE:

RECOMMENDED ON: flat surfaces—ceilings, walls, floors, tabletops

NOT RECOMMENDED ON: small highly carved elements such as ornate mouldings

NUMBER OF PEOPLE: 1 or 2

TOOLS: two 1-inch-wide gloss brushes, 2½-inch brush with long soft bristles (well worn in), large thick-bristled brush, white spirit, clean rags for wiping mistakes, gloves

BASE COAT: satin oil-based paint

GLAZE: *either* about 1 part linseed oil to 3 parts turpentine to a few drops terebine liquid dryer *or* about 6 parts ready-mixed oil glaze to 1 part thinner (see Mixing Paints, Chapter Four)

COLOURS: sample base coat—½ white oil-based paint plus ⅙ chrome green, ⅙ ultramarine blue, 1/12 yellow ochre, and 1/12 raw umber artist's oils

lighter glaze—⅔ chrome green plus ⅓ ultramarine blue and a dash of titanium white artist's oils

darker glaze—⅔ chrome green plus ⅓ ultramarine blue artist's oils

VARNISH: optional (matt finish only)

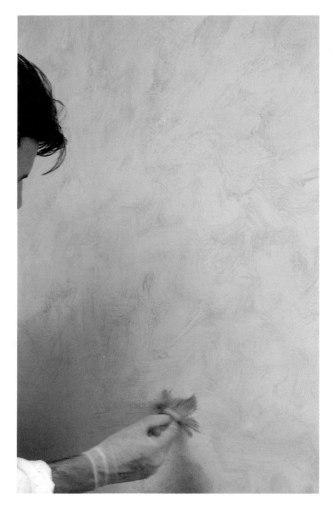

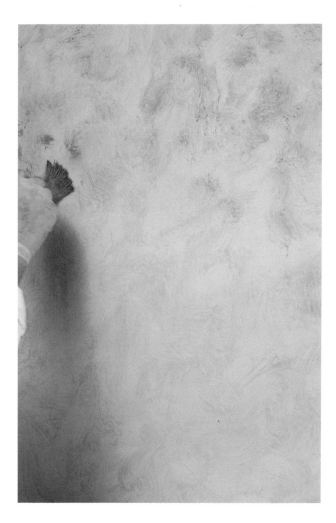

1 With 1-inch-wide brush, apply lighter glaze, splaying bristles to create subtexture as illustrated. Let some base coat show through. Surface should be contrasting and uneven but balanced overall.

2 Apply smaller amount of darker glaze with 1-inch brush in same manner. Some base coat should still show, as well as some lighter glaze.

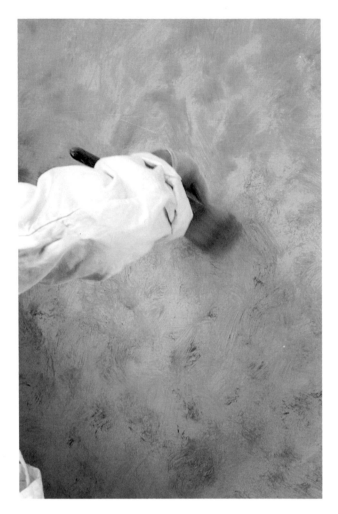

3 Use dry 2½-inch-wide flat bristle brush to smooth and blend glazes while still wet. With wrist, make figure-eight motions, barely touching brush tip to surface to lessen marks. For a more textured look, finish may be left as shown.

4 You can work surface further with large, dry, full-bristled brush.

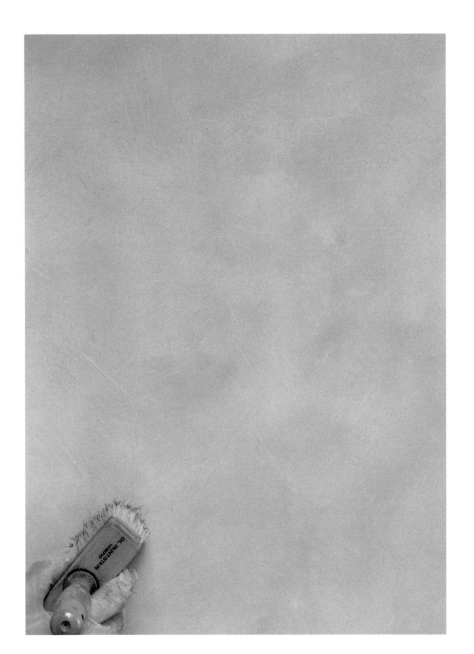

5 Final photo depicts the cloudlike effect after smoothing with brush.

• FADE-AWAY WASHING •

This technique is a much looser, more painterly version of fade-away stippling in Chapter Seven. Refer to that recipe for help in selecting, mixing, and applying glaze colours. Prepare three glazes in harmonizing tones as directed. Note that because the fade-away washing is less precise than stippling, snapping chalklines and penciling in lines dividing wall into bands is optional. Your end result will have lots of character and be excellent for camouflaging surface imperfections.

• R E C I P E •

FADE-AWAY WASHING

LEVEL OF EXPERTISE:

RECOMMENDED ON: flat surfaces only—best displayed on vertical surfaces that you can stand back from, such as walls

NOT RECOMMENDED ON: carved or rounded surfaces, flat areas less than about 3 feet square

NUMBER OF PEOPLE: 2

TOOLS: stepstool, large gloss brush, 2-inch-wide flat soft-bristle brush, chalkline and pencil (optional), gloves

BASE COAT: satin oil-based paint

GLAZE: *either* about 1 part linseed oil to 3 parts turpentine plus few drops terebine liquid dryer *or* about 6 parts ready-mixed oil glaze to 1 part thinner (see Mixing Paints, Chapter Four)

COLOURS: sample base coat—⅓ white oil-based paint plus ⅓ burnt umber, ⅙ yellow ochre, and ⅙ raw sienna with a dash of raw umber artist's oils

dark glaze—½ burnt umber plus ½ raw sienna artist's oils

medium glaze—⅓ dark glaze plus ⅔ clear glaze

light glaze—⅓ medium glaze plus ⅔ clear glaze

VARNISH: optional (matt finish only)

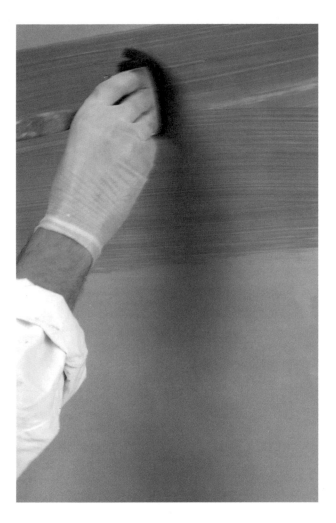

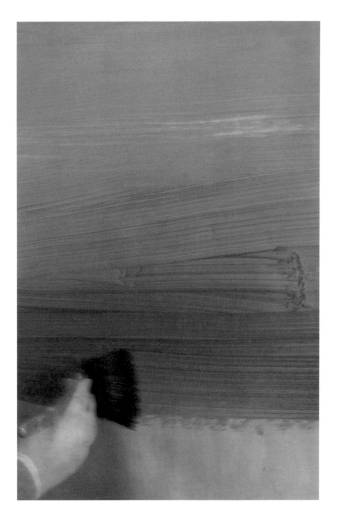

1 Using large gloss brush, paint top band from side to side with lightest glaze. By starting with lightest tone, you avoid having to clean brush before painting other bands.

2 Apply medium glaze from side to side. Do not begin painting where light glaze ends; start toward upper middle of space allotted for medium band (depending on size) and work up so that brush isn't fully charged with paint when it meets the light colour. This helps blend tones. Apply darkest tone from side to side, working up to medium tone in same manner as in preceding step. Never crisscross glaze—it would ruin the fade-away effect.

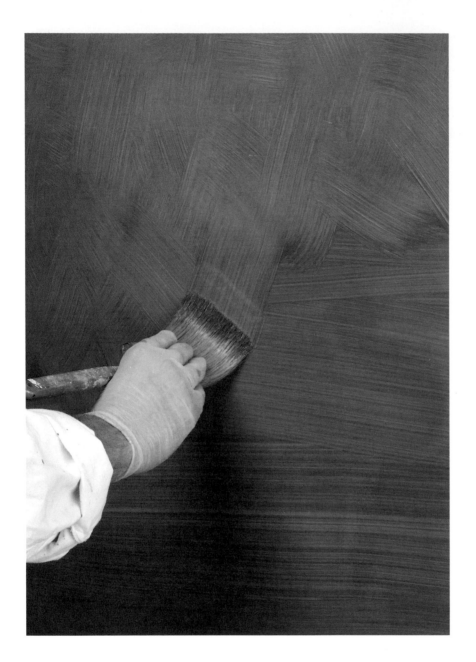

3 With dry, flat 2-or 3-inch-wide brush, form crosshatch or basketweave pattern, making small X-shaped strokes by moving wrist up and down. Start from top of surface and work down in rows to fade light glaze into medium, then medium into dark. (Don't work back up row.) Overlap rows just slightly so that no lines form between.

4 Work on one area until you're satisfied, but don't go back over it later—you'll make light spots. Remember that the more you rework the finish, the paler it will be. Especially with colour washing, don't let small defects bother you. They'll go unnoticed amid the overall effect. Seen here, it exhibits a painterly quality.

CHAPTER NINE

•

SPATTERING

SPATTERING ON
SPATTERING OFF
COMBINATION:
SPATTERING OVER SPONGING IN FIVE COLOURS
STONE-BLOCK EFFECT

SPLASHES OF DOTS ON A BASE COAT FORM THE TECHNIQUE KNOWN AS

spattering. Finishes range from boldly blended bright-coloured paint flecks to arrays of "watermarks" caused by sprinkled thinner to imitations of stone such as porphyry and lapis lazuli.

Although spattering appears random and looks easy to do, it does require planning and experimentation for pleasing textures and colour combinations. Executed finely and evenly, it gives accessories and architectural elements a rich, complex finish. But evenness is hard to attain on large surfaces like walls; they usually include bigger spots and an occasional drip, and they tend to have a contemporary air.

There are many ways to spatter. But whatever method you choose, be prepared for a mess unless you cover everything in the vicinity of what you're painting—including yourself. Take such safety precautions as wearing goggles to keep paint out of your eyes.

You can spatter fastest with an air gun, which you can rent or buy. Rental services offer daily rates for the

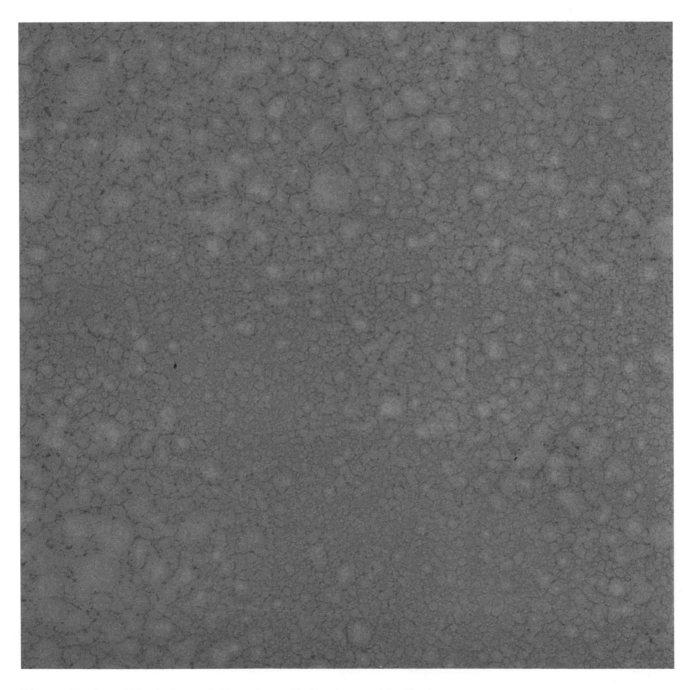

The spattering off technique yields a dramatic "watermark" effect.

air gun, compressor, and special nozzle you need for spattering; you can probably complete a room in a day. But be sure to cover *everything* in the room except what you're spattering with taped down polythene sheeting—you can control the intensity of the gun's spray, but not always its direction.

Air guns are most often used for painting cars, and a book on that subject will give details on basic technique. The firm you rent an air gun from can also tell you how to use it. But, above all, working with this tool takes practice—particularly in triggering it and moving it across a surface for a smooth, even finish. (The movement is reminiscent of a plane taking off and landing.) Air guns usually come with instructions on how to read the meter on the compressor and how to set the compressor to the proper pressure for various kinds of paint. Oil-based paint, emulsion, glaze, and artist's colours can all be used.

Another way to spatter is to hit a paintbrush against a wooden stick or the handle of another brush. For more control, take a stiff-haired brush loaded with paint and hit its bristles with a palette knife, sending out a tiny stream of dots. Or run a palette knife or your thumb over the tips of the bristles of a stencil brush.

For a fine finish on a small horizontal surface like the top of a wooden box, spatter by running a toothbrush over a fine metal screen. Hold the screen horizontally over the surface, dip the toothbrush into the paint, and rub the toothbrush back and forth over the screen.

Many factors influence your results, including the colours you choose, how thickly you spatter, and the consistency of your paint. Experimentation really pays off. Try to thin paint to medium consistency so that it neither blobs nor drips. Experiment with several tones of the same colour at first; then throw in bits of white, black, and a contrasting hue for accents. (Keep in mind that you can adjust colours as you go.) Do some samples in which you cover a lot of your base coat; apply a sparse coating of dots in others.

Spattering works well when masked in some way. For instance, you might tape your surface so that spattering forms stripes or panels. Or, especially on walls in a child's room, you might pin up leaves from trees, arranged as if floating floorward, or paper shapes (a heart or alphabet border, perhaps), then spatter over them in bright colours. When the papers or leaves are removed, silhouettes of the shapes remain on the wall.

In general, the closer you stand to your surface, the finer your spattering will be. Dots get larger if you back up, but you have less control over where paint lands. For dots of the same size, find a distance that gives the results you want and always stay that far from your surface.

• SPATTERING ON •

With its highly contrasting colours, this example of spattering on recalls old Chinese lacquered finishes. Instead of glaze, for this technique you use artist's acrylics thinned with a little water. The opacity of the paint makes the dots stand out from their background. With this technique you can, of course, use any colour combination of base coat and spattering to achieve a broad range of effects, in addition to Chinese lacquer. And along with the paintbrush methods described below, you can spatter on with an air gun with special spattering nozzle or a toothbrush loaded with paint rubbed against a wire net.

Mix paints in small cups or on a palette and test them on paper or cardboard that has been base-coated for hue and consistency. The paint should be of medium consistency. If it's too thick, it will be hard to shake off the brush in fine dots; if it's too thin, it will drip down the surface. Experiment to determine how heavily to load your brush—too much paint will give you blotches, not dots. Dip the brush into the paint so that about three-quarters of its bristles are covered. If the brush drips when removed from the paint, shake it hard against scrap paper until no blotches form and paint dots are the size you want.

• R E C I P E •

SPATTERING ON

LEVEL OF EXPERTISE:

RECOMMENDED ON: accessories, furniture, small or medium-size surfaces

NOT RECOMMENDED ON: ceilings, very large surfaces (especially for initial projects)

NUMBER OF PEOPLE: 1

TOOLS: dust sheets, masking tape, palette, small jars or paper cups, container of water, 1-inch-wide stiff white-bristle brushes, palette knife, wooden stick (or, if desired, air gun or toothbrush and fine wire screen), gloves, goggles

BASE COAT: silk emulsion paint

GLAZE: artist's acrylics thinned with a little water

COLOURS: sample base coat—deep red emulsion paint

glaze—black acrylic

VARNISH: 3 to 4 coats high-gloss polyurethane for Chinese lacquer look; optional for other spattering-on effects

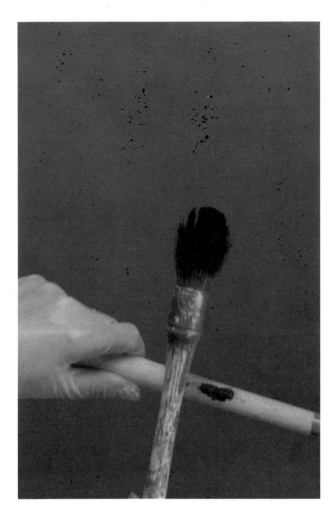

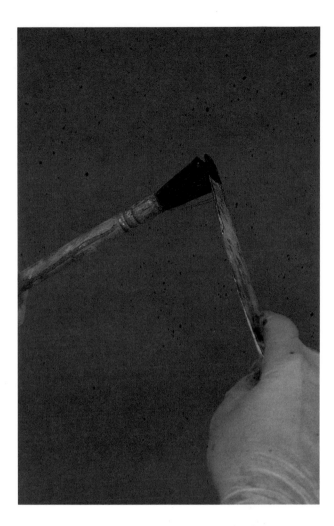

1 One method of spattering is to hit a flat, stiff white-bristle 1-inch-wide brush against wooden handle of another brush to form linear pattern of dots. Move from top to bottom of surface in wide strips so that you don't miss any spots.

2 Vary your pattern by using another spattering technique: Run palette knife over top of stiff-haired brush. This gives you more control and creates more random arrangement of dots. Dark spots on bright base coat provide enough contrast to allow this finish to be seen from a distance. Several coats of high-gloss varnish contribute to its sheen.

• SPATTERING OFF •

Turpentine sprinkled over a stippled oil glaze produced the spattering-off effect pictured here. Practice this technique on cardboard before turning to your surface. The more control you have, the better your results will be. You want drops of turpentine to mark the surface but not run. This makes the technique particularly challenging on vertical surfaces.

Try spattering off with another diluent such as turpentine. Turpentine does not "open up" a surface as much as white spirit. Wear goggles to shield your eyes.

Spatter over glaze that is still wet. If you work with a partner, one person applies and stipples the glaze in sections, and the other spatters them.

• R E C I P E •

SPATTERING OFF

LEVEL OF EXPERTISE:

RECOMMENDED ON: accessories, furniture, small or medium-sized surfaces

NOT RECOMMENDED ON: ceilings or very large surfaces, especially for initial projects

NUMBER OF PEOPLE: 1 or 2

TOOLS: dust sheets, masking tape, gloss brush or roller, stippling brush, white spirit, stencil or flat long-haired brush, palette knife, goggles, gloves

BASE COAT: satin or semigloss oil-based paint

GLAZE: about 1 part linseed oil to 2 parts turpentine plus a few drops of terebine liquid dryer

COLOURS: sample base coat—⅓ white oil-based paint plus ⅓ yellow ochre, ⅙ raw sienna, and ⅙ chrome orange artist's oils

glaze—½ raw umber plus ½ raw sienna artist's oils

VARNISH: optional

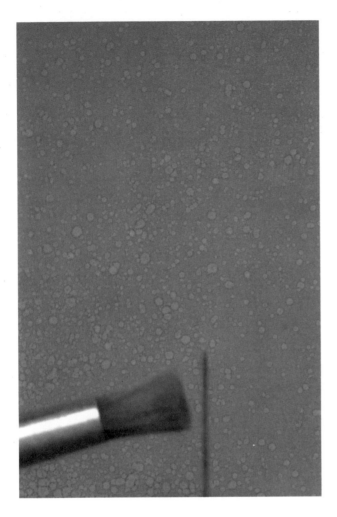

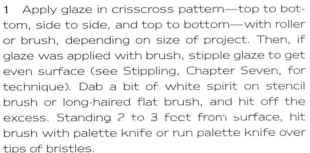

1 Apply glaze in crisscross pattern—top to bottom, side to side, and top to bottom—with roller or brush, depending on size of project. Then, if glaze was applied with brush, stipple glaze to get even surface (see Stippling, Chapter Seven, for technique). Dab a bit of white spirit on stencil brush or long-haired flat brush, and hit off the excess. Standing 2 to 3 feet from surface, hit brush with palette knife or run palette knife over tips of bristles.

2 Close-up shows pattern forming. The more diluent you spatter, the more your pattern opens up. So apply just a little at first—hit brush once in a spot and don't add more until you see the result. The random array of marks give the completed effect of subtle texture when seen from a distance.

COMBINATION:
• SPATTERING OVER SPONGING IN FIVE COLOURS •

This is used in conjunction with two other recipes—spattering on, the first recipe in this chapter, and sponging on (Chapter Five). The sponged-on glaze layer is optional but recommended because it gives the finish an even more textured look than simply spattering on over a base coat. It also lets you do less spattering—a plus, because spattering is time-consuming over large surfaces. A finish that has been sponged and spattered on in colours like those shown is reminiscent of fine stone. You can, however, execute the technique in other colours to produce various effects.

Sponge on your water-based glaze over cured base coat to create textured background, following the step-by-step directions on page 95. With damp sponge, continue working surface until glaze is almost dry. Let surface dry while you complete step 1 below. (It dries quickly because glaze is water-based.)

For spattering on a small surface, arrange drops of artist's acrylics on a palette and mix your colours on the palette with a brush. For a large surface, mix batches of colours in small jars or paper cups.

• R E C I P E •

COMBINATION: SPATTERING OVER SPONGING IN FIVE COLOURS

LEVEL OF EXPERTISE:

RECOMMENDED ON: flat surfaces, mouldings, accessories, or furniture if not high relief

NOT RECOMMENDED ON: ceilings, highly carved elements

NUMBER OF PEOPLE: 1

TOOLS: sea sponges, roller tray, bucket of water, dust sheets, masking tape, container of water, palette or small jars or paper cups, palette knife, stencil brushes or flat stiff long-haired brushes (or, if desired, air gun or toothbrush and fine wire screen), gloves, goggles

BASE COAT: silk emulsion paint

GLAZE: 2 parts acrylic medium to 1 part water for sponged subtexture (optional); artist's acrylics thinned with a little water for spattering

COLOURS: sample base coat—½ white emulsion paint plus ⅙ burnt umber, ⅙ yellow ochre, and ⅙ vermillion red acrylic

sponging glaze—½ burnt umber, ⅓ yellow ochre, ⅙ vermillion red, ⅙ titanium white acrylic

spattering glaze—titanium white, yellow ochre, burnt sienna, raw sienna, burnt umber acrylic

VARNISH: optional

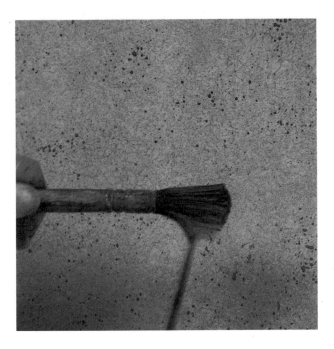

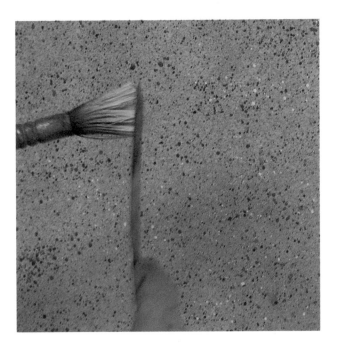

1   On palette are white, yellow ochre, burnt sienna, burnt umber, and raw sienna acrylics. Dip
brush in water (cup attached to palette) and blend
yellow ochre with burnt sienna to get medium
colour, adding a few drops of water, if needed.
Spatter medium colour on surface, following directions on page 166.

2   Mix darker colour using yellow ochre, burnt sienna, and raw sienna, and spatter surface, concentrating on untouched areas.

3   Make darkest colour by
adding burnt umber to previous
colour, and spatter. Then highlight finish by spattering white
mixed with a little yellow ochre.

• STONE-BLOCK EFFECT •

Bring a grand look to a large entry hall, stairwell, or high-ceilinged room by doing walls in stone-block finish. The technique combines spattering on, the first recipe in this chapter, sponging on (Chapter Five), and some special preparation that begins with drawing a layout for a stone wall on paper to scale. ("To scale" means in proportion with your room. For instance, you can represent 1 foot of your wall by 1 inch on your paper—or ½ inch or whatever measurement you choose.) If you were to enlarge the drawing proportionally, it would equal the size of your wall.

There are many traditional layouts for stone. At a bookstore or library, you can find books on construction, architecture, and stone- or brick-laying that provide examples and sometimes sample layouts drawn to scale. Also study photos of old stone buildings and walls for patterns. In this example, alternating rows of vertical lines are aligned as in standard brickwork.

To begin your layout, draw the perimeter of your wall on paper to scale. Then divide the wall into equal horizontal bands. To do this, you must first figure out what size blocks to use. Standard blocks measure 1 foot high by 2 feet long; you may want to vary this according to your wall size. For instance, if you divide your wall into 1-foot-high horizontal bands and end up with an odd-sized (less than 1 foot) band at the bottom of the wall, redistribute the odd space among the other bands, making them slightly higher than 1 foot.

Next, fill in vertical lines across the first horizontal band, placing them about every 2 feet (spacing may vary according to the size of your wall). Try to use only full or half blocks across a row; if you end up with an odd space at the end of a row, redistribute it among the other blocks as you did for the horizontal bands. Then put in vertical lines on the next horizontal band. Place the first line so that it is centered on the block above it. Continue your row of vertical lines, alternating the pattern for the remaining rows.

After completing your layout on paper, reproduce it on the wall. With a partner, snap horizontal chalklines (see box, below). Retrace them lightly with a pencil. Then pencil in vertical lines. Dust off chalk fully. Prepare the room by covering all areas not to be painted; then proceed to step 1.

• USING A CHALKLINE •

Chalklines let you mark easily erased straight lines on large surfaces. You can buy chalklines at home centres, hardware stores, and paint shops. They are small boxes containing 50 to 100 feet of string on a reel. Some of them need to be filled with chalk or talcum powder; others however, come filled with blue chalk that is difficult to wipe off. If you get one of these, empty it out and refill the box with a mix of three-fourths talcum powder and one-fourth blue chalk. This makes the line produced more visible on light surfaces yet easy to remove with a damp cloth.

You need a partner to use a chalkline—one person holds the box, the other person holds the end of the string. Stretch the string along the surface to be marked, pulling the string tight so that it is taut and flat against the surface. Then one person snaps the string hard by pulling it 2 to 3 feet off the surface and letting go so that when the string hits the surface, it leaves a powdery line.

• R E C I P E •

STONE-BLOCK EFFECT

LEVEL OF EXPERTISE:

RECOMMENDED ON: large walls

NOT RECOMMENDED ON: small or carved surfaces

NUMBER OF PEOPLE: 2

TOOLS: chalkline, straightedge, ruler, pencil, ⅛-inch-wide masking tape, step-stool, sea sponges, roller tray, bucket of water, small jars or paper cups, palette knife, stencilling brushes or flat, stiff, long-haired brushes (or air gun, if desired), gloves, goggles

BASE COAT: silk emulsion paint

GLAZE: 2 parts acrylic medium to 1 part water for sponging; artist's acrylics thinned with a little water for spattering

COLOURS: sample base coat—¾ white emulsion, ⅛ yellow ochre, and ⅛ raw umber acrylic

darkest sponging glaze—raw umber, raw sienna, yellow ochre, and a little white acrylic

medium sponging glaze—raw umber, yellow ochre, white acrylic

light sponging glaze—white, raw sienna, yellow ochre, and a little raw umber acrylic

off-white sponging glaze—mostly white acrylic with a little yellow ochre acrylic

spattering glaze—raw umber, yellow ochre, raw sienna, and white acrylic

VARNISH: optional

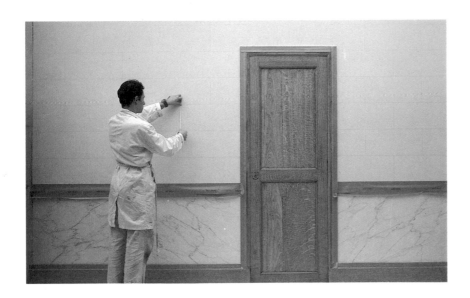

1 Apply ⅛-inch-wide masking tape (or ¼-inch for thicker joinery than shown here) to lines. Place tape consistently either above or below lines and to right or left to keep stones same size. (Be sure to remove all traces of chalk first, or tape won't stick properly and paint may bleed.)

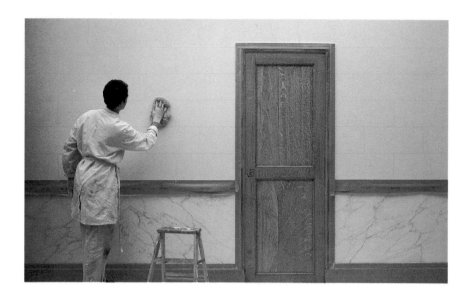

2 Using large sea sponge and medium-coloured glaze, work from side to side in rows, following directions for sponging on (page 94).

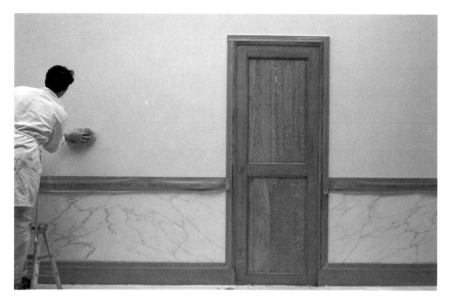

3 With slightly darker glaze, sponge from top to bottom so that glaze layers crisscross but pattern is not visible. Then apply a third glaze layer in a lighter colour from side to side.

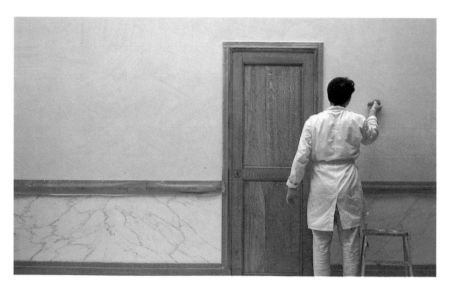

4 When sponging is dry, take well-worn piece of sea sponge with very ragged edges and create light veining by making soft wavy lines, as shown. (See Marbling, Chapter Twelve, for more details.) Use transparent version of one sponging glaze colour. Vary direction of veining, and stop right at tape to make each rectangle look like a separate block of stone.

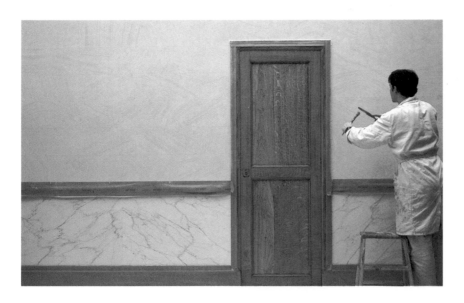

5 Once veining is dry (it dries quickly because glaze is water-based), spatter over it (see first technique in this chapter for instructions) in three or more colours—light, medium, and dark—to create depth. Spattering colours should be darker than sponging colours to simulate impressions in the stone. Stand 2 to 3 feet from your surface and try for fine, even dots.

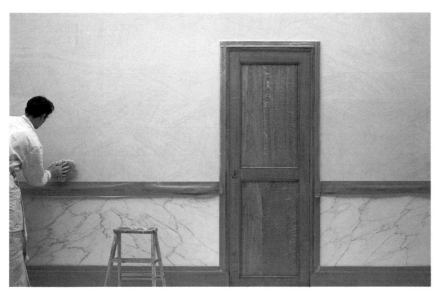

6 When spattering is dry, sponge lightly over entire wall with off-white glaze to tone down veining and unify effect.

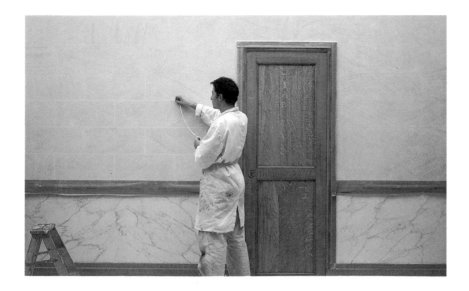

7 After wall is completely dry, peel back tape slowly, as shown. (Don't pull tape off fast because paint may come off.)

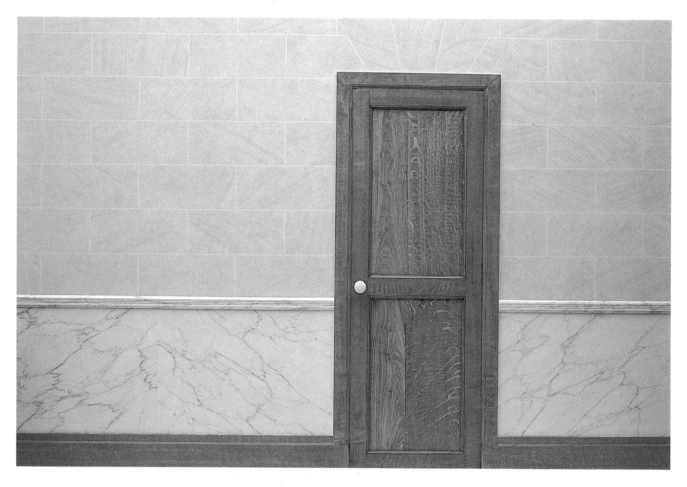

Fine complements to the stone-block effect are the marbleized dado and the oak-grained door and trim. The traditional wood and stone combine formality with a rusticity in a manner that might suit a country house.

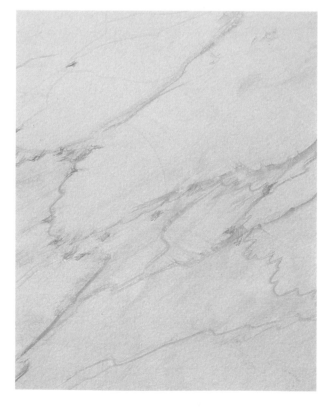

The dado simulates three slabs of white marble arranged in herringbone pattern. (The slabs are for authenticity—real marble wouldn't come in a piece as large as the entire dado.) Create the slabs by dividing the dado into three sections, then doing the first slab and letting it dry. Tape the edge of the first slab and do the second. Repeat this procedure for the third section. To learn the white marbling technique, see page 204. The version shown here includes more veining.

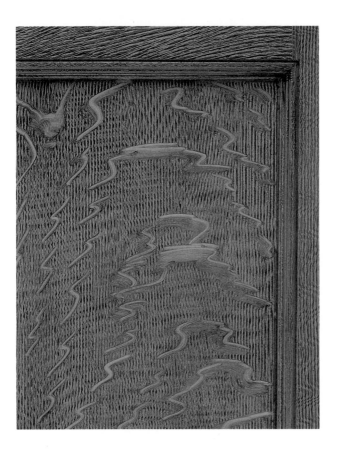

Step-by-step instructions for the oak graining that decorates this door appear on page 230. Professional painters do doors in a special order, starting with the panels—turn to Preparing to Paint, Chapter Three, for photos of this method.

Close-up illustrates how glaze layers and spattered acrylics blend to create stonelike finish.

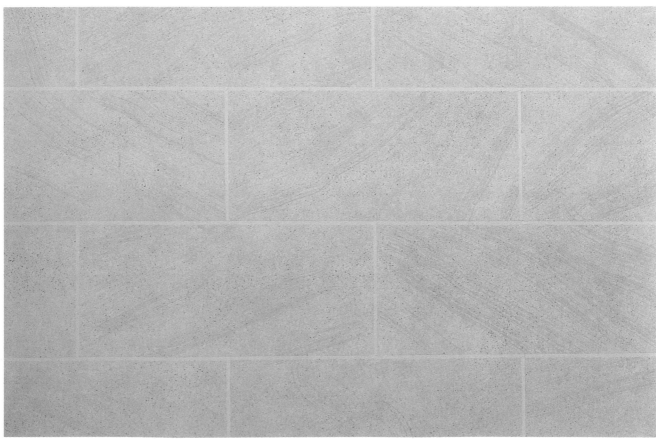

CHAPTER TEN

•

DRAGGING

DRAGGING WITH STEEL WOOL
DRAGGING WITH A HARD-BRISTLE BRUSH
COMBING

A CLASSIC TECHNIQUE POPULAR IN THE EIGHTEENTH CENTURY, DRAG-

ging derives from wood-graining methods, and it sometimes employs the same tools in a different way. In dragging, you apply glaze over a base coat, then remove it by sweeping over it with a dry brush, graining comb, steel wool, or another tool that will leave an imprint. You can make simple versions of dragging tools yourself—see page 187.

Effects range from elegant to homespun, depending on the tools and colours you pick. Experiment to see how various tools handle and how they work on your surface. For instance, graining combs or combs cut from plastic or cardboard need a flat surface in good condition for pleasing results—they catch on every bump and leave marks. But steel wool or a long-haired brush can be effective on a rougher surface.

Take care to prime, base-coat, and glaze the surface evenly and thoroughly. For big surfaces, roll on the glaze, then "pre-drag" it with a wide flat brush.

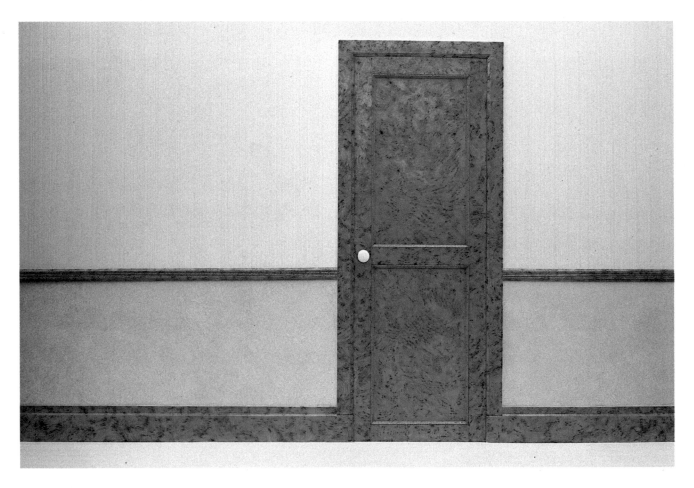

In dragging, it is particularly important to work on fresh glaze that will come off easily. You will also have to keep a "wet edge." This means the dragged glaze on one strip must still be wet when you start dragging the next strip. So enlist a partner. One person will glaze a 3-foot-wide vertical strip; the other will drag it.

Don't drag right to the far edge of each glazed strip. Stop dragging 3 to 6 inches from the edge, let the other person glaze the next strip, then drag through the space into the newly glazed row so that no line forms where rows touch. Try not to stop dragging in mid-row. After each pass, wipe the glaze from your tool with a clean rag.

WALL: Featured on the wall above the chair rail is dragging done with a stiff nylon brush. The technique is executed here in an off-white hue over a light blue base coat. DADO: A combination of ragging and cheeseclothing—pinkish-white over a rose background—graces the dado. DOOR & TRIM: Burr wood graining enlivens the door and architrave.

• DRAGGING WITH STEEL WOOL •

You can produce this finely textured effect by dragging a steel-wool pad through your glaze. Steel wool comes in several sizes from fine to coarse. Medium-coarse was used in this example.

Be sure to wear gloves to protect your hands from steel wool and goggles to shield your eyes.

Apply the glaze with a brush. Work in a crisscross pattern—top to bottom, side to side, top to bottom. Brush strokes should be visible; they form a subtexture over which to drag. Work with a partner—one person applies the glaze in 2- to 3-foot-wide strips, the other drags it with steel wool.

• R E C I P E •

DRAGGING WITH STEEL WOOL

LEVEL OF EXPERTISE:

RECOMMENDED ON: almost all surfaces

NOT RECOMMENDED ON: highly carved mouldings and other elements

NUMBER OF PEOPLE: 2

TOOLS: large gloss brush, medium-coarse steel-wool pads, clean rags, gloves, goggles

BASE COAT: satin oil-based paint

GLAZE: about 6 parts ready-mixed oil glaze to 1 part thinner (see Mixing Paints, Chapter Four)

COLOURS: sample base coat—⅔ white oil-based paint plus ⅙ raw umber, ⅙ yellow ochre, and ⅙ oxide of chrome artist's oils

glaze—⅔ raw sienna and ⅓ ultramarine blue artist's oils

VARNISH: optional

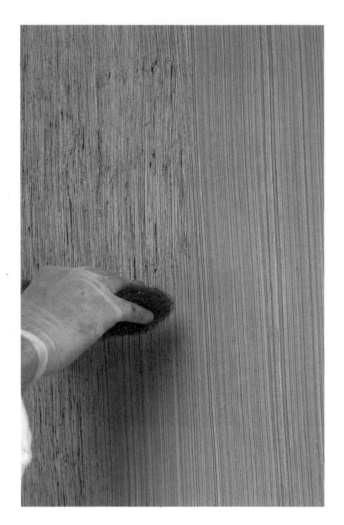

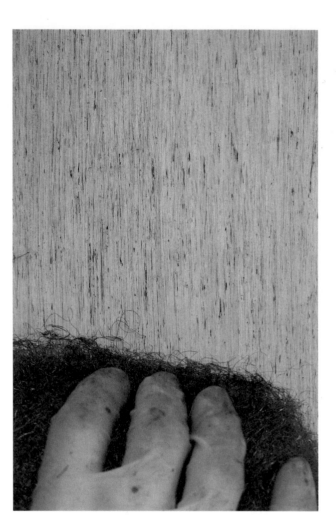

1   After pre-dragging the glaze, grasp steel-wool pad with thumb on bottom and fingers on top. Hold at an angle and drag 6 to 12 inches in several short strokes. Lift pad, and run it down strip again; then wipe pad and continue dragging another 6- to 12-inch strip below the first. (Unlike dragging with a brush, this technique enables you to stop in the middle of a strip without leaving a mark.)

2   Close-up focuses on coarse graining. If you don't get enough definition, don't wait till surface is completed, but quickly rework finish within the 2- to 3-foot section just glazed. Keep turning and wiping pad; once saturated, replace with a clean one. Remember that the more you work over glaze, the lighter the finish will be.

3 Graining appears subtler from a distance, as the completed effect illustrates.

• DRAGGING WITH A HARD-BRISTLE BRUSH •

Practice pays off with this traditional method of dragging. The finish is deep and lustrous, particularly when done with a very transparent glaze several tones darker than the base coat. Note that the more contrast between glaze and base-coat colours, the more evident the striped effect and the more obvious any imperfections.

This technique is much easier on small areas such as moulding, doors, and furniture than on, say, walls, because dragging a straight floor-to-ceiling strip is difficult—especially while getting on and off a stepstool. To keep dragging straight on walls, you can use a level to draw light guidelines in pencil every foot. Or you can tape a plumbline to a cornice and move the line as you go.

Drag with a stiff long-haired brush about 4 inches wide. Line up your first stroke with the edge of the wall. To prevent curving, keep your arm straight, always the same distance from the wall. Bend your knees as you work down the surface in long movements. Use the lowest ladder or stepstool possible so that you get fewer jolts from moving down steps. Stand back from your work frequently and readjust alignment as needed.

The way your brush touches the wall is important. In dragging, you press the brush flat against the wall, and the middle of the bristles produces the imprint (the tips of the bristles are usually too soft). For dragging at the top and bottom of walls, mask ceiling or cornice moulding and skirting to get a clean edge. If necessary, push harder on the brush at the top and bottom of the wall to create an imprint. (If the glaze starts gathering in those spots, lighten your pressure.)

If your base coat and glaze are close in hue, you might just wipe a clean line along moulding edges with a cloth to form a plain, even border.

• R E C I P E •

DRAGGING WITH A HARD-BRISTLE BRUSH

LEVEL OF EXPERTISE:

RECOMMENDED ON: only very flat vertical or horizontal surfaces

NOT RECOMMENDED ON: ceilings, mouldings, surfaces in poor condition

NUMBER OF PEOPLE: 2

TOOLS: gloss brush or roller, flat 4-inch -wide hard-bristled brush, special dragging brush (optional) called a 'flogger,' white spirit for cleanup, clean rags, gloves

BASE COAT: satin oil-based

GLAZE: about 6 parts ready-mixed oil glaze to 2 parts turpentine (see Mixing Paints, Chapter Four)

COLOURS: sample base coat—⅔ white oil-based paint plus ⅓ ultramarine blue and a dash of yellow ochre

glaze—⅓ Prussian blue plus ⅔ ultramarine blue artist's oils

VARNISH: optional

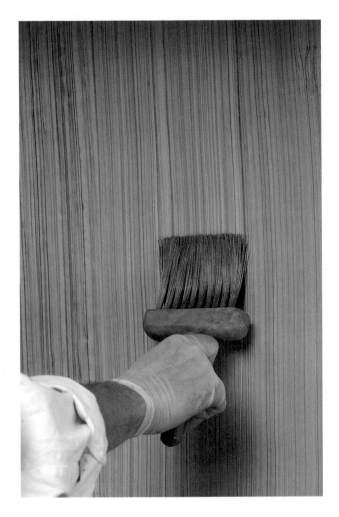

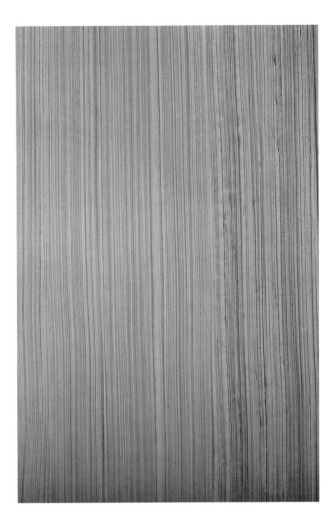

1 Apply glaze evenly in crisscross fashion—top to bottom, side to side, top to bottom—with brush or roller, depending on project's size. Apply glaze in 3-foot-wide sections. Then drag over glaze with stiff-haired brush, wiping brush on cloth after each pass. Note how brush is held and positioned on wall. Stop after this step for finely dragged finish. For coarser effect, re-drag surface with special dragging brush, holding brush as shown.

2 To keep pattern straight, pick either very dark or light line in strip just dragged and align brush with it for next strip. But note that dragged glaze dries even faster than brushed-on glaze. Re-drag surface in 3-foot-wide sections; don't wait until you have completed an entire wall.

• COMBING •

Replete with handcrafted appeal, combing offers a lively finish, seen to best effect in contrasting colours or diverse tones as shown here. However, in strong hues the effect is busy, and imperfections are more noticeable; you may prefer it on small surfaces and furnishings. Try pale neutrals or pastels for larger areas.

Several combing patterns appear here—crisscross, basketweave, moiré, and Colonial graining. Experiment with these in various colours for a wide range of effects, or invent your own patterns.

A challenge with combing is that you can't go back over your work. And because it is more exacting, it is best done on a flat surface in good condition. Work from a top corner—left if you're right-handed; right if you're left-handed.

You can use steel wood-graining combs, which come in sets containing various sizes. There are also rubber graining combs, but they are harder to find. Or devise your own tools from heavy cardboard or plastic, as explained in the first preparation step below.

• R E C I P E •

COMBING

LEVEL OF EXPERTISE:

RECOMMENDED ON: very smooth, flat surfaces of small to medium size, especially furniture, dados, and accessories

NOT RECOMMENDED ON: ceilings, carved mouldings and other ornate elements

NUMBER OF PEOPLE: 1 or 2

TOOLS: combs (plastic, rubber, metal, cardboard), stippling brush, clean rags, gloves

BASE COAT: oil-based paint

GLAZE: about 6 parts ready-mixed oil glaze to 1 part thinner (see Mixing Paints, Chapter Four)

COLOURS: sample base coat—⅔ yellow ochre and ²⁄₉ red ochre artist's oils plus ⅑ white oil-based paint

glaze—½ red ochre and ½ raw umber artist's oils

VARNISH: optional

· PREPARATION ·

1 Make your own comb by cutting V-shaped notches (easier to cut than U-shaped) into the flat edge of half of a plastic lid. You can space notches evenly or unevenly and have teeth of various sizes. Don't make teeth too big, however, or excess paint will build up in gaps and form dark lines. Plastic must be flexible enough to comb without raking or scoring the surface. If plastic proves too soft for combing, staple or glue a strip of cardboard to the back just above teeth.

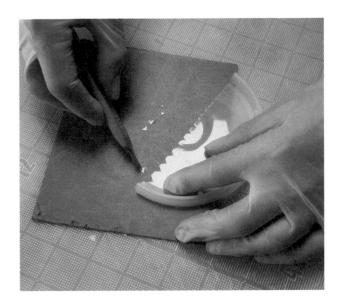

2 Brush on glaze from top to bottom, then side to side, and top to bottom. Stipple surface with flat brush to obliterate brush strokes and form subtexture.

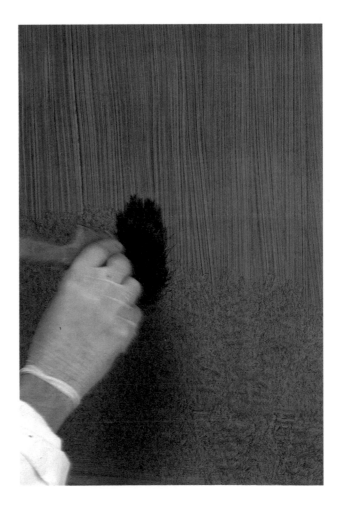

• CRISSCROSS •

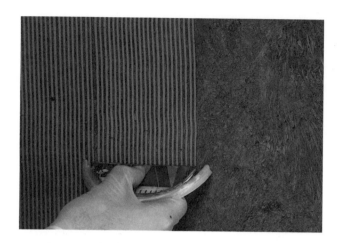

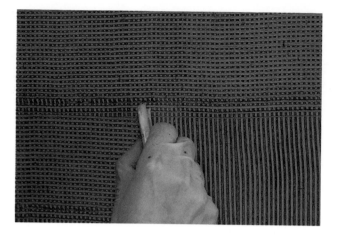

1 Drag glaze with comb. Hold comb as shown and keep arm outstretched. (Mark vertical guidelines on wall beforehand, if necessary.) Clean comb after each pass. Don't overlap rows; try to align rows so that gap between each pair of rows is same width. Don't stop in mid-row, or mark will show. See dragging with a hard-bristle brush (page 184) for additional instructions. Leave pattern as is, or follow next step for crisscross effect.

2 Top vertical lines with straight horizontal rows, following tips in step 1. You can't mark guidelines here, however, so don't expect a perfect pattern. The effect should appear handcrafted.

• BASKETWEAVE •

1 Start from top corner (right one if left-handed, left one if right-handed). Comb down to form square. Next to it, comb across to make second square. Continue alternating across row. Align second row directly below first, beginning with square combed across. Note that work is easier to keep straight than other combing techniques because you do short strokes and can adjust with squares below and alongside.

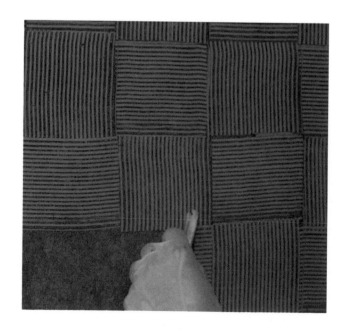

· MOIRÉ ·

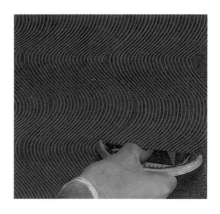 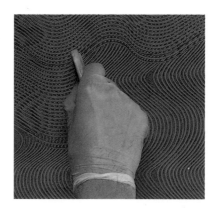 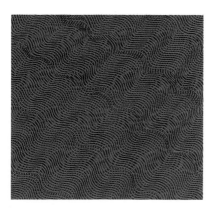

1 Comb glaze in wavy vertical rows. You can't align rows beforehand; just follow previous row as closely as possible, keeping gap between rows same width. Keep comb at a 45 degree angle to surface and move arm, not wrist, from left to right as you move down. Leave pattern as is, or do next step for moiré effect.

2 Comb wavy horizontal rows over vertical pattern. Note that effect is busy and gives a unique look. It perhaps looks best on a small piece like a wooden trunk.

3 To vary effect, comb diagonally over vertical rows, as photo illustrates.

· COLONIAL AMERICAN GRAINING ·

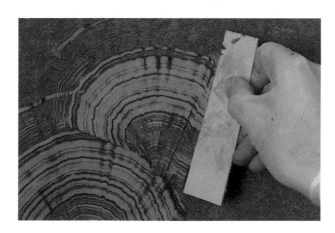 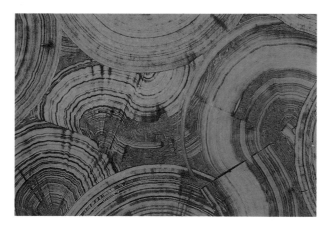

1 Comb with thick cardboard strip. Experiment with cardboard notched and unnotched. For effect shown, notches proved unnecessary. Cardboard held at angle and skipped slightly over surface created a naive graining effect. Make three-quarter circles, overlapping them. Work from wrist, using backhand and forehand motions. Vary movement to form wavy lines as well.

2 Traditionally found on paneling, doors, and furnishings, this effect duplicates naive wood graining and lends a folk-art feel.

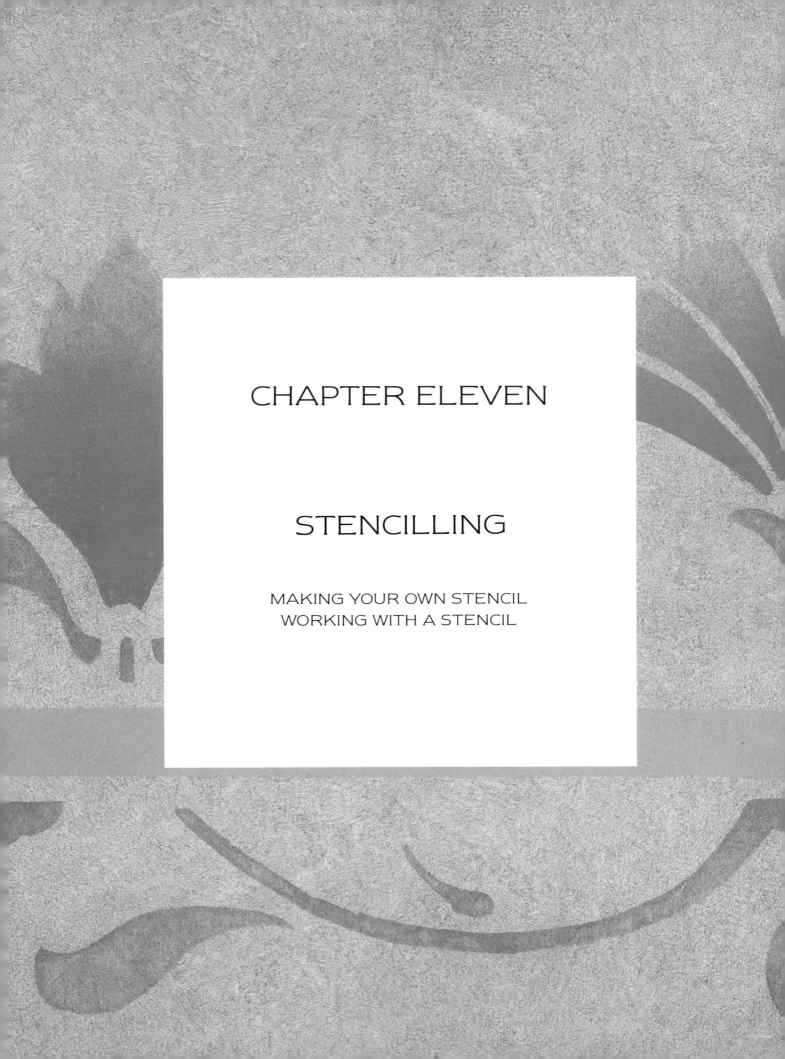

CHAPTER ELEVEN

STENCILLING

MAKING YOUR OWN STENCIL
WORKING WITH A STENCIL

WHEN YOU THINK OF STENCILLING, PERHAPS COLONIAL AMERICAN

motifs—such as the pineapple, symbol of welcome, or garlands of fruit and foliage—and colours—slate blue, rust, mustard, dark green—come to mind first. But don't stop there in considering how this technique can embellish your interiors. A little research will turn up motifs including Egyptian, classical, Chinese, Japanese, Mexican, Indian, Pompeiian, Art Deco, Victorian, modern, child-like, and more. For ideas, you can look in books on art and interior design or visit museums and decorator show houses. Select a motif that suits the character of your room and the period of your decor.

You don't have to be an artist to excel at this technique. You can trace your designs from an array of sources, including books and magazines on art, interior design, and architectural ornament. You will also find easy-to-reproduce designs on pottery, wallpaper, rugs and fabrics.

Stencilling is as much at home on walls as it is on floors, ceilings, furnishings, and fabrics. It can be a single motif or a repeating pattern. With it, you can emphasize or substitute for architectural elements. For instance, you might place a border at chair-rail or cornice height or create frames around windows and doors. Or you could centre a single motif on wall panels, cabinet doors, or dresser drawers. And instead of covering fine wood flooring with rugs or carpeting, consider enlivening it with a stencilled design.

Designs range from simple to complex. You can have one colour or as many as twenty-five. You need a separate stencil for each colour, however; so the more colours you do, the more time-consuming the process will be. To keep a project from overwhelming you, consider starting with a simple motif and adding to it over time.

You can buy precut stencils today (see source list), but to indulge your creativity, you might want to get a design specially suited to your decor and save money by producing your own stencil, following the instructions in the next recipe. High-level drawing skills aren't required: Stencilling shapes are usually simplified. Instead of drawing, you can trace a motif—from fabric, say—or find one in a book of stencils (see following recipe).

Stencils can be made from various materials including acetate, Mylar, thin posterboard, and special stencil paper. (Stencil paper is used in the following examples. Made of hot-pressed heavy paper, it is particularly recommended because it doesn't tear easily.) Over your stencil, you can spray, sponge, or brush paint onto a surface.

Cut out stencils with care. Use a craft knife, and practice first, especially for rounded shapes. Note that each motif comprises smaller shapes linked by "bridges," narrow strips that hold the details of the stencil together. If you trace your pattern from a stencil book, the bridges will already be in place, but if you adapt a pattern, you'll have to make your own. Decide how to simplify the shape and break it down to its basic elements. Place the bridges where they give your shape the most definition.

The way you combine motifs and colors gives a personalized feel to stenciling. How you apply the paint also distinguishes it. You can add shading or use a fade-away effect to create depth. And avoid

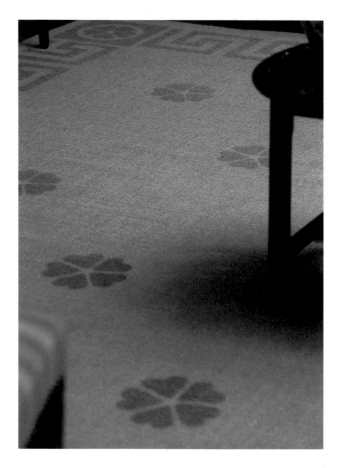

A sisal rug is stencilled with a Greek-key pattern.

a mistake common with this technique: Use as little paint as possible so that it doesn't bleed under the stencil and ruin the design.

Stencil over your base coat or glaze the surface with another decorative painting technique first, depending on the effect you desire. In either case, your surface must be dry before you begin stencilling. See Mixing Paints, Chapter Four, to learn how to mix a base coat and glaze. Learn to apply a base coat in Preparing to Paint, Chapter Three. Turn to the glazing technique you've chosen for a step-by-step guide.

• MAKING YOUR OWN STENCIL •

You can create your own pattern, adapt a motif from antique fabric or wallpaper, or find an example you like in a book of stencils. The stencil shown here came from *Victorian Stencils: Design and Decoration*, from the Dover Pictorial Archives Series.

You will probably need to enlarge a stencil from a book on a photocopy machine. You'll probably have to do this in stages—enlarge a page from the book as much as possible, then put the photocopy on the machine and enlarge that. Repeat this process until you have the size you want. If you don't have access to an enlarging machine, take the page from the book to a photocopy shop and have it enlarged. In this example the motif was enlarged from about 3 inches to 5 inches high.

You must make a stencil for each colour in your design (three in this example). A crucial part of stencilling several colours is aligning all the stencils. You do this by means of careful measuring and a system of registration marks.

As shown here, first take your enlarged photocopy and draw a straight line along the top and bottom of the pattern. Next make several triangular registration marks along the lines (see step 1 below for placement). Then run off about five copies of your enlarged pattern—one for each colour plus a few extras. Finally, cut out registration marks on three copies and set the extras aside.

Now cut three pieces of stencil paper to the size of your pattern and trace a pencil line 1 inch from the bottom on each.

• R E C I P E •

MAKING YOUR OWN STENCIL

LEVEL OF EXPERTISE:

TOOLS: several photocopies of your design (enlarged or reduced to size desired), tracing paper, coloured markers, rubber or plastic cutting mat (or wood board or heavy cardboard), craft knife with disposable blades, stencil paper (or acetate, Mylar, or thick cardboard), pencil, ruler, shellac, disposable roller, roller tray, artist's adhesive spray, masking tape, newspaper, drawing pins

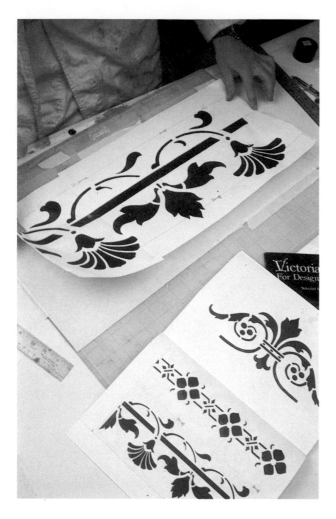

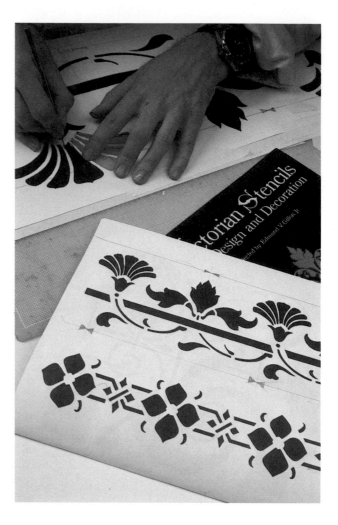

1 Tape a piece of stencil paper to cutting mat. Spray artist's adhesive on back of photocopy, following instructions on can and heeding safety precautions. Press photocopy onto stencil paper, aligning bottom on photocopy with line on stencil paper, which is visible through "windows" created by cutout registration marks.

2 Before cutting, determine the colour scheme for the pattern. Place tracing paper over photocopy and experiment with different schemes for the pattern using coloured markers. Hold tracing paper over the surface you plan on stencilling to approximate the completed effect. Then, once you've decided on your colour scheme—remembering that you must create a stencil for each colour—cut out all parts in first colour on stencil with a craft knife. Cut registration marks as well and incise V-shaped notches at ends of bottom line. Press down firmly through two layers. Take care not to cut any of the "bridges"—thin ties that link shapes of stencil. And cut corners precisely—don't let knife slip past where lines of corners meet—so that paint doesn't seep under stencil. It's a good idea to practice cutting on scrap paper.

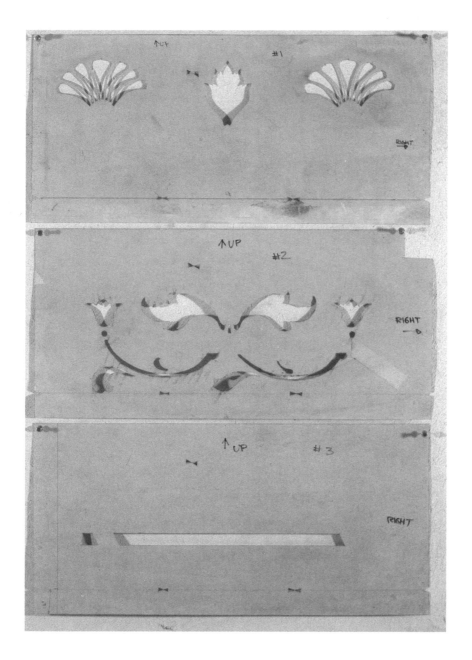

3 Number first stencil and label it "up" and "right" to avoid holding stencil the wrong way when you paint. Repeat steps 1 to 3 for second and third stencil, with new photocopies and pieces of stencil paper, making sure to align all registration marks accurately. Shellac stencils to strengthen them and make them easy to clean. Using disposable roller, apply two coats of shellac on each side (each coat dries in about 10 minutes). To dry, tack stencils to a wall with drawing pins for about an hour.

• WORKING WITH A STENCIL •

This example features a multicoloured border stencilled over a wall that has been cheeseclothed. (Colours for the cheeseclothing appear on the recipe for cheeseclothing, in Cloth Distressing, Chapter Six; see the accompanying step-by-step directions.) Other finishes that look attractive with stencilling are stippling (Chapter Seven) and colour washing (Chapter Eight). The use of a fade-away technique on the flowers contributes sophistication to this design.

Make samples of your textured base coat. Stencil on the samples in the colours you mix to preview the final effect. You'll see that colours look different when applied through a stencil rather than brushed on, because stencilling requires a thinner layer of paint. The appearance of colours also varies when they are viewed in combination.

Mix your stencil colours in small jars and cover them, because paint dries fast. Set up a palette with dabs of colours on it and work from that.

• R E C I P E •

WORKING WITH A STENCIL

LEVEL OF EXPERTISE:

RECOMMENDED ON: flat surfaces, rounded surfaces like columns

NOT RECOMMENDED ON: mouldings and other carved surfaces

NUMBER OF PEOPLE: 1 or 2

TOOLS: glazing brush, muttoncloth or cheesecloth, roller tray, board or palette, gloves, small lidded jars, spirit level, chalk, artist's spray adhesive, masking tape, newspapers, small, medium, and large stencil brushes or one brush for each colour you are using, paper towels, container of white spirit for cleanup

BASE COAT: satin oil-based paint

GLAZE: for cheeseclothing—about 6 parts ready-mixed oil glaze to 1 part thinner

for stencilling—artist's acrylics thinned with bit of water

COLOURS: sample base coat—$\frac{2}{3}$ white oil-based paint plus $\frac{1}{6}$ raw sienna, $\frac{1}{6}$ burnt umber, and a dash of chrome yellow artist's oils

glaze for cheeseclothing—$\frac{1}{2}$ burnt umber, $\frac{1}{3}$ raw umber, and $\frac{1}{6}$ burnt sienna artist's oils

stencilling—orange—$\frac{1}{2}$ vermillion red, $\frac{1}{3}$ chrome orange, $\frac{1}{6}$ chrome yellow, and a dash of white artist's oils

brown—$\frac{1}{2}$ raw umber, $\frac{1}{3}$ raw sienna, $\frac{1}{6}$ chrome orange, and a dash of white artist's oils

green—veronese green, $\frac{1}{3}$ raw sienna, and $\frac{1}{6}$ white artist's oils

VARNISH: optional (matt finish suggested)

1 Using a spirit level, draw chalk guidelines over cheese-clothed background at height at which you want border to appear. Gently and evenly spray back of stencil with removable artist's mounting adhesive. Make sure bridges are secure so that they don't lift and let paint seep under. Press stencil firmly onto wall, aligning bottom guidelines on stencil with line chalked on wall, using "bow-tie" shaped registration marks. Put two strips of masking tape on top and bottom of stencil.

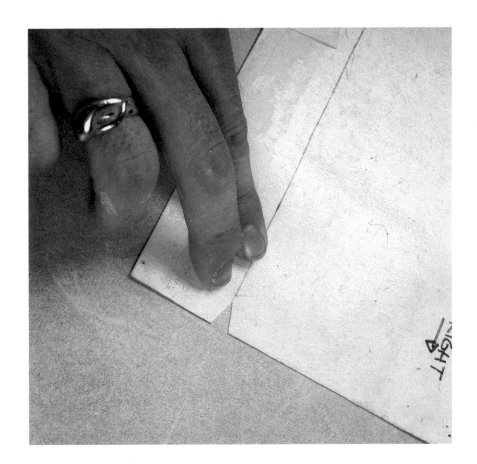

2 Dab stencil brush into first stencil colour. Rub brush on palette to coat evenly. Discharge paint on paper towel till tip of brush is almost dry. Always paint registration marks first—this lets you realign stencil easily if it falls during printing. Of course, you don't want marks that are not part of the design on the wall; lift stencil from the bottom, and place pieces of tape on wall under each mark to protect surface and paint registration marks on tape. Strips of tape on top act as hinges and keep stencil in place.

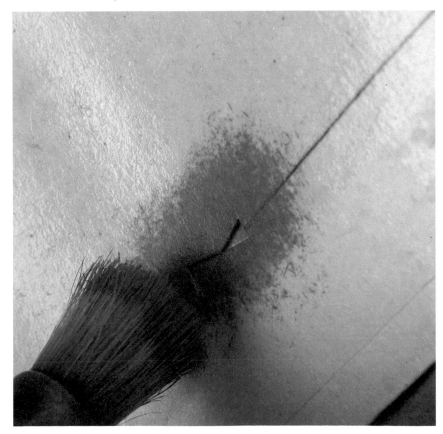

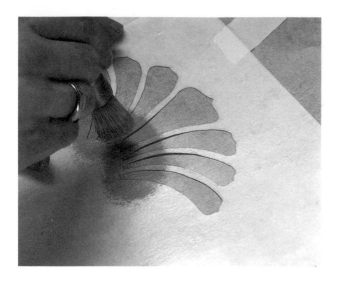

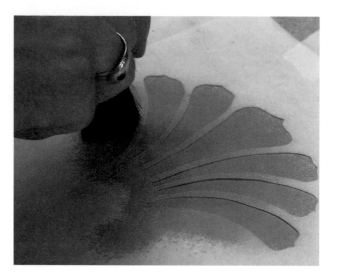

3 Apply first colour either to largest area or to the shape at centre of design. Here, colour is applied first to the flowers, adapting fade-away stippling technique (Chapter Seven) to small scale. Working with small stencil brush in light dabbing motion, concentrate paint on base of pattern.

4 Dab base quickly until brush is almost free of paint, then move from side to side up pattern. Lighten your touch as you go, but keep touch firm enough to get full outline, even at top. Don't work back down. Instead, lift brush, pick up a little more paint, and dab base again to make it opaque.

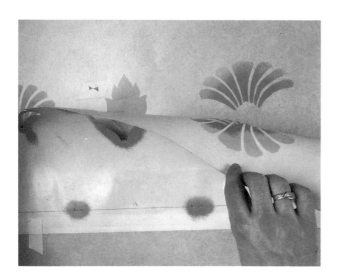

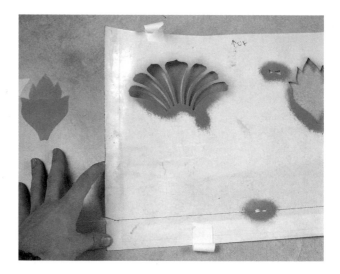

5 Lift stencil from bottom to check that all parts in first colour have been completed.

6 Remove stencil and reposition next to first imprint, aligning as shown. Continue printing and moving stencil to end of row. Wipe stencil, if necessary, with dry paper towel after every two or three prints. (Notice registration marks on tape.) Always make sure to do all of one colour—even if stenciling continues in another room—before starting the next colour. Clean first stencil with thinner, let dry, and store.

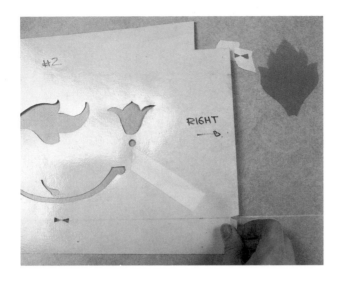

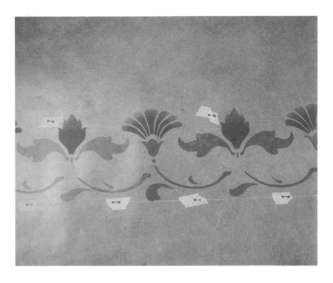

7 Align second stencil, using registration marks. Tape it and paint over registration marks in second colour. For complex designs requiring many stencils, this method helps you keep track of which colour you're up to. In this example, stencil stems and leaves of flowers with your second colour.

8 Lift stencil and check that all elements slated for second hue are done. Move stencil, repeating the process across the row. A light touch and almost paint-free brush contribute to the delicate colour of foliage in this example.

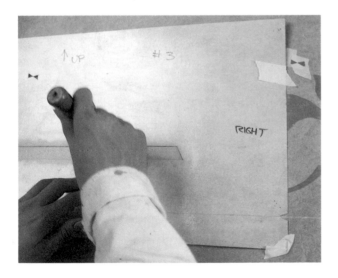

9 Align third stencil and apply last colour. Repeat process across row.

10 The fade-away effect gives depth to flowers in this Victorian border.

CHAPTER TWELVE

·

MARBLING

WHITE MARBLE
RED MARBLE
GREEN MARBLE
APPLICATION:
YELLOW SIENNA MARBLE ON A COLUMN
APPLICATION:
MARBLING A FLOOR

YOU CAN SUGGEST THE CLASSIC BEAUTY OF MARBLE WITH THESE
decorative-painting techniques. Among the many varieties of marble, you will easily find one with colours and
patterns to please you and suit your decor. Each variety has special characteristics. Study pieces of marble or
photos of it to become familiar with its characteristics. You might also look at paintings by Old Masters to see
how they executed this faux finish. Because there are so many kinds of marble, there's no point in copying an
example exactly, unless you want to match your surface to an existing piece of marble—skirtings to a marble
fireplace surround already in the room, for example. Once you understand the basics, you can invent your
own authentic-looking patterns and colours.

For best effect, use the marbling technique sparingly. Doing only the skirting and cornice can dignify a
room. And place marble where you would expect to find it, unless you want an incongruous effect. You
wouldn't expect to see this heavy material on a door, for instance, but you've probably admired it on panels,

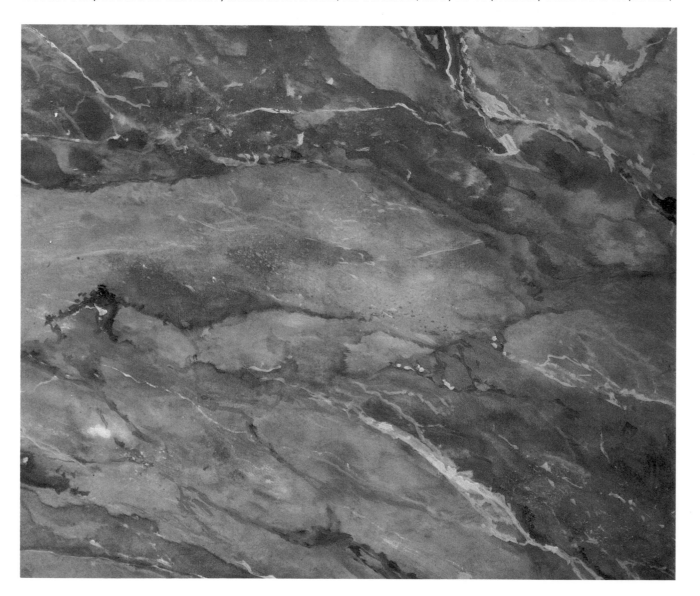

The key to successful marbling is to study the veining patterns and colours of actual marble.

tabletops, accessories, dressing tables, and bath surrounds. You wouldn't expect to see an entire wall of marble, except perhaps in an especially spacious and luxurious room—and even then it wouldn't be one solid piece but panels or blocks of several types or colours, because marble is usually cut into 4-by-8-foot blocks.

See the illustration, page 60, for help in dividing a wall into panels. You can also divide a wall into blocks arranged like standard brickwork; for directions, see the stone-block effect at the end of Chapter Nine. Note that, unlike bricks, marble blocks are set so that their joinery is barely visible; no mortar shows between the blocks.

Found in many parts of the world, marble is limestone naturally transformed over thousands of years by heat and pressure. It is polished to give it a shiny finish. Two main families of marble are breccia and veined. Breccia is made up of stone that has been broken into many small fragments and then reformed, with sediment filling the spaces between fragments. The fragments are angular and irregular in size, shape, and colour. Veined marble is one piece of stone with cracks running through its layers; residue fills the cracks, forming its characteristic veins. Learning more about how various marbles are formed can give you a better idea of how patterns develop.

For the marbling techniques that follow, it is crucial to devise the patterns carefully and mix the colours to perfection. Study the drawings that accompany each recipe and examine the finished examples pictured here to get a feel for the technique. Before you begin marbling, do several sketches of your pattern to gain confidence so that when you paint on your surface, your movements will be quick and sure. Veining is hard to do realistically at first. You might want to try veining with a feather instead of a brush to achieve light, varied strokes.

Marbling is a gradual process of adding more and more shapes and veining in many subtly mixed tones of colours. Bear in mind that for many marbles, too much contrast between tones may make the effect too intense. Keep your base coat, textured glaze, pattern, and veining close in either hue, intensity, or value to tie the effect together.

Varnishing completes a marbleized effect, but for a pale-coloured marble, be sure to use a varnish that will yellow as little as possible. Two coats of varnish will make good protection for walls; use three coats for tabletops and four coats for floors. But keep in mind that the more coats you use, the more the varnish may yellow. In the case of a white marble, you may have to compromise by getting less protection to preserve the look of your finish.

These finishes can be challenging, but you don't have to create only realistic effects. The techniques make great decorative finishes even if they just approximate the type of marble on which you based your design.

Practice and study will lead to more authentic results. But even if your first attempts have more folk-art appeal than realism, they can still blend well with many settings.

Before marbling, prepare your surfaces well. The technique needs a surface in good condition to best approximate the cold smoothness of stone. (When you apply gloss varnish over the effect, surface imperfections will stand out.)

For small surfaces, you can just set up the paint colours you'll need for the pattern and veining on a palette with a cup of water attached. But for larger surfaces, mix glazes in plastic containers, fill another container with water, and have a palette of colours handy for veining and details.

Your base coat must be cured before you begin the step-by-step procedure. The chart accompanying your technique will tell you which kind of base coat to use. See Mixing Paints, Chapter Four, to learn how to blend a base coat. See Preparing to Paint, Chapter Three, to learn how to apply it.

• WHITE MARBLE •

White marble is a breccia marble, composed of many irregular shapes. The drawing on this page shows a fragmented pattern. Study it, as well as the final photo, and do several drawings and samples before painting a pattern on your surface to ensure that your motions will be quick and fluid. Note that the larger your surface, the larger the shapes in the pattern should be.

Squeeze artist's acrylics in black, white, raw umber, ultramarine blue, and yellow ochre onto a palette. In the centre of the palette, mix all colours except black with enough water to form a light, watery neutral hue. If your surface is large, however, mix the colours and water in a plastic container instead. Now go to step 1.

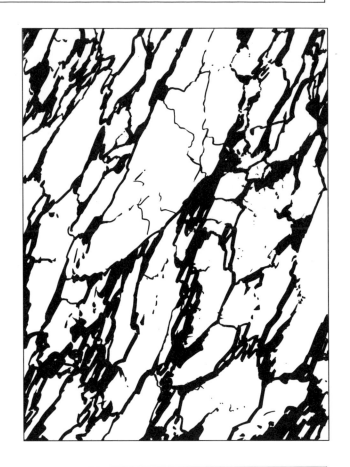

• R E C I P E •

WHITE MARBLE

LEVEL OF EXPERTISE:

RECOMMENDED ON: floors, panels, tabletops, mouldings, accessories

NOT RECOMMENDED ON: very large surfaces (unless divided into panels) or highly carved elements

NUMBER OF PEOPLE: 1

TOOLS: palette, container of water, container for glaze (optional), small well-worn sea sponges, chamois cloth, flat long-haired brush, fine round pointed brush, badger-hair brush

BASE COAT: silk emulsion

GLAZE: artist's acrylics and water

COLOURS: sample base coat—⅞ white emulsion plus 1/16 yellow ochre and 1/16 black acrylic

glaze for first sponging—⅓ titanium white, ⅓ burnt umber, ⅓ ultramarine blue, and a dash of black acrylic

palette colours—white, raw umber, ultramarine blue, yellow ochre, and black acrylic

VARNISH: satin or gloss acrylic varnish or non-yellowing polyurethane

1 Dip small sea sponge into neutral hue. Dab sponge in paint and drag it over surface to create textured ground. Make finish more irregular than you would in standard sponging; leave a few parts untouched. As you work, occasionally dab sponge into paint on palette so that you get bits of pure colours on sponge—a dash of black, then ochre, and so forth. This creates subtle variations on the surface. Stand back and examine the surface at intervals. Smooth with light feathering motions where colour changes are too pronounced. Let dry.

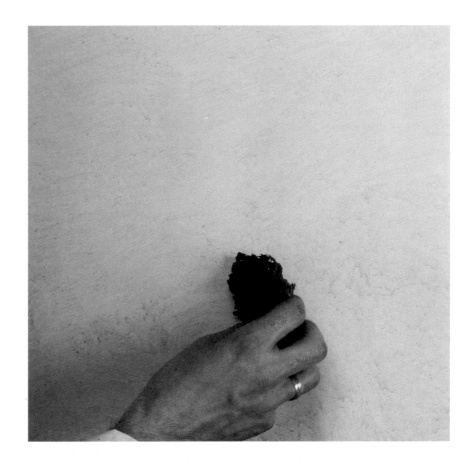

2 On palette or in container, mix white, ultramarine blue, raw umber, and a little black with water. Using a small, flat long-haired brush, paint major light shapes of marble that are close in value to your base coat (refer to drawing shown here and to your sketches).

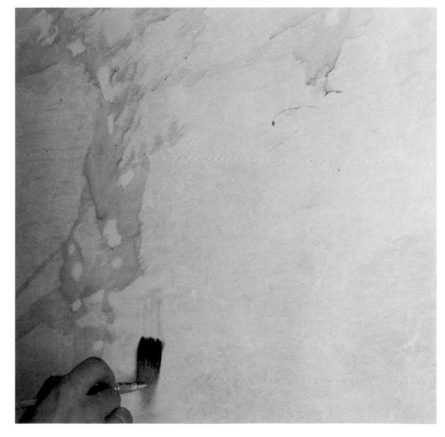

3 Smooth and feather surface with badger-hair brush. Then with chamois leather wipe off small spots within large grey shapes to make a more complex pattern.

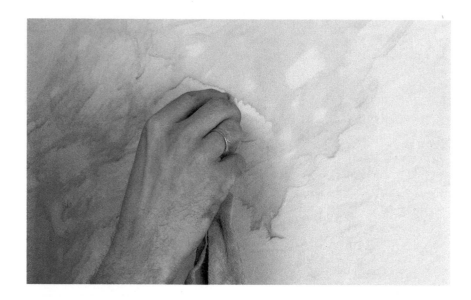

4 Combine raw umber, ultramarine blue, black, and drops of ochre and white with water. Using fine round pointed brush, paint veining (for tips on technique, see below). Hold brush relatively far back on handle as shown. As in step 1, pick up bits of pure colour to get variation— sometimes use just raw umber, sometimes ochre, and so on. For more colour changes, keep working with brush till it runs out of paint. Don't outline shapes precisely. Have some veins cross; make others bisect large masses. In few areas, add dots.

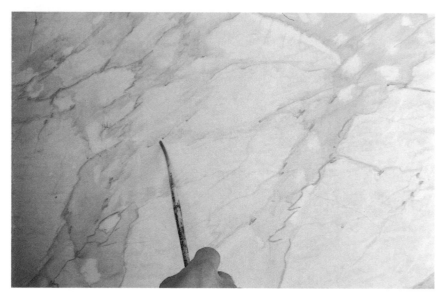

5 Using a well-worn sponge with frayed edges, dab and drag watered-down white acrylic over surface to create depth. Vary touch so that paint is semiopaque in some areas, very transparent in others.

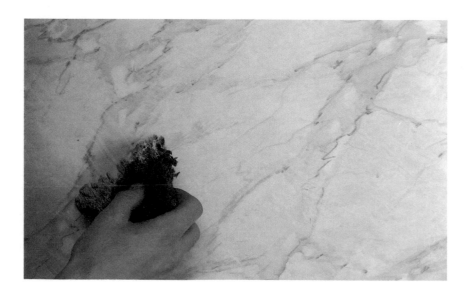

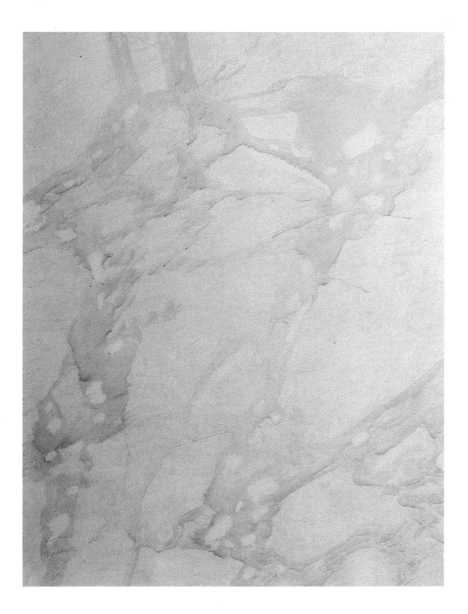

6 Varnish has been applied to the marbleized finish. (Remember: choose varnish that yellows as little as possible, especially for white marble.) Close examination reveals a subtle, complex surface; some veins are pure colours—ochre, raw umber, and so forth.

• TIPS FOR VEINING •

1. Variety is the key. Give each vein its own character. Vary its tone. You can make paint slightly lighter or darker by changing the amount of water you add to it or the amount you pick up on your brush. Vary your pressure on the brush to produce veins in many different widths.

2. Think about the material you are replicating as you work; you want to capture the fragmented look of marble. Veins should look somewhat like fine cracks. Veins should "tremble," or squiggle slightly. They shouldn't be straight lines, parallel and evenly spaced, or broken into a regular series of dots. Avoid having veins cross at one point like a star.

• RED MARBLE •

Before you begin, study the drawing of the marble pattern in the illustration and examine the finished effect to familiarize yourself with its characteristics. Practice drawing patterns on paper, then try using a brush on paper before painting your surface.

• R E C I P E •

RED MARBLE

LEVEL OF EXPERTISE:

RECOMMENDED ON: floors, panels, tabletops, mouldings, accessories

NOT RECOMMENDED ON: very large surfaces (unless divided into panels), highly carved elements

NUMBER OF PEOPLE: 1

TOOLS: small well-worn sea sponges, palette, container of water, containers for glaze (optional), small round brush, fine pointed long-haired brushes, flat long-haired lettering brush

BASE COAT: silk emulsion

GLAZE: artist's acrylics plus water

COLOURS: sample base coat—white emulsion sponging glazes—¾ titanium white, plus ⅛ ultramarine blue, ⅛ raw umber, and a dash of black acrylic

red glaze—red oxide plus a little burnt sienna, vermillion red, and chrome orange acrylic

palette colours—white, black, burnt umber, raw umber, and ultramarine blue acrylic

VARNISH: satin or gloss acrylic varnish or polyurethane

1 Dab and drag sponge over surface to form textured ground, as in step 1 of white marble technique, above. Use palette of white, ultramarine blue, raw umber, and black acrylics plus water to create pale blend. Pick up bits of pure colour on sponge as you work, and smooth when completed. Let dry; paint will dry fast because it is water-based.

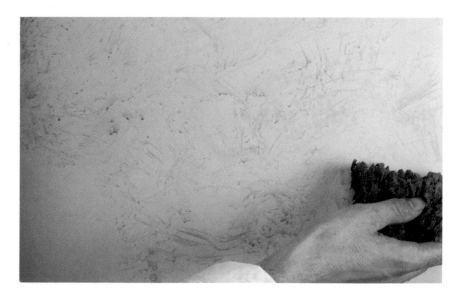

2 Repeat process with darker mix of same colours. (either add a little blue or black acrylic to glaze, or remix colours and add less water this time.) Apply more randomly so that some of base coat and first sponging are visible. Let dry.

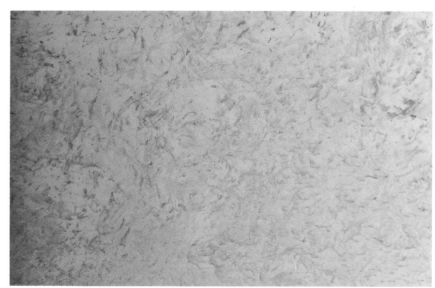

3 Combine red oxide; dabs of burnt sienna, vermillion red, and chrome orange; and just a little water. Make big enough batch to cover surface. Paint marble pattern with flat, long-haired lettering brush on about three-quarters of surface. Apply two coats in some areas for depth.

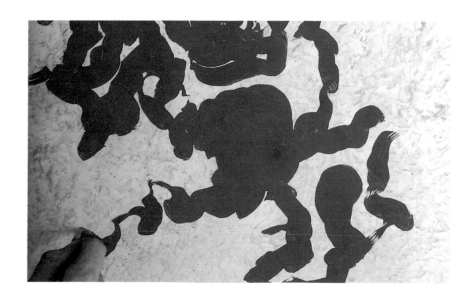

4 Make very transparent glaze of burnt umber and water. Sponge mainly over red areas— white areas already have sponged texture. Then mix slightly darker glaze of burnt umber and a little black; make glaze more opaque by adding less water.

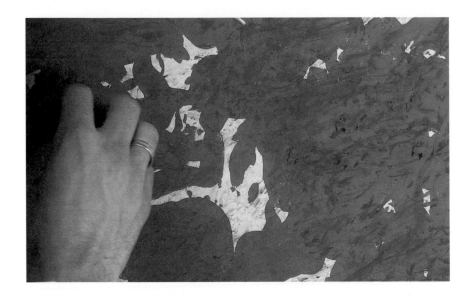

5 Mix a more opaque glaze of white plus a little black, ultramarine blue, and raw umber to get light grey-white. Apply with the corner of a sponge over entire surface. Set aside glaze for use in step 7 below. With fine pointed brush, add light veining in pure raw umber acrylic. Make wavy lines in various directions, some crossing others.

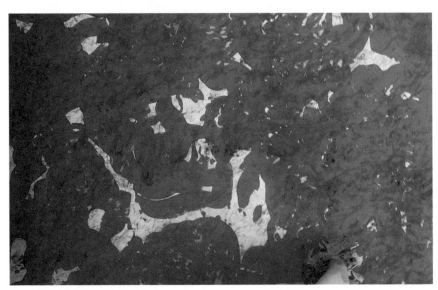

6 Add white to lighten grey-white glaze sponged on in step 5. With fine pointed brush, outline one side of most grey shapes to create shadow and depth. Vary thickness and tone of strokes. Then paint over some grey shapes with very transparent grey glaze.

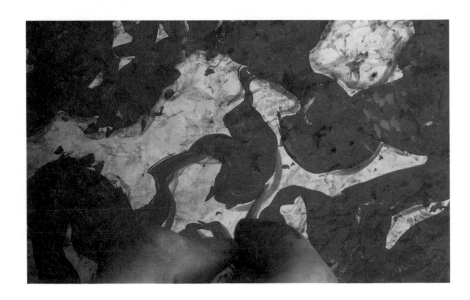

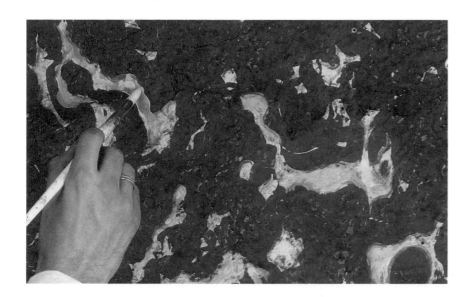

7 With round brush, outline some grey areas in same manner as in step 6, using white glaze tinted with yellow ochre.

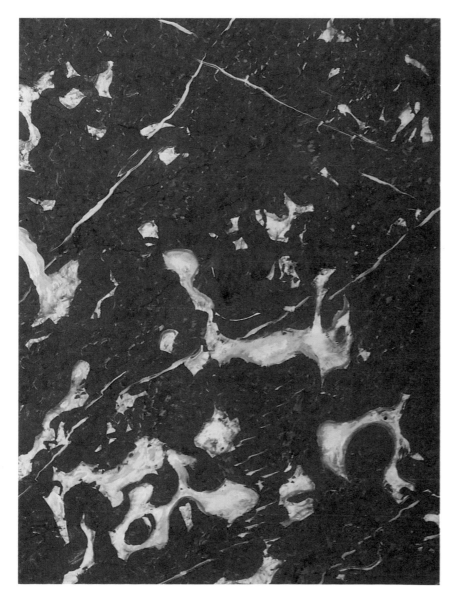

8 With fine pointed brush, vein in broken stepped lines of various sizes across surface as shown. With brush, pick up burnt umber and raw umber, each thinned with a little water, from palette to introduce subtle colour changes. Once varnished, the finished surface takes on the polished sheen of marble.

• GREEN MARBLE •

Although painted in oils here, this marble can be done in acrylics, too. For its background, it employs a finish shown in an earlier chapter—ragging off and cheeseclothing: light over dark (end of Chapter Six). The background colour is mainly black tinted with green plus a little white. Follow the step-by-step procedure for that technique and let your surface dry. Make a transparent glaze of 2 parts turpentine to 1 part boiled linseed oil. Rub the glaze over your surface with a clean cloth. Now proceed to step 1.

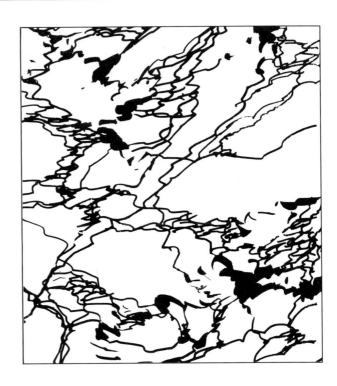

• R E C I P E •

GREEN MARBLE

LEVEL OF EXPERTISE:

RECOMMENDED ON: floors, panels, tabletops, moulding, accessories

NOT RECOMMENDED ON: very large surfaces (unless divided into panels), highly carved elements

NUMBER OF PEOPLE: 1

TOOLS: glazing brush, cheesecloth, roller tray, gloves, cotton rags, palette knife, round brush, fine short-haired white-bristle brushes, 1-inch-wide long-haired white-bristle brush, spalter brush or high quality gloss brush, palette, containers for glaze (optional), turpentine

BASE COAT: satin oil-based paint

GLAZE: 2 parts turpentine to 1 part boiled linseed oil

COLOURS: sample base coat—½ black oil-based paint plus ¼ emerald green plus ¼ chrome green artist's oils

glaze and palette colours—white, black, ultramarine or Prussian blue, raw sienna, yellow ochre, oxide of chrome, alizarin crimson artist's oils

VARNISH: satin or gloss oil-based varnish

Note: For this technique, you complete half of finish, then let surface dry overnight (see step 4); so be sure you set aside enough time to complete your project.

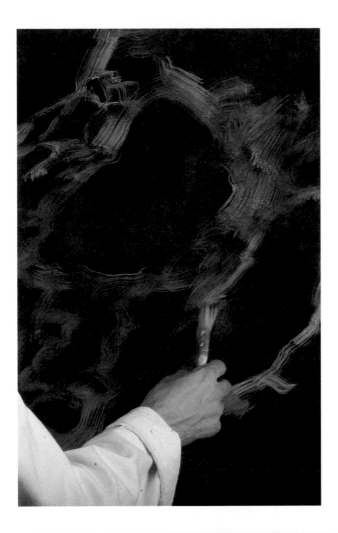

1 Mix a light, transparent tone by adding white plus a little oxide of chrome, raw sienna, and ultramarine blue artists oils to glaze described above. With 1-inch-wide long-haired brush, paint marble pattern as in drawing, opposite page.

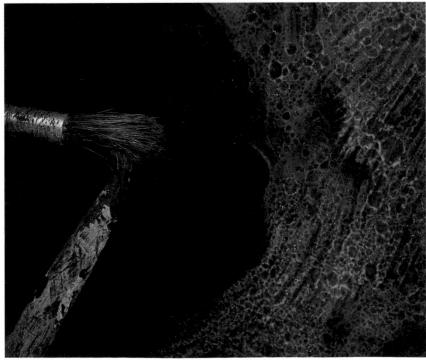

2 With brush and palette knife, spatter off (page 168) with paint thinner to form tiny shapes within light-colour glazed areas. Spatter a little at a time, waiting to see results before proceeding. Then wrap cloth around finger and wipe off small areas on glaze to create more shapes and to add depth.

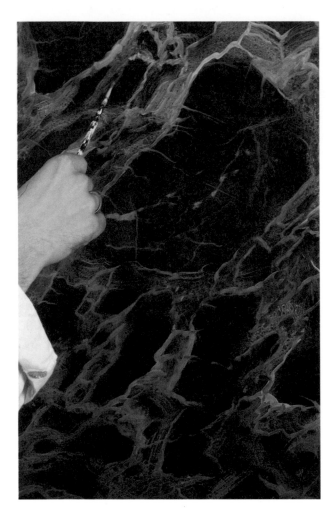

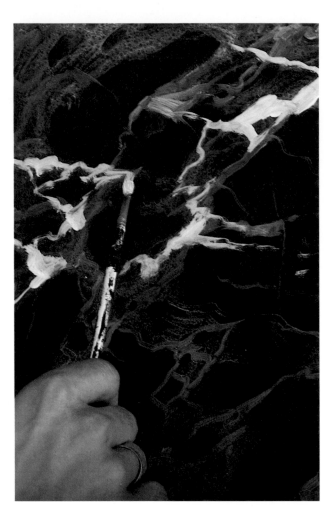

3 Vein surface with fine short-haired brush in colours a little darker than background. Mix these colours on palette from combinations of raw sienna, white, ultramarine blue, yellow ochre, and oxide of chrome: first, white plus raw sienna and ultramarine blue; next, white plus yellow ochre and oxide of chrome; then white plus oxide of chrome and raw sienna. Continue creating more colours by mixing paints on palette in other combinations and in varying amounts, and vein with these mixtures. Pick up some pure colour on your brush as you work. Paint until brush runs dry; this will alter colours and increase depth. Don't outline shapes closely. Vary shapes, sizes, and colours of veins extensively.

4 Tint white with a bit of green and do some veining. Add ochre to paint and vein some more. Partly outline major shapes, varying width of lines. Add some broken stepped lines across surface. Then smooth some areas with spalter brush or high quality gloss brush and let dry overnight. The next day, make clear glaze, as described in introduction above, and rub on the surface with cloth.

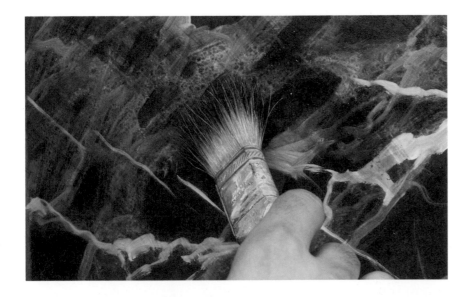

5 Create three transparent glazes using clear glaze and the following colours: (1) blue and raw sienna; (2) oxide of chrome, black, and a little blue; and (3) alizarin crimson and a little black. Apply them with flat brush, varying strokes—in some places, splay bristles; in other, sweep lightly over surface with diagonal strokes. Alternate colours in some places, overlap them in others. Create several colour combinations using prussian blue, oxide of chrome, and black (mix the first colour with more black, the second with more blue, and so forth). Spatter paint over wet glazes, creating colours as you go. See page 166, for spattering directions. Highlight some veins with white.

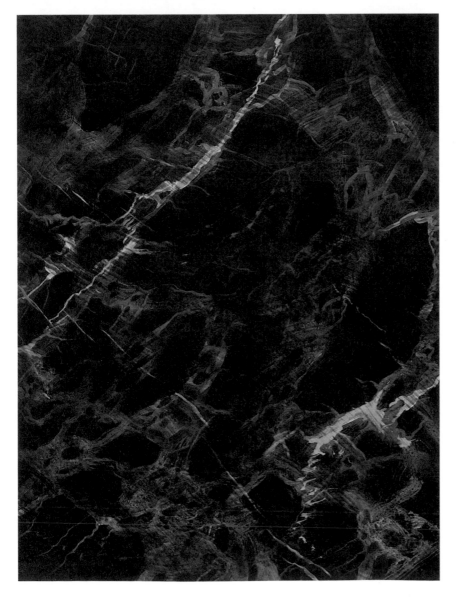

6 Photo shows the finished effect after three coats of varnish.

APPLICATION:
• YELLOW SIENNA MARBLE ON A COLUMN •

Originally an old painted wood column, this marbled treasure was first sanded, filled, primed, and then base-coated with three layers of yellow satin emulsion.

Move around the column as you work so that you keep track of how your finish looks from all sides. Avoid painting veins so that they wrap around the column and their ends meet. Follow the drawing at right for pattern.

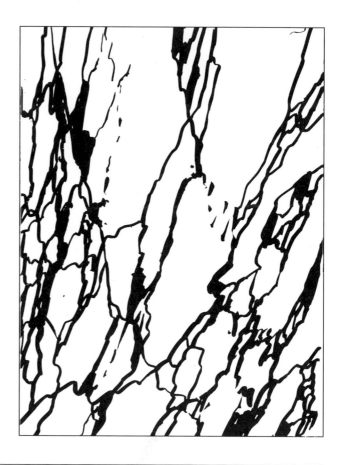

• R E C I P E •

YELLOW SIENNA MARBLE ON A COLUMN

LEVEL OF EXPERTISE:

RECOMMENDED ON: columns, floors, panels, tabletops, mouldings, accessories

NOT RECOMMENDED ON: very large surfaces like walls (unless divided into panels), carved elements

NUMBER OF PEOPLE: 1

TOOLS: small well-worn sea sponges, palette, containers for glaze (optional), container of water, badger-hair brush, fine long-haired brushes, flat brushes, and round brushes (fitches)

BASE COAT: semigloss emulsion paint

GLAZE: artist's acrylics and a little water

COLOURS: sample base coat—⅔ white emulsion to ⅓ chrome yellow acrylic

glaze and palette colours—white, chrome yellow, yellow ochre, chrome orange, vermillion red, raw sienna, chrome oxide green medium, ultramarine blue acrylic

VARNISH: satin or gloss acrylic varnish or non-yellowing polyurethane

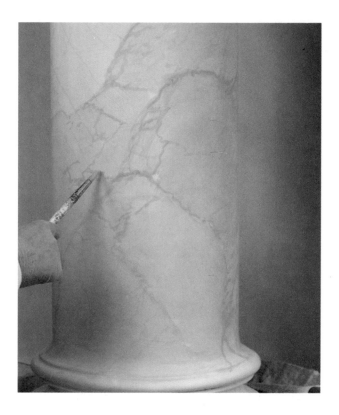

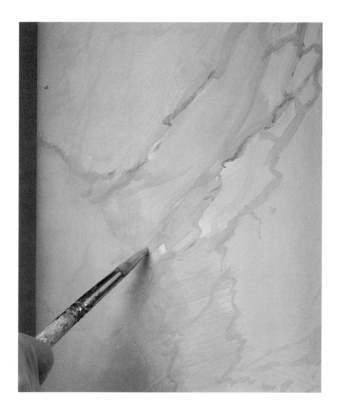

1 With very transparent glaze of ochre yellow acrylic and water, paint main shapes of marble pattern with 2-inch-wide flat brush, leaving large areas of base coat visible. Then, using medium round nylon brush, vein over surface, as shown, with same glaze.

2 Do more veining in various colours, mixing paints on palette (see recipe for colours) as you go to get wide range of hues—one with more white, another with more ochre, and so forth. Use mainly yellow ochre, chrome yellow, chrome orange, and raw sienna. Keep veining until brush is free of paint. Work around column, building up an intricate system of veins.

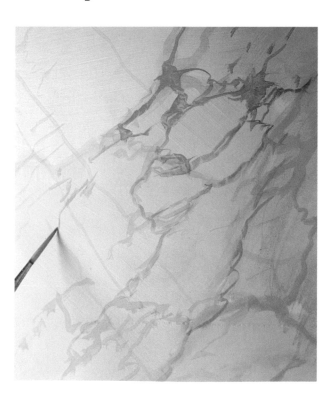

3 With finer brush, vein in stronger colours, including vermillion, raw sienna, chrome orange, chrome yellow, and a little yellow ochre. Make lines sharper and add more detail. Make some veins transparent green, as shown.

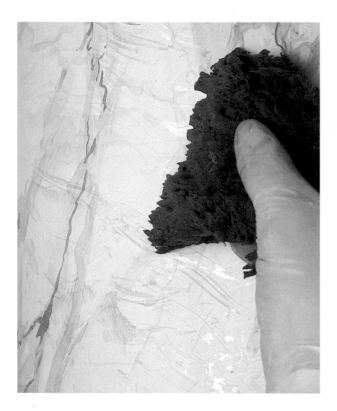

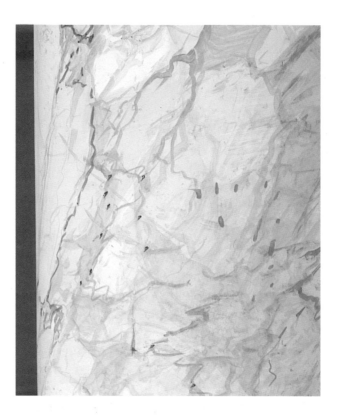

4 With sponge, dab very transparent glazes of ochre yellow, raw sienna, and red ochre around column. Drag sponge, blurring and smoothing, as you apply.

5 With flat short-haired brush, paint even stronger colours, such as crimson, blue, and raw sienna, at intersections of some veins. Also add dots and a few darker veins.

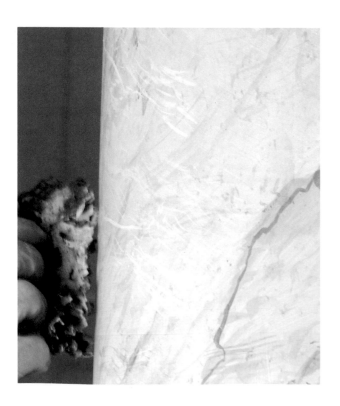

6 Dab pure white acrylic thinned with water over the entire column, dragging and smoothing as you work.

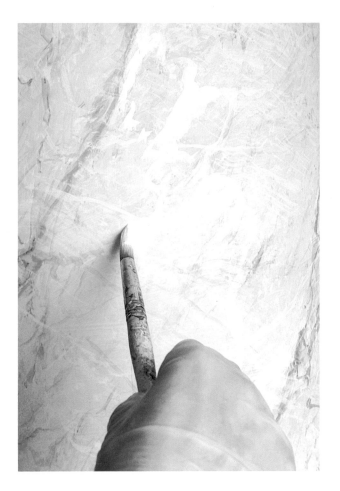

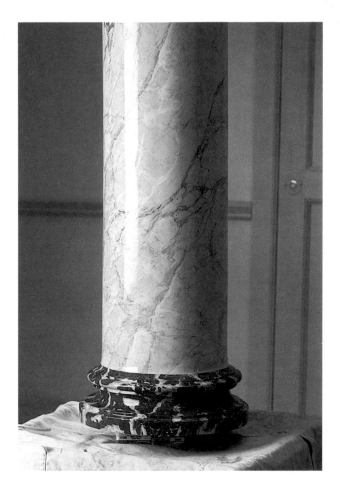

7 Use flat brush of medium thickness to do veins in white acrylic thinned with a little water, then in opaque white acrylic.

8 For base, follow directions for red marble, above. On a small area like this, make many squiggles for best results. When possible, study real marble for inspiration. Once paint dries, coat the column with satin or gloss oil-based varnish.

APPLICATION:
• MARBLING A FLOOR •

Created for the March, 1989, Kips Bay Designer Show House in New York City, this faux marble floor contributes richness and elegance to a stairway landing designed by Richard L. Neas of Manhattan.

The floor was stripped with a sander, then primed with oil-based primer and base-coated with two layers of white eggshell. Drying times between paint layers were carefully respected to build a sound foundation over which to marbleize.

Once the design was conceived, a scale drawing was made of the floor on graph paper so that one square on the paper represented one tile of the floor. The drawing showed the layout of the floor and gave exact measurements for each tile and border to make the design easy to reproduce. Samples were made to ensure that colours and patterns would work well together.

• R E C I P E •

MARBLING A FLOOR

LEVEL OF EXPERTISE:

PEOPLE: 2

TOOLS: small well-worn sea sponges, flat soft-haired brush, badger-hair brush, palette, containers for glazes, containers of water, fine long- and short-haired brushes for veining

BASE COAT: semigloss emulsion

COLOURS: sample base coat for white taupe marble—white emulsion

palette colours—titanium white, black, raw umber, ultramarine blue, yellow ochre, and oxide of chrome acrylic

sample base coat for red ochre inlaid marble—½ red ochre, ½ burnt sienna, and a dash of titanium white acrylic

glaze for red ochre—red vermillion, red ochre, and yellow ochre acrylic

VARNISH: satin polyurethane

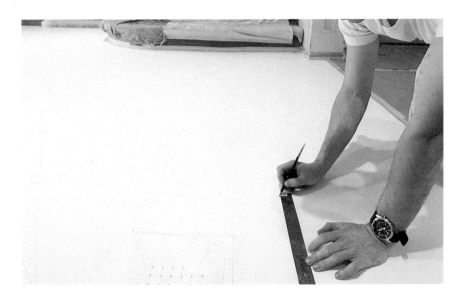

1 Following drawing, mark grid on floor using a straightedge.

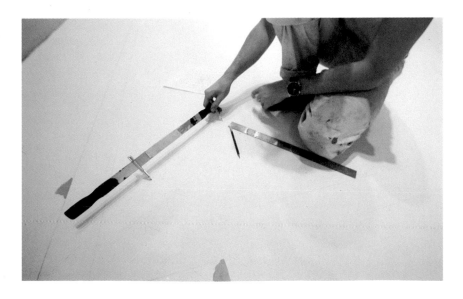

2 Snap chalklines on floor (see page 172 for instructions on how to use a chalkline), trace over them in pencil, and pick up all chalk with sponge—you will have to tape over these lines, and tape won't stick securely over chalk. Note sample of floor taped to wall as guide.

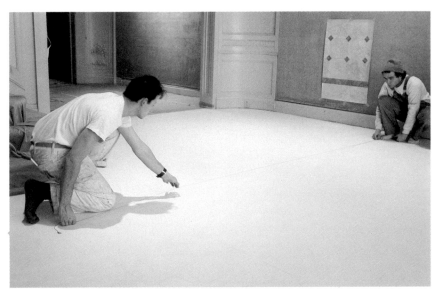

3 Use beam compass to form rounded corners of design.

4 Begin with stone border. For technique, see stone-block effect, page 172. Tape edges of border. Divide border into several sections. This lends authenticity to the end result, since stone comes in slabs, not in room-sized lengths. For this border, mix three pale earth-tone glazes in plastic containers; sponge one on each of three sections for natural look. Then set up palette of earth tones, and begin veining atop glazes, blending in more colours as you go.

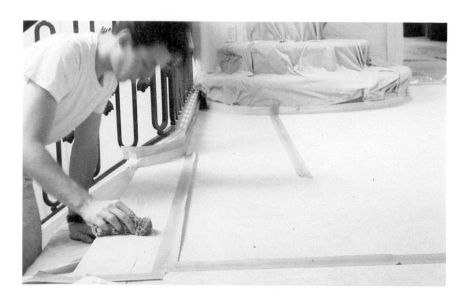

5 Let border dry; cover with plastic. One person tapes edges of darker marble border next to stone, then base-coats border and begins taping light-marble perimeter and first interior rows of squares. Other person completes perimeter—following directions for white marble, above, but using warmer colours (see recipe for marbling a floor)—then moves inside and paints every other square in first interior rows. When dry, paint alternate squares. When alternate squares are dry, tape inner edges of next interior rows. One person paints next rows. Other person removes tape from sections once dry and begins taping medallions.

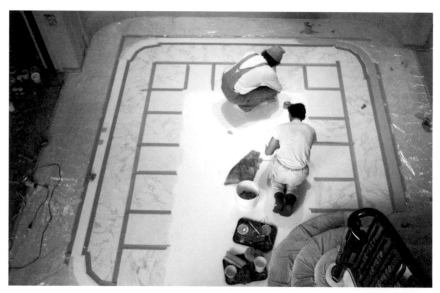

6 Once the base coat of darker border is dry, one person forms breccia marble pattern atop it by painting main marble shapes with flat brush in very transparent glaze of red ochre and burnt sienna. Then veins are added in white acrylic. Follow white marble above, but change colours.

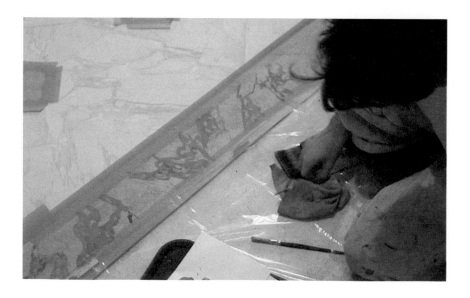

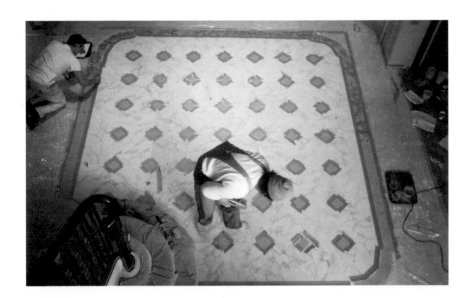

7 One person finishes taping medallions and base-coats them while other person completes border. After medallions are dry, they are marbleized as in step 6.

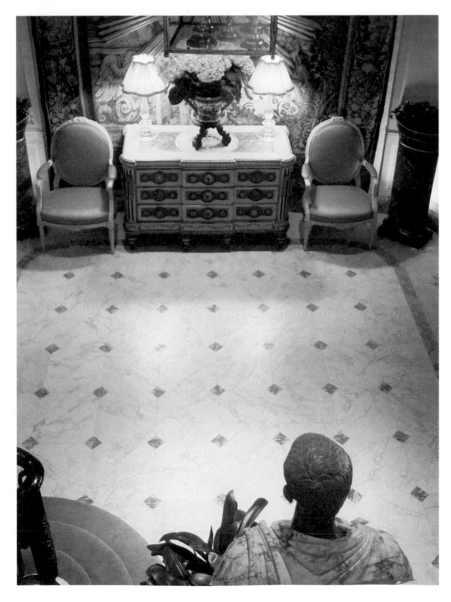

8 Once medallions are dry, remove all tape from floor. Retape a few squares and brush over them with transparent glaze of yellow ochre and raw umber, feathering lightly. Tiles in varying tones "age" the floor and give it a natural look. Varnish floor with four coats of satin polyurethane (not gloss—it causes a glare).

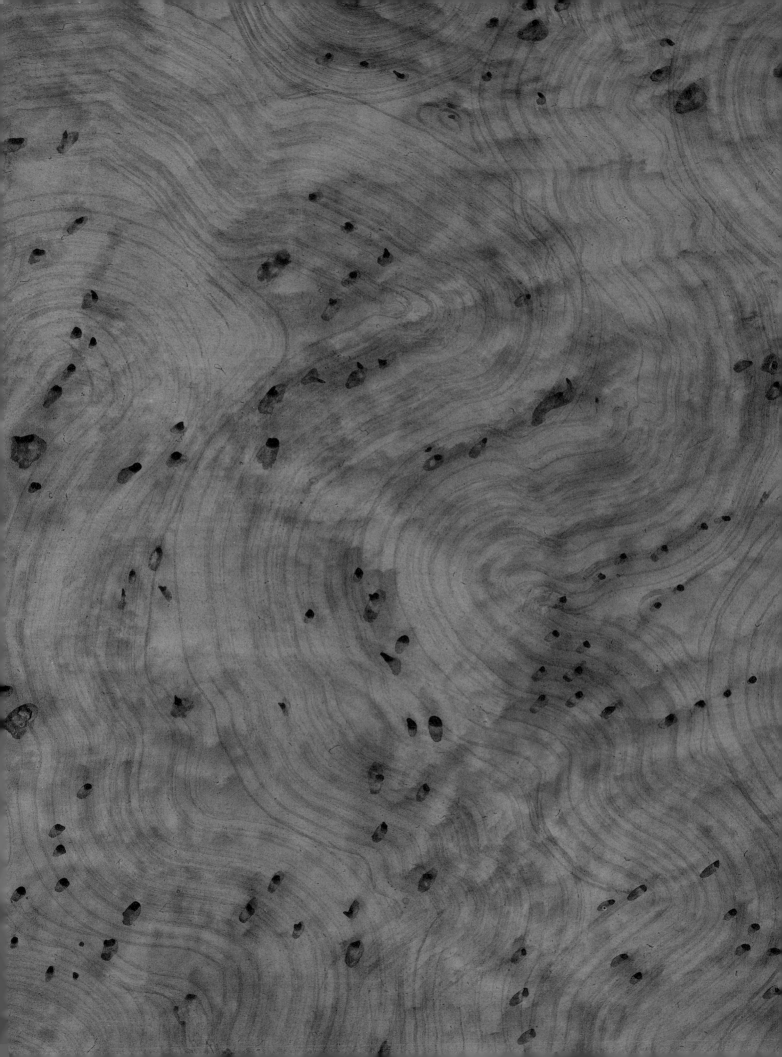

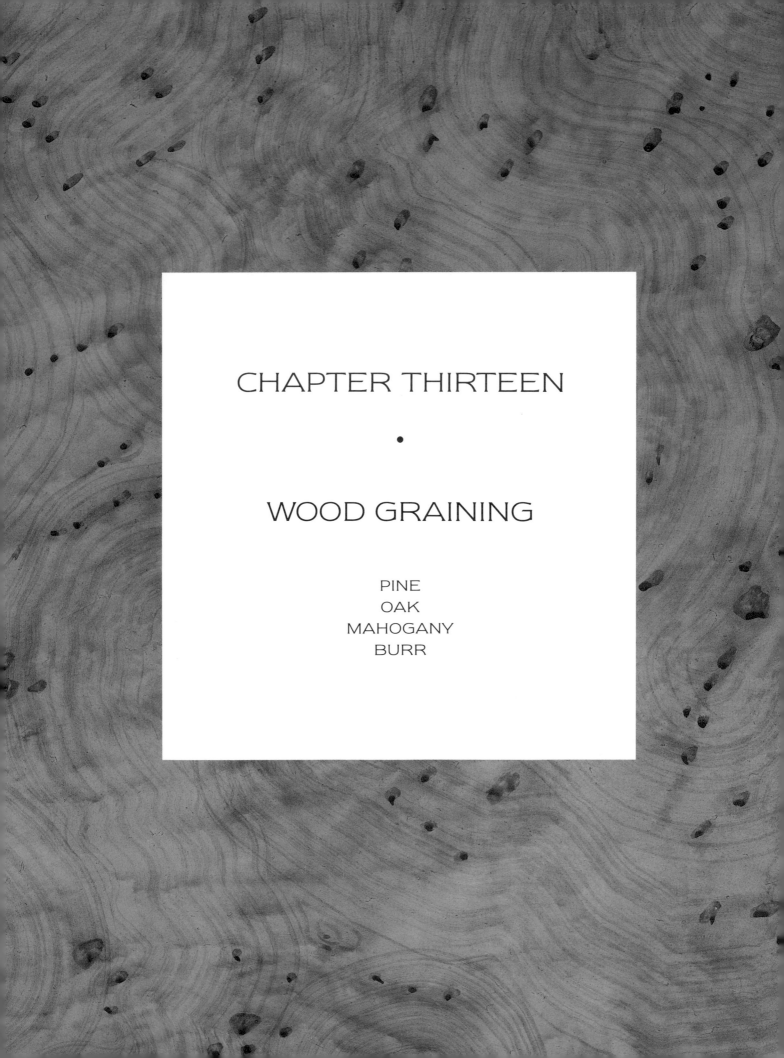

CHAPTER THIRTEEN

·

WOOD GRAINING

PINE
OAK
MAHOGANY
BURR

CREATING WOOD GRAINING THAT LOOKS AUTHENTIC IS AN ART THAT

takes years to master. With practice, the simplified approach presented here will give you pleasing (though not always the most realistic) finishes.

Like marble, wood comes in many types, and each has its own pattern. In addition, the graining pattern on a piece of wood depends on how the tree it came from grew and the part of the log from which it was cut.

The centre of the log is called heartwood; boards cut from this section feature figured graining—pairs of inverted V's, sometimes gathered around a knot. The outer rings are called sapwood; boards from this section display straight graining. Oak logs are often quartersawn, or cut in quarters and then into boards that show short squiggly marks across their straight graining.

Careful attention to colour and pattern are vital in reproducing wood. Study the drawings and photos that accompany these techniques and, whenever possible, have a piece of the wood you're reproducing beside you as you work. Pay close attention to the direction of the grain.

Invest time in practice. Make samples, experimenting with colours and painted details such as knots and burrs. A few specialty tools are required for wood graining—steel combs, pencil dragger brushes, badger-hair softeners. Get comfortable with them before tackling your first project.

Wood graining has long been used to imitate expensive and exotic woods. You can also use it when you get a new piece of furniture and want to match its finish to a piece already in the room. In renovating an old house, you might grain new trim or doors to match older elements in rare and much more costly woods. Or you may want to grain in a colour—say, a Colonial American blue—to imitate old painted wood. And you might combine several of the effects presented in this chapter into a wood-inlay design for a floor or a tabletop.

Dragging and combing (Chapter Ten) are two decorative finishes that developed from wood graining. You may want to try them first to get a feel for some of the tools and techniques.

For most wood-graining projects, your base coat and glazes should be close in tone, and the base coat should always be lighter than the glaze. Accompanying the step-by-step procedures are recipes that note what kind of base coat to use. Chapter Four tells you how to mix a base coat; Chapter Three tells how to apply one. Make sure your base coat is fully cured before glazing over it.

Drawing at right shows the pattern of figured pine graining.

• PINE •

The best kind of graining to try first is pine. One of the most common woods, it is easy to recognize and probably the simplest to produce.

Two brushes will aid you in graining: the spalter (or a high quality gloss brush) and the pencil dragger. Both are available through mail order (see source list) as well as in specialty paint stores and art supply shops.

The painted pine pictured here exhibits two types of graining—figured and straight. You will use both acrylic and oil glaze in this technique. Begin by applying acrylic glaze in crisscross fashion—top to bottom, side to side, top to bottom. Smooth glaze with a spalter; then go to step 1.

• R E C I P E •

PINE

LEVEL OF EXPERTISE:

RECOMMENDED ON: doors, panelling, cabinetry, mouldings, furniture, accessories

NOT RECOMMENDED ON: intricately carved mouldings, furniture or accessories, whole wall (unless divided into panels)

NUMBER OF PEOPLE: 1

TOOLS: fine flat brushes, large and small spalter (or high quality gloss brushes) and pencil dragger brushes, glazing brush, cotton cloth

BASE COAT: satin emulsion paint

GLAZE: 1—about 2 parts acrylic medium to 1 part water

2—about 6 parts ready-mixed oil glaze to about 1 part thinner (see Mixing Paints, Chapter Four)

COLOURS: sample base coat—½ white latex paint plus ⅓ raw sienna, $\frac{1}{12}$ raw umber, and $\frac{1}{12}$ yellow ochre acrylic

glaze 1— ¾ raw sienna and ¼ burnt sienna acrylic

glaze 2—transparent

VARNISH: satin or semigloss oil varnish

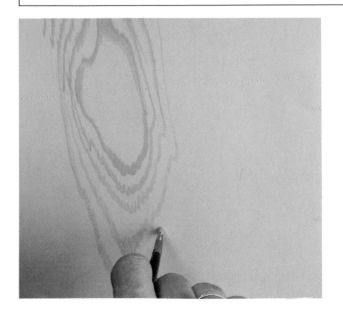

1 Mix artist's acrylics in small container and paint figured graining with small brush. See drawing for pattern or copy directly from figured pine board. Make lines tight around center of figures, then thicker and more elongated as you move out.

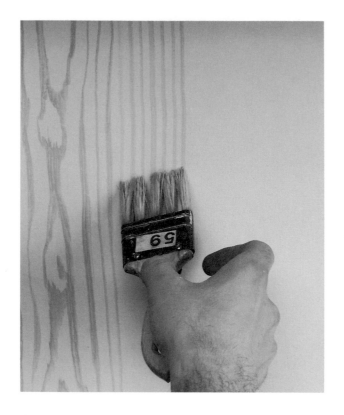

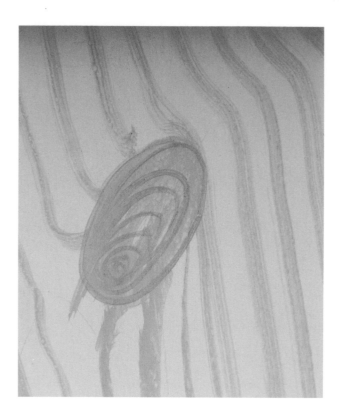

2 After painting every few lines, fan out glaze with spalter to get splayed-out effect on edges. With pencil dragger, paint straight graining along sides of figures, following outline.

3 Paint knots in same colour glaze as graining. Form oval shape angled upward. Once oval dries, paint inner lines with same glaze—but use less water so that colour will be darker. Make circles meet at one edge, as shown. Once knots and graining are dry, reglaze surface with wet and even coat of transparent oil glaze. (graining dries fast because paint is water-based.)

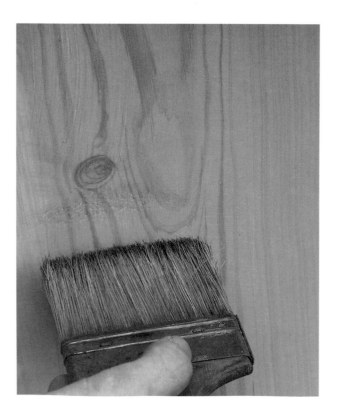

4 With spalter, bring a little wet glaze under and above knots to create shading and shadows.

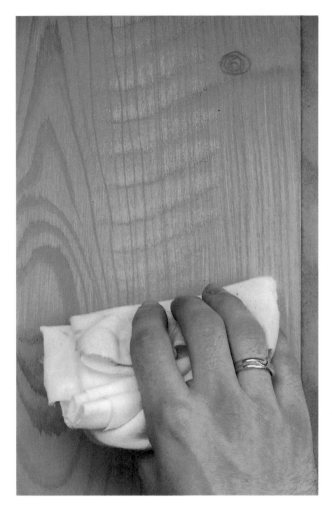

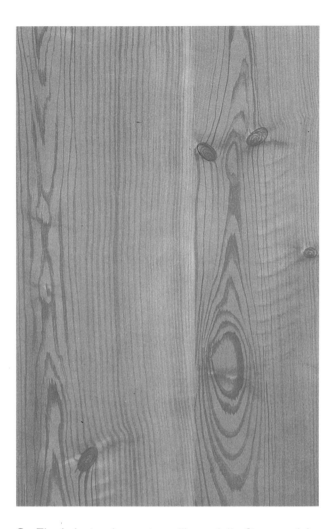

5 Fold a cotton cloth into a 4- by 6-inch rectangle. Holding it with thumb down and fingers on top, add more shading below knots and near figures. Make patting motion to form pattern shown; then feather out with spalter.

6 Final photo shows two "boards" after varnishings. To get contrast in tones, glaze second board with slightly darker version of oil glaze in step 3. (To get clean edge, tape first board after it dries, then paint second.) Or cover both boards with slightly darker oil glaze, then wipe most of glaze from one board (taking care to keep sharp edge) so that board looks faded.

• OAK •

Steel combs create the graining in this oak technique. The combs come in sets, usually three large, three medium, and three small; gear the size of the comb to the size of your surface. Within each size, there are wide-, medium-, and narrow-toothed combs. Note that one side of the comb is smoother than the other; use them smooth side down. Because decorative painting is becoming increasingly popular, you may find comb sets in art shops or craft stores; or you can order them by mail (see source list).

Practice is invaluable with wood-graining techniques. Examine the drawings of oak graining and the finished effect as well as pieces and photos of wood. The steps below explain three different types of oak graining.

Glaze some samples and try combing them to see how your colours look and to gain experience with the tools. Adjust the colour and consistency of your glaze, if necessary, then apply it evenly to your surface in crisscross pattern—top to bottom, side to side, top to bottom. While glaze is still wet, begin graining.

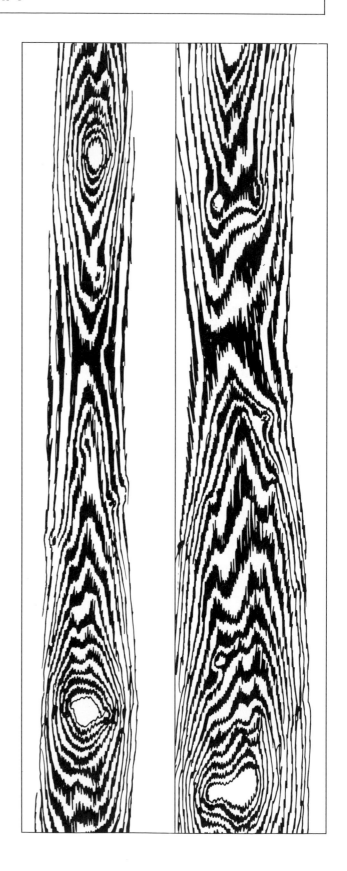

Drawing at right shows the pattern of heartwood oak graining, page 234.

• R E C I P E •

OAK

LEVEL OF EXPERTISE:

RECOMMENDED ON: doors, panels, cabinetry, mouldings, furniture, accessories

NOT RECOMMENDED ON: highly carved mouldings and other elements, whole walls (unless divided into panels)

NUMBER OF PEOPLE: 1

TOOLS: set of steel combs, large and small spalter brushes (or high quality gloss brushes), gloss brush, fine flat brushes, small piece of hessian, lint-free cotton cloth, turpentine, gloves

BASE COAT: semigloss oil-based paint

GLAZE: about 6 parts ready-mixed oil glaze to 1 part thinner (see Mixing Paints, Chapter Four)

COLOURS: sample base coat—⅓ yellow ochre, ⅓ burnt umber, and ⅙ raw umber artist's oils plus ⅙ white oil-based paint

glaze—½ burnt umber, ⅓ yellow ochre, and ⅙ raw umber artist's oils

VARNISH: satin or semigloss oil-based varnish

• SAPWOOD (STRAIGHT GRAINING) •

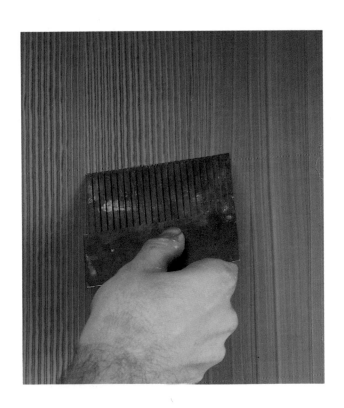

1   Grain surface first with large comb that has the widest teeth. Hold comb at 45-degree angle, thumb on top and fingers on bottom. Smoother side of comb should face down. Wipe comb after each pass.

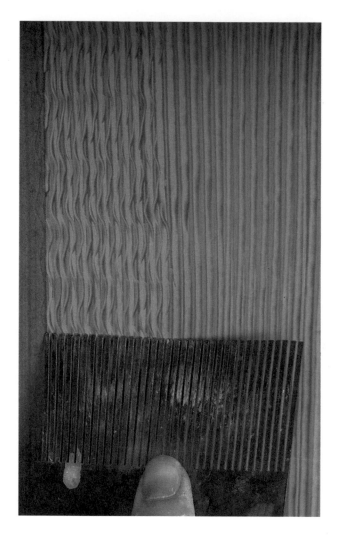

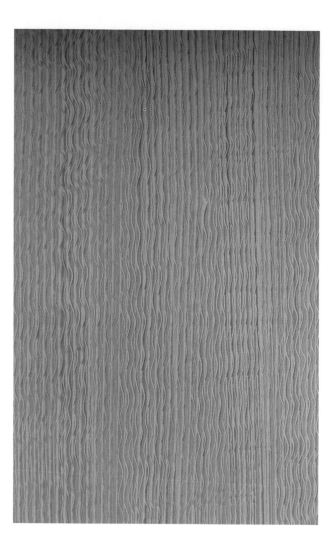

2 While glaze is still wet, grain surface again with medium-tooth comb, this time making slightly wavy lines.

3 On parts of surface, you will have straight graining, as shown here. For other parts, use straight graining as a base and, while glaze is still wet, follow steps for quartersawn and heart-wood, below.

• QUARTERSAWN •

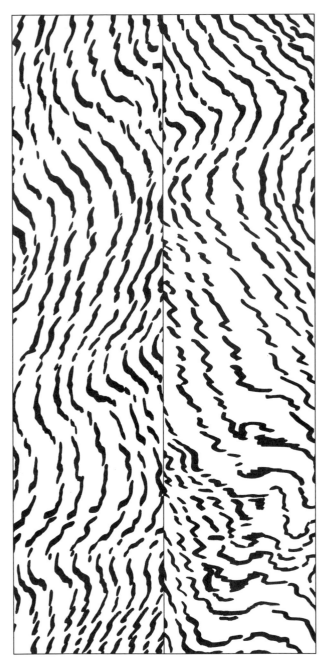

Drawing above shows the pattern of quarter-sawn oak graining.

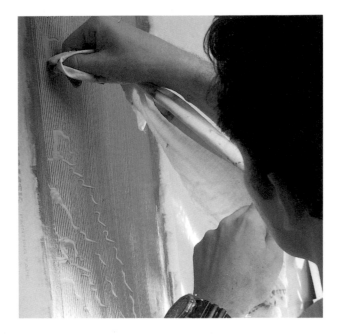

1 Wrap corner of cloth (about 4 by 12 inches) around thumbnail (or palette knife if your nails are short), as shown. Wipe glaze in Z-shaped pattern, as in drawing, turning cloth to clean spot often.

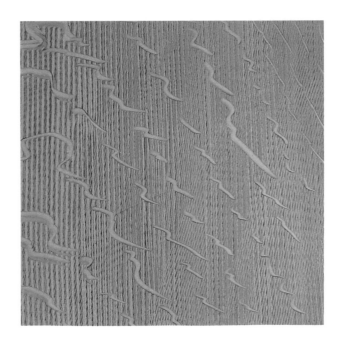

2 Dashes should vary in length and width, and should flow diagonally across surface.

• HEARTWOOD •

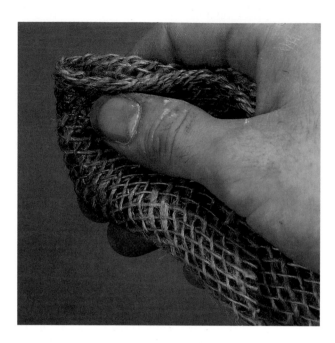

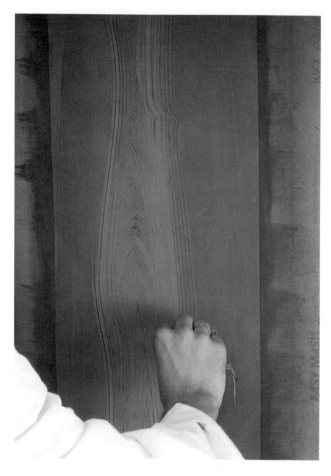

1 Cut piece of hessian about 6 inches square (old, worn hessian is best). Trim loose edges so that they don't get into glaze. Fold piece in quarters to get sharp corner, as shown.

2 Draw figured graining in glaze with hessian (see drawing). Make pairs of inverted-V strokes to form "hearts" of wood. Keep graining tight near centres of hearts, longer and narrower as you move away. V-shaped strokes should be thicker at middle than at ends. With inverted-V motion, wipe some glaze from centers of hearts.

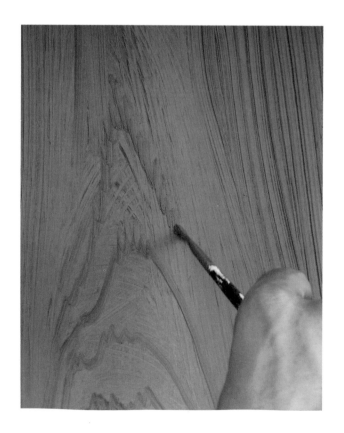

3 With well-worn brush, paint over pattern with glaze in inverted-V motion. Note that brush is held near end of handle. Feather and smooth glaze, working from hearts out with small spalter brush.

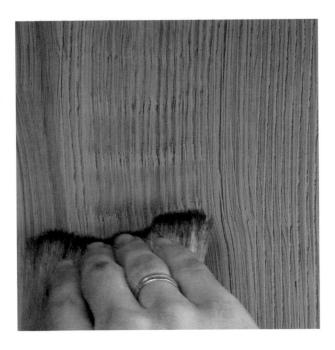

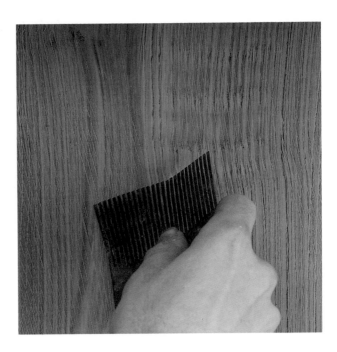

4 Holding spalter by bristles, as shown, drag and lift brush down surface to make pattern of horizontal lines in some areas.

5 Using large comb with widest teeth, grain along sides of pattern, following outline. Trace to end of each heart; then move comb in and grain in space between hearts (the joinery).

6 Final photo shows two oak "boards" after varnishing—the one at left is heartwood, the one at right is quartersawn. Note the small knots that were added after straight graining.

• MAHOGANY •

The mahogany technique also requires two glazings. Because you will be using oil-based paints, you must let your surface dry before applying the second glaze. The example shows one "panel" with straight graining and another featuring forked mahogany—the type of graining found where a trunk divided into two shoots.

Apply the glaze in crisscross pattern. Working from top to bottom, add more glaze in some areas to vary colour values.

• R E C I P E •

MAHOGANY

LEVEL OF EXPERTISE:

RECOMMENDED ON: doors, panels, cabinetry, mouldings, furniture, accessories

NOT RECOMMENDED ON: highly carved moulding and other elements, whole walls unless divided into panels

NUMBER OF PEOPLE: 1

TOOLS: large and small spalter brushes (or high quality gloss brushes), gloss brush, fine flat brushes, small round brush, container of turpentine, cotton cloth, gloves

BASE COAT: satin oil-based paint

GLAZE: about 6 parts ready-mixed oil glaze to 1 part thinner (see Mixing Paints, Chapter Four)

COLOURS: sample base coat—⅓ white oil-based paint, ⅓ yellow ochre, and ⅓ red ochre artist's oils

glaze—⅓ alizarin crimson, ⅓ burnt sienna, and ⅓ raw umber artist's oils

VARNISH: satin or semigloss oil-based varnish

• STRAIGHT GRAINING •

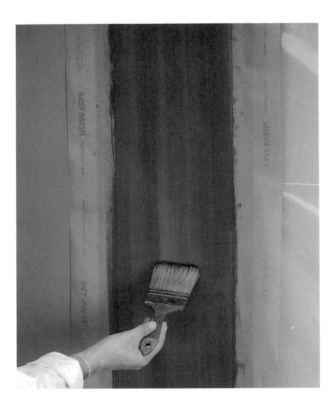

1   Feather the surface up and down with spalter brush to smooth and soften it.

2   Fold cotton cloth into small rectangle. Hold cloth with thumb underneath and fingers spread apart on top, and drag it down surface. (Cloth lifts glaze only where fingers touch the surface.) Do second stroke next to first, and continue across surface. Vary position of fingers so that you can't count number of strokes made. (Strokes don't have to be perfectly straight—they should follow the same direction, but might be slightly angled.)

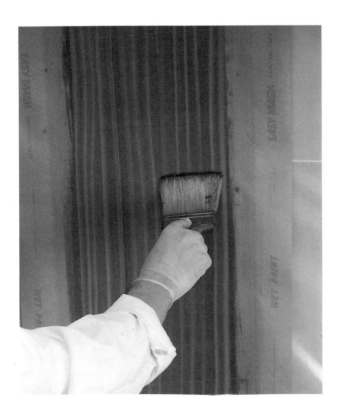

3   After dragging whole surface, smooth it with large spalter; work from top to bottom, not from side to side. Let dry overnight, then reglaze, following step 6, below.

• FORKED MAHOGANY •

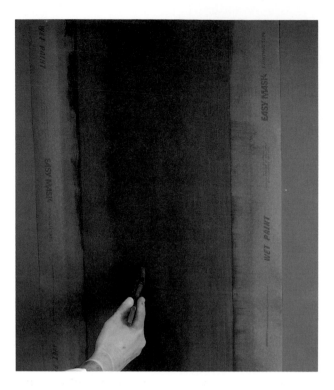

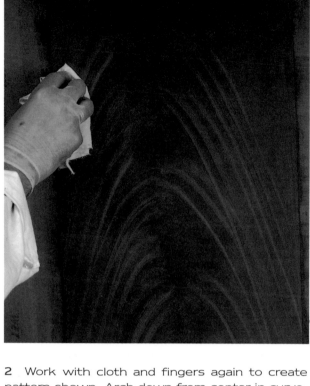

1 Glaze surface, making dark strip down center and keeping sides light. To darken centre, apply more glaze.

2 Work with cloth and fingers again to create pattern shown. Arch down from center in curve, alternating strokes on either side of dark strip. Smooth with spalter, following the pattern formed by your fingers.

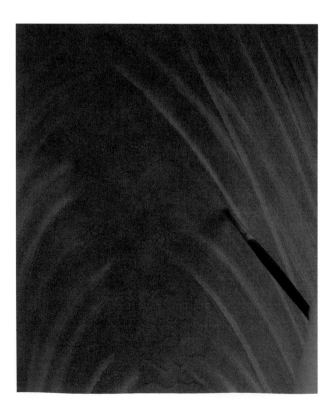

3 With small, flat brush (a well-worn brush works best), paint thin darker line along finger stroke on one side, cross center with thin wavy line, then pick up finger stroke on other side and follow it. Feather strokes gently from center to outside edges to soften. Let dry overnight.

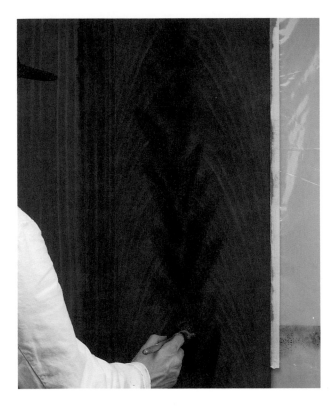

4 Using same glaze as in step 1, reglaze forked mahogany "panel." Then, create pattern shown in center of panel with small strokes of round brush. Darken glaze slightly with dash of artists oils, if needed.

5 With cloth and fingers, alternate strokes from side to side in an arching movement. Start at the outside, arch over and then down the centre (forming the shape of a cane). Then feather strokes with spalter, following the same pattern.

6 When forked mahogany panel dries, reglaze straight-grained panel, then feather evenly with spalter. (For variety, glaze this panel in slightly darker colour.) Three coats of varnish give a polished look to this rich wood finish.

• BURR •

Cut from domed growths on trunks of trees, burred wood is rare and not found in large pieces. For realistic effect, you wouldn't use this technique on large surfaces such as walls. The wood is popular for fine furniture and accessories, door panels and trim, and faux burr would best suit these surfaces, too. Most tree species produce burrs; burr elm, walnut, and tulipwood are favorite finishes. Like the technique for pine, this technique requires both oil- and water-based glaze.

• R E C I P E •

BURR

LEVEL OF EXPERTISE:

RECOMMENDED ON: very small flat areas, best where traditionally found—tabletops, small panels, furniture, accessories

NOT RECOMMENDED ON: walls, highly carved surfaces

NUMBER OF PEOPLE: 1

TOOLS: Well-worn piece of sea sponge, badger-hair brush, spalter (or high quality gloss brush) and pencil dragger brushes, glazing brushes, fine long-haired brush, palette, container of water, gloves

BASE COAT: silk emulsion paint

GLAZE: 1—1½ part acrylic medium to 4 parts water plus artist's acrylics

2—about 6 parts ready-mixed oil glaze to 1 part thinner (see Mixing Paints, Chapter Four)

COLOURS: base coat—⅓ white emulsion plus ⅓ yellow ochre and ⅓ red ochre acrylic

glaze   1—raw umber acrylic

glaze   2—transparent

VARNISH: satin or semigloss

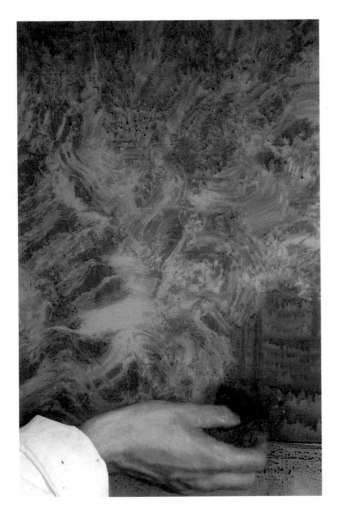

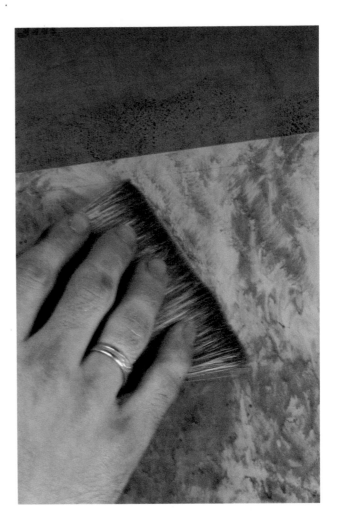

1 Apply water-based glaze in loose criss-cross pattern with large brush. Glaze should be wet, almost runny. Dampen frayed piece of sponge with water, then pick up glaze (see sponge washing, page 151, for tips). To create depth, turn and swirl sponge in some areas, let base coat show through in others, and leave some areas untouched.

2 Holding spalter brush as shown, make rows of short horizontal marks in some areas. Then smooth surface with badger-hair brush.

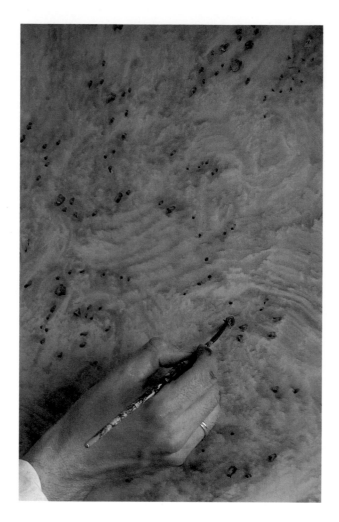

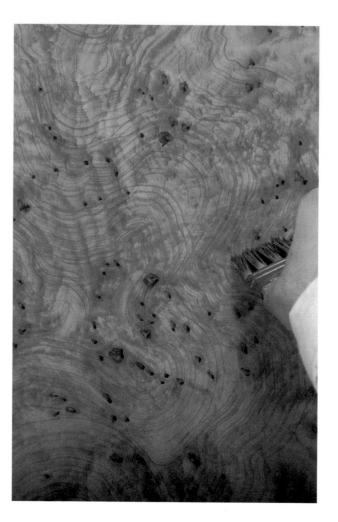

3 With fine-pointed long-haired brush, paint tiny burrs in darker areas only. Make burrs almond-shaped, varying in size from about ¼ inch to ½ inch.

4 Use pencil dragger to add veining. In centre of palette, mix paint and water with spalter to watery consistency. Don't dip more than tip of brush into paint or veining will be too thick. Shake off excess paint and flatten brush against palette, if necessary. Vein in rounded wavy lines, following pattern created by sponge. Make some variations, but don't let lines cross pattern.

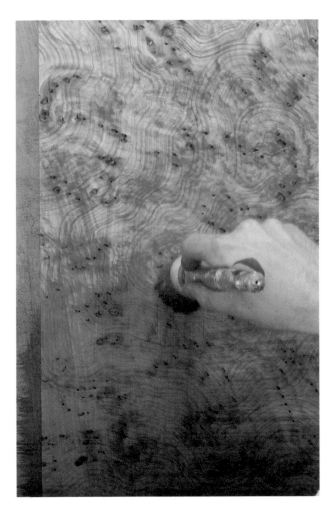

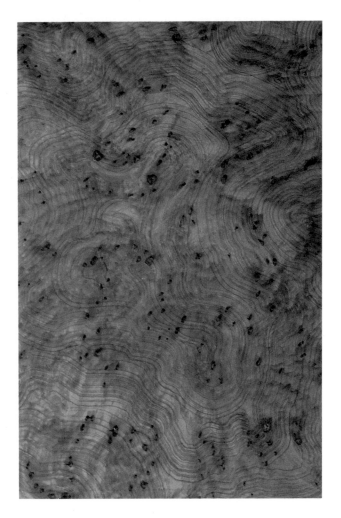

5 Once veining has dried (this happens quickly because paint is water-based), paint over surface with oil-based glaze. Then smooth with spalter.

6 After varnishing, the finished effect displays its rich surface texture.

APPENDIX

•

BIBLIOGRAPHY
SOURCES
INDEX

· BIBLIOGRAPHY ·

The Art of Marbling, Stuart Spencer, Macdonald Orbis (1988)

The Artists' Handbook of Materials and Techniques, Ralph Mayer, Faber (1951)

Fantasy Finishes, Davies Keeling Trowbridge, Macdonald Orbis (1989)

Lyn Le Grice's Art of Stencilling, Viking (1986)

Paintability, Jocasta Innes, Weidenfeld & Nicolson (1986)

Paint Magic, Jocasta Innes, Windward (1981)

Simple Painted Furniture, Annie Sloan, Dorling Kindersley (1989)

The Stencilled House, Lyn Le Grice, Dorling Kindersley (1988)

· SOURCES ·

SUPPLIES AND TOOLS

Allied Reprographics
2nd floor
39 Liverpool Street
Sydney NSW 2000
Tel: (02) 267 6937

Art Basics Pty Ltd
916 Victoria Road
West Ryde NSW 2114
Tel: (02) 807 2359

Artistcare (Aust) Pty Ltd
83-85 Whiting Street
Artarmon NSW 2064
Tel: (02) 437 4222

Artistcare (Aust) Pty Ltd
52 Baxter Street
Fortitude Valley QLD 4006
Tel: (07) 252 8099

Artistcare (Aust) Pty Ltd
214 Gouger Street
Adelaide SA 5000
Tel: (08) 211 8883

Artistcare (Aust) Pty Ltd
101 York Street
South Melbourne VIC 3205
Tel: (03) 699 6188

Francheville (Aust) Pty Ltd
1–5 Perry Street
Collingwood VIC 3066
Tel: (03) 416 0611

Jasco Pty Ltd
118–122 Bowden Street
Meadowbank NSW 2114
Tel: (02) 807 1555

Oxford Art Supplies
221 Oxford Street
Darlinghurst NSW 2010
Tel: (02) 360 4066

HOUSE PAINT, GLAZE AND VARNISH
MANUFACTURERS

Berger & British Paints
15 Gow Street
Padstow NSW 2211
Tel: (02) 796 9777

Cabot's Wood Stains
3/2 Aquatic Drive
Frenchs Forest NSW 2086
Tel: (02) 451 1600

Cabot's Wood Stains
1330 Ferntree Gully Road
Scoresby VIC 3179
Tel: (03) 765 2222

Croda Paints
21 Seven Hills Road
Seven Hills NSW 2147
Tel: (02) 674 1122

Croda Paints
42-48 Cochranes Road
Moorabbin VIC 3189
Tel: (03) 553 1844

Dulux Australia
McNaughton Road
Clayton VIC 3168
Tel: (03) 542 5678

Evergard Industries Pty Ltd
Corner Rufus & Duffy Streets
Epping VIC 3076
Tel: (03) 401 2266

Feast Watson Pty Ltd
82-86 Bay Street
Botany NSW 2019
Tel: (02) 316 6444

Hodgson's Dye Agencies Pty Ltd
56 Bay Street
Broadway NSW 2007
Tel: (02) 211 4633

Pascol Paints Australia Pty Ltd
472-474 Gardners Road
Alexandria NSW 2015
Tel: (02) 669 2266

Sikkens Wood Finishes
184-186 Campbell Street
Surry Hills NSW 2010
Tel: (02) 360 4500

Taubmans Pty Ltd
7 Birmingham Avenue
Villawood NSW 2163
Tel: (02) 727 1200

• INDEX •

Page numbers in italic indicate illustrations

CONVERSION CHART

Use this chart to convert imperial measurements (used throughout this book) to metric measurements.

Inches to millimetres, centimetres

⅛ in = 3 mm
¼ in = 6 mm
½ in = 1.27 cm
1 in   = 2.54 cm
5 in   = 12.7 cm
10 in = 25.4 cm
20 in = 50.8 cm
40 in = 101.6 cm

Feet to metres

1 ft   = 0.30 m
5 ft   = 1.52 m
10 ft   = 3.04 m
50 ft   = 15.2 m
100 ft = 30.4 m

Square feet to square metres

1 sq ft   = 0.09 sq m
75 sq ft   = 6.97 sq m
300 sq ft = 27.87 sq m

Gallons to litres

1 gallon   = 4.54 l
5 gallons = 22.73 l